The Antipedo Baptists of Georgetown County, South Carolina

1710–2010

For Matt

Dad

The Antipedo Baptists
of
Georgetown County, South Carolina
1710–2010

Roy Talbert, Jr., and Meggan A. Farish

THE UNIVERSITY OF SOUTH CAROLINA PRESS

© 2015 University of South Carolina

Published by the University of South Carolina Press
Columbia, South Carolina 29208

www.sc.edu/uscpress

Manufactured in the United States of America

24 23 22 21 20 19 18 17 16 15
10 9 8 7 6 5 4 3 2 1

Library of Congress Cataloging-in-Publication Data
Talbert, Roy.
The Antipedo Baptists of Georgetown County, South Carolina,
1710-2010 / Roy Talbert, Jr., and Meggan A. Farish.
pages cm
Includes bibliographical references and index.
ISBN 978-1-61117-420-5 (hardbound : alk. paper) — ISBN 978-1-61117-421-2 (ebook)
1. Baptists—South Carolina—Georgetown County—History. 2. Georgetown
County (S.C.)—Church history. 3. First Baptist Church (Georgetown, S.C.)—
History. 4. Georgetown (S.C.)—Church history. I. Title.
BX6248.S6T35 2014
286'.175789—dc23
2014011489

This book was printed on recycled paper with 30 percent
postconsumer waste content.

For Virginia Bruorton Skinner

Contents

Illustrations

Acknowledgments

This work was made possible by financial support from the Georgetown Baptist Historical Society and, at Coastal Carolina University, the Lawrence B. and Jane P. Clark Chair endowment. We are also grateful for the kind assistance and generous lending policies of many libraries and archives, especially the South Carolina State Archives, South Caroliniana Library, Furman University, and the Georgetown Public Library. Without free access to the large collection housed at the Georgetown First Baptist Church, this work could not have been completed. We owe a special debt to J. Glenwood Clayton, longtime Furman archivist and editor of the *Journal of the South Carolina Baptist Historical Society*. The assistant to the Clark Chair, Isaac Dusenbury, proved invaluable with his research and digital-age skills, as did Stephanie Freeman, business manager of the Department of History at Coastal Carolina University. For the kindness of the members and staff of the First Baptist Church and for the hospitality of the gracious citizens of Georgetown, we shall always be grateful.

Introduction

THIS IS THE STORY of what is today the First Baptist Church of beautiful and historic Georgetown, South Carolina. In 1710 there was no church and no town—simply a wild, unsettled place called Winyah. This work provides a brief overview of the origins of the Baptist faith and practices and then traces William Screven's journey from Somerset, England, to Kittery, Maine, to Charleston, South Carolina, and finally to Winyah. His historical significance, simply stated, is that he brought Baptist beliefs to the South and organized the First Baptist Church of Charleston before moving to modern-day Georgetown. Screven's youngest son, Elisha, is equally important—he named and laid out the town of Georgetown, South Carolina's third-oldest port. Elisha also helped found the first non-Anglican church in the area, an interdenominational meeting house the Baptists shared with the Presbyterians and Independents. That meeting house was on the Black River, up from Georgetown in rich indigo country, and by the eve of the Revolution another jointly shared edifice had been built in Georgetown.

The three denominations were joined by a common purpose—their dissent from the established Anglican Church. Their role in the American Revolution, where religious toleration was key to their agenda, is significant. It is possible that had the British allowed freedom of worship, the Revolution may have taken a different turn in South Carolina. Sources indicate that South Carolina's experience was similar to that of Virginia, as recently interpreted by John A. Ragosta in his 2010 *Wellspring of Liberty: How Virginia's Religious Dissenters Helped Win the American Revolution and Secured Religious Liberty.* The early South Carolina Baptist leaders of that age—Oliver Hart, Richard Furman, and Edmund Botsford—were all involved in the war. Moreover, they had direct connections with Georgetown, nurturing the Baptists there. Botsford, known to historians for his writings on slavery, became the longtime pastor of the Baptist church in Georgetown, officially organized in 1794 as the Antipedo Baptist Church. *Antipedo baptism* is the archaic term for opposition to infant baptism, and, beyond the several historical markers in Georgetown, it is now rarely used.

Georgetown District, as it was known until after the Civil War, was a complicated place. The port, while it bustled, exhibited more than its share of social ills, and all religious denominations had a difficult time surviving. The racial demographics were startling—the district had the highest black-to-white ratio in the state, at its peak approaching 90 percent. With practically nine out of ten people African American, and very few free people of color, the vast majority were slaves. While many slaveholders were Episcopalians, most of their slaves were Baptists and Methodists. This work, therefore, includes the development of the oldest African American Baptist Church in Georgetown, Bethesda, which, immediately after the Civil War, sprang from the slave members of the Antipedo Baptist Church. Bethesda's first meetings were held in a building formerly owned by the antebellum church.

The Revolution hit Georgetown hard, and the Civil War struck Georgetown even harder. It took the Baptist church more than two decades to recover from the latter, and its struggle is part and parcel of the general New South movement. It was not until World War II that the town and its churches began to achieve their dreams. Since then, what began as the Antipedo church has become the progenitor of all Southern Baptist congregations in Georgetown. Among the many tourist attractions in the old town are the various monuments to those early Baptist leaders. William Screven himself is buried there, forever ensuring Georgetown a prominent place in Southern Baptist history.

Because Baptists have a much looser hierarchy, their church records are typically not as complete as those of the Episcopalians and Methodists. The most important Baptist sources are the minutes of individual churches. The survival rates of these documents depend on the experiences of each church, and a few have remarkably intact minutes. In the case of Georgetown there are excellent records from 1805 to 1821, but from that point until 1909 none has been discovered. Baptist churches are organized into associations and are expected to send by letter annual reports, which are frequently quoted or summarized in the association minutes. Here Georgetown's records are somewhat more complete. For several years in the antebellum period and throughout the Civil War and Reconstruction, Georgetown Baptists were able to send neither a letter nor a delegate to the association. Baptists met in annual conventions at the state level, and the minutes from those meetings are especially valuable after the Civil War. By the early twentieth century, records at all levels—local, association, and state—are in fine shape, containing details of church organizations, budgets, pastors, and staff. The principal housing place for such records is Furman University's extensive collection of church, association, and convention minutes. Land records are difficult to find, especially in the lowcountry. For the colonial period, deeds or indentures are well preserved and are available at the South Carolina State Archives. From independence onward, most of Georgetown District's records were lost in the Civil War. Local newspapers also vary in survivability from town to town. While many have been lost, Georgetown County Library has a valuable collection, although in the antebellum period there are few references to the church activities of any denomination. Beginning with the New South, however, newspaper editors were eager to report religious events. Building a new church, holding a revival, or welcoming a new pastor were all chronicled in great detail.

The present work also benefits from the earlier efforts of Baptist historians. Most significant is Leah Townsend's 1935 *South Carolina Baptists, 1670–1805,* which was extended by Joe Madison King's 1964 *A History of South Carolina Baptists.* South Carolina Baptists were the subject of Robert A. Baker's 1982 *Adventures in Faith: The First 300 Years of the First Baptist Church, Charleston, South Carolina,* and he became a particularly good friend of the Georgetown church. General Georgetown history was admirably covered by George C. Rogers, Jr., in his 1970 *History of Georgetown County,* which set new standards for local history. We also relied heavily on Charles Joyner's highly acclaimed 1984 *Down by the Riverside: A South Carolina Slave Community,* an analysis of slavery on the Waccamaw Neck. While neither of these books was intended as church history, Rogers is informative regarding the Methodists, and most of the slaves studied by Joyner were owned by Episcopalians. Our search of the Works Progress Administration's slave narratives in the Pee Dee, analyzed so brilliantly by Joyner, reaffirms his conclusion that there is very little discussion of any denomination in the interviews aside from postslavery African American churches.

The greatest help for this study came from efforts of the pastors and members of the First Baptist Church of Georgetown. Led by church historian Virginia Skinner, they have researched and collected a significant body of archival material. Spurred by the anticipation of the church's tricentennial celebration in 2010, the church had those valuable sources beautifully preserved. From all these sources we have attempted to put together something more than a strictly institutional history, hoping to tell the story of Georgetown's churches, especially the Baptists, within the larger context of social, economic, and political history.

ONE

From Somerset to Kittery

THE MOST SIGNIFICANT historical baptism is that of Jesus Christ, who went down to the Jordan River to be baptized by John the Baptist. Many cultures, particularly the Hebrews, had well-established rituals involving water, usually as part of a purifying preparatory exercise. This was essentially John's message—be baptized and cleansed to "prepare the way for the Lord" (Matt. 3:3 [KJV]). It is likely that Jesus' baptism involved immersion since the Gospel of Mark describes him as "straightway coming up out of the water" (1:10). In the early church, baptism was a mandatory requirement for converts. Little is known about the church of the first century, but archeological evidence suggests that immersion was the most prominent form of baptism, with other methods such as effusion and sprinkling becoming commonplace at a later time.[1] Baptism was also an important part of the Great Commission, which urged Christians to "Go ye therefore, and teach all nations, baptizing them in the name of the Father and of the Son and of the Holy Spirit" (Matt. 28:19). As Christianity spread during the early centuries, most of those baptized were adult converts, although some families were baptized together.

By the Middle Ages, with Western Europe thoroughly Christianized by the Roman Catholic Church, infant baptism had become the most common practice. With the church the primary institution in Europe, people identified themselves not so much by nationality as by being Christian. The result was a church that became rich, powerful, and decadent. In 1517 Martin Luther issued his famous Ninety-Five Theses, setting ablaze the Reformation that, in so many respects, went far beyond his immediate goals. The Lutheran Church itself became an established institution. While Luther rejected many of the sacraments of Catholicism, his was still a conservative viewpoint, never imagining the fires of religious enthusiasm that flared so quickly after he took his stand. It was a complicated and violent period involving politics, class warfare, and religious persecution. By the 1520s Northern Europe in particular was racked with violence. The desire for religious reform eventually sparked serfs to rebellion and culminated in the German Peasants' War of 1524. Luther's doctrine was at least partially blamed for the uprisings, which were suppressed by 1526.[2]

The defeated rebels of the Peasants' War and others found refuge in many small but vocal sects. Some groups not only cast off everything reminiscent of the "old religion" but also rejected civil government. One sect that adopted these principles were the Anabaptists, a term meaning rebaptizer. Anabaptists are usually linked to Switzerland and German states, but they appeared in various places, including Austria, Italy, and France. Association with Anabaptists carried a stigma that brought severe persecution. It was considered much easier to burn Anabaptists than to convert them.

It is difficult to trace the migration of the Anabaptists from northern Europe to the British Isles, but those who fled to England often found themselves still subject to persecution. As early as the 1530s, however, there was an organized Anabaptist Church in London. Some scholars link Anabaptists with Baptists since both groups lived in the same areas of England and shared several core beliefs, but Anabaptism slowly declined, and the Baptist faith, as we know it today, has a different set of origins.[3] Whether or not Baptists were directly related to Anabaptists remains debatable, but Baptists did evolve out of the various Separatist, Nonconformist, or Dissenter groups scattered throughout England and the Continent. Over time several branches of the Baptist faith emerged. The first were General Baptists. In the study of their history two names appear frequently: John Smyth and Thomas Helwys. Smyth, an ordained minister of the Church of England, became a Separatist about 1607 and left England for Amsterdam with John Robinson and his congregation. Smyth was largely responsible for the basic principles of the General Baptists, namely vicarious atonement for all through the death and resurrection of Christ, which officially drew the line separating General Baptists and Calvinists. The latter stressed predestination and the doctrine of the elect. Helwys, who immigrated with Smyth to Amsterdam and was baptized by him, later established his own church when Smyth aligned with the Mennonites. Helwys and his congregation returned to London in 1612 to establish the first General Baptist Church.[4]

A second division of Baptists was known as the Particular Baptists, whose origins can be traced to a Separatist church in London. As early as the 1620s their members began to study the nature of baptism in the New Testament and came to the conclusion that infant baptism was unscriptural. In 1638 Henry Jessey, a former minister of the Separatist church, broke away with several other members of the congregation and called themselves Antipedo Baptists, a term that literally means "anti-infant" baptism. A few years later the church adopted immersion as the sole means of baptism, and by the 1640s the General Baptists followed suit. Particular Baptists are best remembered for following Calvinist principles, including predestination. Apart from their differences over the possibility of salvation, the General and Particular Baptists and many other

Separatists shared common principles—their devotion to an independent congregation and a limited baptism to those who had made a profession of faith.[5]

What allowed Baptists to begin to mature was the peculiar religious climate in England. Beginning with Henry VIII, the country endured a transformation from Catholicism to Protestantism. Except for a short period of persecution during the reign of Catholic Mary I, Anglicanism emerged as the established church. Mary's successor, Elizabeth I, was more concerned with the loyalty of her subjects than with their devotion to one faith, and she promoted a policy of toleration. Her attempt to unite the country politically, however, fractured it religiously. The existence of multiple faiths became increasingly problematic, and Elizabeth decided to persecute extremists on both sides.[6]

The Stuarts exacerbated England's religious issues when James I took the throne in 1603. He advocated strict conformity to the Church of England and the Book of Common Prayer and made few concessions to Dissenters. His son, Charles I, embraced Arminianism, a faith that rejected the Calvinist doctrine of predestination and endorsed good works and religious rituals in order to win salvation. A religion reminiscent of Catholicism and the atrocities of Bloody Mary's reign helped to widen the gap separating Charles from his English subjects, and he faced Parliament vehemently opposed to both his political and religious ideas. By 1642 the English Civil Wars had officially begun.[7]

As the country prepared for battle, Baptists, along with other Nonconformists, filled the ranks of Oliver Cromwell's army. Siding with Cromwell, these groups hoped that religious persecution would end in victory. They were at least partially correct, but several tracts printed from 1642 to 1644 associated Baptists with the radical sixteenth-century Anabaptists in Munster. The Particular Baptists responded to that charge with the 1644 London Confession of Faith.[8] The threat of physical punishment and imprisonment temporarily subsided when Parliament granted limited religious toleration in 1647, and as a result more religious factions emerged. Baptists became one among many branches of Protestantism to flourish, each espousing various biblical interpretations.[9]

The Restoration of 1660 brought an end to Protestant toleration when Charles II took the throne. The Act of Uniformity, Test Act, Conventicle Act, and Five Mile Act marked a new era of persecution against Nonconformists, with punishments ranging from fines and imprisonment to burning and beheading. Roughly seventy-five thousand faced persecution, eight thousand of whom were executed. Nevertheless, Baptist membership continued to grow, with some two hundred churches established in England during this time.[10]

Meanwhile, a new window of opportunity opened across the Atlantic as Nonconformists settled North America to escape oppression. Puritan minister

Roger Williams was one such immigrant. Arriving in Massachusetts Bay in 1631, he was offered a position as pastor of the newly organized church in Boston but refused because he felt the Puritans had not definitively severed ties with the Church of England. Williams's strict beliefs about separating church and state resulted in his banishment from the colony by the General Court of Massachusetts in 1636. He and others subsequently moved southwest of Massachusetts Bay and purchased land from the Narragansett Indians to establish Providence, Rhode Island. Williams formed a Baptist church within three years, signaling the beginning of the Baptist presence in America.[11]

Although the Dissenters who came to the New World advocated religious freedom for themselves, few practiced tolerance for others. While the phenomenon was not limited to Massachusetts Bay, the colony acquired a particularly notorious reputation. The Puritans who migrated there in 1629 drifted away from their Anglican roots and moved toward Congregationalism, refusing to tolerate other religious sects. Since church and state were still connected, nonconformity resulted in disenfranchisement, stripping Dissenters of their political voice. Furthermore, Massachusetts Bay claimed to have jurisdiction over the territory that became Maine and New Hampshire. James I had granted the same land to two different parties, and debates over who had the rightful claim ensued for years until Massachusetts Bay enveloped New Hampshire in 1643 and Maine in 1652, extending its authority into the two colonies. Nevertheless, Baptist immigrants were firmly grounded in their faith, and congregations sprouted up across New England.[12] The First Baptist Church of Boston was established in 1665 after ten years of underground activity; however, the faithful did not escape the notice of authorities and moved frequently. Other congregations could not organize into formal churches, but private correspondence shows that Baptist leaders held meetings in their homes in Massachusetts Bay, New Hampshire, and Maine.[13]

One area of particular interest to this study is Kittery, Maine. Some historians cite Hanserd Knollys, possibly the first Particular Baptist preacher in America, as an early figure promoting the Baptist faith in Kittery. In the 1660s Nicholas Shapleigh used his home to hold Baptist services and paid a Puritan minister to lead worship. About that same time Massachusetts Bay issued an edict extending religious jurisdiction into Maine and New Hampshire. Attendance and financial support of the official church became mandatory, and it was more difficult for Baptists to remain in hiding.[14]

With persecution escalating in England, Baptists and other Dissenters escaped to the colonies, including a man by the name of William Screven. Nothing is known of his early life beyond the fact that he was born in Somerton, Somersetshire, in 1629.[15] In June of 1652 the records from the Luppet Baptist

Church in Devon list two "gifted brethren" baptized by Thomas Collier, one of whom was William Screven.[16] Screven soon began preaching and baptized several people. In 1656 he signed the Somerset Confession of Faith, likely written by Collier and adopted by Baptist churches in Somerset, Wilts, Gloucester, Devon, and Dorset.[17] These principles helped erase the barrier between General and Particular Baptists through agreement on some doctrinal practices, especially Antipedo baptism.[18] Throughout the course of his ministry, Screven continued the trend of integrating these two Baptist sects.

Sometime after 1660 Screven left England for America, probably to escape the persecution brought on by the restoration of Charles II. Screven's first documented presence in America came in 1668, when he witnessed a deed in Salisbury, Massachusetts. In the spring of the following year he apprenticed himself for four years to George Carr, a local shipwright. When his stint ended in 1673, he earned a living as a shipwright and purchased ten acres of land in Kittery, Maine. Screven married Bridgett Cutt, daughter of Robert Cutt, a former member of the British Parliament and an early settler of New Hampshire.[19] Over the course of their marriage William and Bridgett raised a total of thirteen children: Mercy, Sarah, Bridgett, Elizabeth, Patience, Samuel, Robert, Joshua, William, Joseph, Permanous, Aaron, and Elisha.[20]

While Screven was making a home in Kittery, his activities came under the scrutiny of Massachusetts Bay officials. On July 6, 1675, he was ordered before the grand jury for failure to attend Puritan services, but the charges were dropped after he explained that he had been at services in Portsmouth.[21] Screven saw no reason to be alarmed about being a practicing Baptist, and he participated in local affairs, becoming constable for lower Kittery in 1676 and serving on the grand jury in 1678 and 1679.[22]

Just as it seemed Screven had escaped the watchful eye of the Puritans, Massachusetts Bay purchased the Maine patent and sealed the fate of Dissenters. As Joshua Millet stated in his *History of the Baptists in Maine,* "the Congregationalists were recognized by law as the Standing Order. They viewed the Baptists in the light of religious fanatics, and regarded their doctrines and influences as deleterious to the welfare of both society and religion."[23] Screven could have chosen to step out of public life and hide his convictions, but he remained active in his civil and religious duties. In 1679 he signed a petition to the king, seeking relief from Massachusetts Bay's intolerance. No progress was made, and Screven endorsed another petition requesting royal control of Maine; however, the Crown did not take action right away.[24]

A year later Screven took a curious step, raising questions among scholars about his identity. The records of the First Baptist Church of Boston show that on July 21, 1681, William Screven, his wife Bridgett, and Humphrey

Churchwood were baptized.[25] Nineteenth-century authors dismissed the idea that there could have been two William Screvens.[26] In the early twentieth century Henry Burrage, a New England Baptist clergyman and historian, offered a different view—two generations of William Screvens, the English father baptized in the Luppet Baptist Church and who signed the Somerset Confession of Faith, and his son, the American William Screven, Baptist leader in Maine.[27]

This idea was accepted until the Baptist historian Robert Baker began his monumental research in the 1960s. While Baker never fully discredited Burrage's theory, he offered reasonable evidence that the William Screven living in Maine was the same William Screven who lived and was baptized in England. Baker contends that a second baptism should not be dismissed. Taking England's history into consideration, it is possible that the church in Somerton no longer existed due to persecution, and the Boston church may have asked Screven to be baptized again for accreditation purposes. There are early references to people receiving baptism a second time once they arrived in the New World because of the method of baptism they had originally received (effusion or immersion) or to signify their faith in a new land. It seems more likely that the William Screven in America was the same "gifted brethren" who fled England.[28]

Screven became an ordained minister in 1682 by request of the Kittery Baptists, who considered him a "beloved brother . . . gifted and endued, with the spirit of veterans to preach the gospel."[29] Boston agreed immediately, calling Screven "a man whom God hath qualified and furnished with the gifts of his Holy Spirit and grace."[30] Screven was in Boston when Humphrey Churchwood, a prominent member of the Kittery congregation, wrote to the First Baptist Church in 1682, pleading for Screven to return to Kittery as "his long absence from us, has given great advantage to our adversaries." The magistrate was threatening to impose a penalty of five shillings on several congregation members for attending Baptist religious services.[31] Screven, so outspoken about his Antipedo Baptist beliefs, refused to allow one of his children to be sprinkled, and he was ordered before the Provincial Council at York on account of his "blasfeamous speeches about the holy ordinance of baptisme" and for claiming that "Infant Baptisme . . . was an ordinance of the Devill."[32] When Screven refused to pay the fine, he was sent to jail. He remained there for one month, after which the Court of Pleas fined him ten pounds and ordered him never to preach again in the province. That June he swore to the General Assembly that he would leave Maine immediately.[33]

Screven remained in Maine despite his promise. He wrote to Boston asking that a church be established in Kittery.[34] Isaac Hull, Thomas Skinner, and Phillip Squire responded: "We doe therefore in ye name of ye Lord Jesus &

by the Appointmtt of his Church deliver them to be A Church of Christ in ye faith and order of ye Gospel."[35] They then traveled from Boston to Kittery to ordain Screven as pastor and Churchwood as deacon.[36] Once Screven had successfully instituted a church at Kittery, the Court of Sessions summoned him in October 1683, and the following year the Court of Pleas demanded that Screven come before the General Assembly.[37]

Since there is no record of Screven's appearance at either court, scholars have speculated that he left Kittery as early as 1683 and made his relocation to Charleston, South Carolina.[38] More-recent discoveries have shed light on the activities of the Kittery church and suggest that Screven remained in Maine until the mid-1690s. Current scholarship gives 1696 as the date of Screven's permanent settlement in South Carolina, the first year his name appears on record as having purchased land in the colony.[39] From 1684 to 1696 Screven remained an active member of the Kittery community. He purchased land, appraised estates, and served as commissioner, representative, foreman of the grand jury, and moderator of Kittery. He was also a witness in several contracts.[40] Scholars have speculated that the William Screven who remained in Maine was Screven's son, William, Jr., but the latter would have been too young to be involved in government affairs. It is also clear that the land purchased in Maine between 1684 and 1696 was in the father's name. When William Screven's son Robert sold the property in 1704, he secured power of attorney solely from his father and not his brother. What steered Screven's biographers to attribute these roles to his son was the lack of religious work on record. No letters or church documents exist to prove Screven was still preaching in Kittery, nor is there any evidence that he was prosecuted by authorities for remaining in Maine when he had been ordered out by the court. Rapid developments in England, however, had altered his status for the better. The Glorious Revolution and the subsequent crowning of William and Mary in 1689 resulted in the Toleration Act, which granted legal status to Dissenters, including Baptists. It was also during this time that complete royal control was finalized in Massachusetts, Maine, and New Hampshire, lifting the Puritan hold over those colonies and, with it, persecution of Baptists.[41]

Although religious intolerance had softened, Screven and the Kittery church had several reasons to move to Charleston in 1696.[42] For one, Indian raids in Maine were becoming more frequent. Another factor was Maine's financial crisis. When Screven was commissioner for Kittery, he petitioned the court in 1694 to excuse the town from paying taxes, a request that was granted that year and the year after.[43] South Carolina also had a reputation for welcoming Dissenters. Since the 1680s the lords proprietors had actively promoted their settlement in the colony. Screven would have undoubtedly considered a government amiable to Baptists a great advantage.[44]

Some of Screven's acquaintances had already taken the opportunity to move to South Carolina and may have convinced him to join them. It is likely that Bridgett's family, so closely connected with Barbados, spoke with Screven about the advantages of living in South Carolina and encouraged him to move. Screven also had family ties with the influential Elliott family, who, years earlier, had migrated from England to the colony. There is, as well, the connection of the Axtells. Several members of Screven's congregation were related to Lady Axtell, a well-known Baptist in South Carolina and the mother of Joseph Blake, governor of the colony when Screven arrived. Another important South Carolina contact for Screven was the powerful Landgrave Thomas Smith, who is said to have helped the Baptists get established in the Charleston area. Later the Screvens and Smiths owned adjoining plantations, and William's grandson James married Mary Hyrne Smith, the daughter of the second Landgrave Thomas Smith.[45] Screven's move seems hardly accidental, and the links between Kittery and South Carolina were far from tenuous.

The exact date of Screven's relocation to South Carolina is unknown, but he and at least thirty men and women secured land in the colony by late 1696.[46] Land records show that Screven owned a home in Charleston as well as land in the interior.[47] It is also clear that he remained active as a shipwright while ministering to his congregation, who first met at Somerton and then moved to Charleston in 1698. The church, which is still flourishing today, cites its founding date as 1682, the year Kittery was established. That venerable institution is now known as the First Baptist Church of Charleston, the mother church of Southern Baptists.[48]

TWO

Charleston

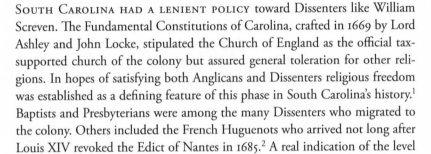

SOUTH CAROLINA HAD A LENIENT POLICY toward Dissenters like William Screven. The Fundamental Constitutions of Carolina, crafted in 1669 by Lord Ashley and John Locke, stipulated the Church of England as the official tax-supported church of the colony but assured general toleration for other religions. In hopes of satisfying both Anglicans and Dissenters religious freedom was established as a defining feature of this phase in South Carolina's history.[1] Baptists and Presbyterians were among the many Dissenters who migrated to the colony. Others included the French Huguenots who arrived not long after Louis XIV revoked the Edict of Nantes in 1685.[2] A real indication of the level of toleration was the influx of Sephardic Jews driven out of Spain during the Inquisition. The only religion prohibited in South Carolina was Catholicism, making the colony the most tolerant, next to Rhode Island.[3]

The ability to worship openly, however, came at a price and was entangled in the larger question of colonial governance. Anglicans opposed the proprietors and favored Crown rule, while the proprietors encouraged immigration, enticing Dissenters with promises of religious freedom. From the beginning, religious freedom was a bargaining chip in the proprietors' efforts to increase their authority and to encourage immigration. To make matters worse, the Fundamental Constitutions were never ratified, giving Anglicans the opportunity to challenge the proprietors' actions. It was only a matter of time before the Church of England became the one and only "church" in the colony.[4]

Governor Joseph Blake's death in 1700 and the subsequent promotion of the Anglican James Moore to the governorship signaled an end to the relative peace that existed between Anglicans and Dissenters. Joseph Morton, Jr., Dissenter and senior landgrave, should have succeeded Blake, but Moore objected on grounds that Morton held both proprietary and royal positions. The Grand Council and proprietors agreed and soon after selected Moore governor, although he was never confirmed. Moore used his new power to invade Spanish Florida and attack St. Augustine in 1702, an endeavor that failed miserably and left the colony in considerable debt.[5] The following year he presented a bill before the General Assembly to allot four thousand pounds for another invasion, but the opposing Dissenters withdrew. When they returned the following day, the Anglicans refused to recognize the Dissenters' rights as members of the body.[6]

The details of what happened next are difficult to determine. According to some reports, the Dissenters were attacked by a mob in the streets of Charleston when the assembly adjourned. Daniel Defoe, author of *Robinson Crusoe* and *Moll Flanders,* championed the Dissenters' cause. His brief, written on their behalf and printed in London in 1705, offers the most vivid description of these supposed events. Defoe claimed Moore had been elected unjustly and had "acquir'd and obtain'd the Government of this Province by Fraud, Flattery and trifling Exceptions." Defoe recalled the prominent Dissenters who had been assaulted, including Landgrave Thomas Smith who "was set upon by Lieutenant Colonel George Dearsly, who . . . swore he would Kill him, and if he had not been prevented, would have done the said Smith some considerable Mischief to the endangering of his life."[7] While Defoe's inflammatory piece is likely propaganda, his account illuminates the building tensions between the two parties.

Nathaniel Johnson, an Anglican, was commissioned as governor in 1703. Johnson was influenced by Samuel Thomas, a missionary of the Society for the Propagation of the Gospel in Foreign Parts. Thomas worked closely with the governor to turn the tide in favor of the Anglicans. While there is no direct evidence of a conspiracy, Thomas was outspoken against Dissenters, especially Baptists. In a 1702 letter to London, he grumbled, "Here are many Anabaptists in these parts, there being Preachers of that sort here, chuse rather to hear them than none. I hope in God I may establish many and bring back some."[8]

On April 26, 1704, Johnson called an emergency meeting of the assembly. Since many Dissenters lived in the backcountry, they did not arrive in Charleston in time to stop "An Act for the more effectual Preservation of the Government of this Province," more commonly referred to as the Exclusion Act. This new law made conformity to the Church of England compulsory for membership in the Commons House of Assembly, officially removing Dissenters from their official posts. With the 1705 Church Act the Church of England became established in South Carolina and the Book of Common Prayer the official form of worship. In retaliation Dissenters sent representatives to London, and Queen Anne ordered the proprietors to disallow both acts. Johnson received word in 1706 of the Crown's ruling and had no choice but to order the assembly to repeal them. Shortly thereafter, however, he persuaded the legislature to replace the old laws with the 1706 Church Act, restoring Anglicanism as the tax-supported religion of South Carolina.[9]

The assembly's decision is curious given the considerable number of Dissenters living in South Carolina in comparison to the number of Anglicans. In 1710 contemporaries estimated that Presbyterians, Huguenots, Congregationalists, Baptists, and Quakers comprised roughly 60 percent of the population.[10] Perhaps the unwillingness of Dissenters to find common ground impeded their ability to fight Johnson, but ultimately it was their taxes that contributed to the salaries of Anglican ministers and the construction of their churches. The only legal marriages were those performed by Anglican priests, and the parishes themselves were political entities. The act also denied Dissenters the privilege of incorporating their churches. Although many protested, religious equality would not be restored in South Carolina until 1778.[11]

While this drama unfolded, William Screven was attempting to unite the Kittery and Charleston Baptists. Sometime in the late 1690s both groups integrated and met at William Chapman's house on King Street.[12] A major milestone in the church's history came on July 18, 1699, when William Elliott donated lot 62 on Church Street to the "people distinguished by the name of Antipeado Baptists." William Sadler, John Raven, Thomas Bulline, Thomas Graves, and John Elliott were the initial trustees.[13] According to the early Baptist historian Morgan Edwards, the lot measured 230 by 100 feet, and the building itself was 47 by 37 feet.[14] A hurricane swept through Charleston in 1752 and destroyed the church records, so an exact date for the building itself is not known. This facility, probably a wooden structure, was the first Baptist meeting house in the South, and, according to one author, the neighborhood surrounding the church earned the name Baptist Town.[15]

Rather surprisingly, Screven and his congregation do not appear to have been overtly persecuted. No court fined or imprisoned him, nor was he barred from preaching.[16] While Screven went largely unnoticed by civil authorities, other Dissenters did not hesitate to speak out against his ministry. Joseph Lord, a Congregationalist preacher from Dorchester, Massachusetts, was Screven's most vocal opponent. Lord had migrated to South Carolina with his congregation in 1695, just before Screven's arrival. Upon returning to South Carolina from a visit to New England, Lord wrote his northern brethren on February 21, 1699:

> When I came up to Dorchester I found that a certain Anabaptist teacher (named Scrivan), who came from New England, had taken advantage of my absence to insinuate unto some of the people about us, and to endeavor to make proselytes, not by public preaching of his own tenets, nor by disputations, but by employing some of his most officious and trusty adherents to gain upon such as they had interest in, and thereby to set an

example to others that are too apt to be led by any thing that is new. And he had like to have prevailed: but for Mr. Cotton's and my coming has a little obstructed them.[17]

In the fall of 1702 Hugh Adams, a local minister, issued a challenge to debate Screven on matters of doctrine. When the seventy-three-year-old Screven declined due to illness, both Lord and Adams felt the Baptist preacher was lying to avoid confrontation. Lord claimed that "the Anabaptists are much at a loss what excuse to make for the man that has been much extolled by them; for it is believed by many his sickness was feigned."[18] Adams alleged that Screven was "pretending to be a mighty preacher of the Anabaptist error" and that the "Said Anabaptist Prater . . . in his Shame and Confusion Retired about 50 miles out of Town into the Countrey, not appearing again There for about 4 months."[19] The tension between Screven and other Dissenters did not wane. About 1713 an Anglican minister witnessed an argument between Screven and a Presbyterian, describing the former as "a Ship Carpenter, ye Anabaptist Teacher at Charleston; between whom & Mr. Livingston, there has been a sharp contention, concerning some of the town Presbyterians seduced by him."[20]

Screven did not allow such opposition to hinder his ministry, which continued to grow in and around Charleston. Missionaries sent to the colony in 1700 by the Society for the Propagation of the Gospel in Foreign Parts complained about the many Baptists thwarting their efforts to gain converts. One official, Nicholas Trott, lamented, "We are here very much infected with the sect of the Anabaptists."[21] Governor Nathaniel Johnson substantiated Trott's observation; in 1708 he estimated that as many as 10 percent of the 4,180 white persons in Charleston were Baptists.[22]

Screven was able to garner new converts, but what do we know of his congregation? First and foremost, Baptists were bound by their belief in adult baptism. Second, all Baptists insisted that baptism should be by immersion. There were also major doctrinal issues about salvation, along with questions concerning church authority and the order of worship. With regard to organization, Baptists ultimately rejected governance by ruling elders and remained committed to autonomous congregations. The nature of worship was a particularly sensitive issue. Hymn singing was a source of debate from the seventeenth century forward. The austerity and simplicity of their services would be quite unfamiliar to the modern visitor. Many early meetings were held outdoors, sometimes in structures made of boughs and called brush arbors or in private homes.[23] The Charleston Baptists used these temporarily facilities until they erected a meeting house.

A major concern that divided the Baptists of Screven's day, and for some time thereafter, was the laying on of hands. This ritual stemmed from the very early churches, where the bones of martyrs were believed to transfer power when touched. In the 1670s a leading Baptist minister in London, Benjamin Keach, advocated laying on of hands, and his son, Elias, included the provision when, in 1697, he amended the 1689 London Confession of Faith, a Particular Baptist document. Tradition has it that Screven opposed the practice, and in 1700 the Charleston church excluded the articles regarding laying on of hands and ruling elders. There is debate among scholars over Screven's precise doctrines. It seems clear that the Kittery church accepted the 1689 London Confession and brought it to South Carolina. We know that one of Screven's last requests was that his congregation find a minister who shared his Particular Baptist beliefs.[24]

Some Baptists in Screven's congregation did not agree with him. Charleston had its share of General Baptists, and perhaps he was willing to make compromises in an effort to maintain harmony between the two groups.[25] From existing evidence, we know that Screven did not close the doors to his Antipedo brethren, and numerous General Baptists found a place in the congregation. William Elliott, who donated the lot where the church was built, is said to have been a General Baptist. In 1702 the Assembly of General Baptist Churches in England passed a resolution to buy books for "our Brethren of the Baptist perswation and of the Generall Faith who haue their abroad in Carolina." The church had initially asked for a minister, probably searching for an able replacement for the aging Screven, but the assembly could not fill their request.[26]

The rapport between the General and Particular Baptists did not continue long after Screven's death, and within a quarter of a century a deep schism developed that nearly destroyed the church. In 1736 the General Baptists withdrew and began meeting at Stono. That same year the Ashley River group left. Ten years later, in litigation over the ownership of the meeting house, Thomas Simmons, then pastor of the church, and Francis Gracia, a deacon, recalled the fellowship that had existed during Screven's tenure: "Although the two Sects differed upon the Point of the Decrees of God yet they did not think that a sufficient Reason to break the Communion of the said church until the unhappy Differences which of late Years arose in the said church by some of the Members both of the Calvinist and Arminian Persuasion carrying the peculiar Tenets of their Doctrine to too great a length."[27] After much deliberation the provincial legislature ruled in 1745 that both the General and Particular Baptists had an equal right to the building.[28] Many of the Particular members could not come to terms with the decision and constructed their own meeting house the following year. This was a very dark time for the First Baptist Church of Charleston. Not only did the body split, but the Edisto Island community, to whom Screven had ministered and where he had baptized several new converts, separated and formed their own congregation at Euhaw in 1746.[29]

An aging Screven had hoped to be relieved of his many pastoral responsibilities, and in 1707 England sent a Reverend White to help, a man about whom we know very little, except that he died soon after arriving.[30] Ministers were scarce in the New World. Even the church in Boston pleaded with Screven to return, but he declined. Serving the church that had ordained him may have had some appeal, but Screven responded, "My prayers are to God for you, though I am not with you, nor can I come to you, as I was inclined to do if I could; our help being taken from us: for our Minister that came from England is dead, and I can by no means be spared." Instead, Screven advised his Boston brethren to employ Ellis Callender, one of their members.[31]

In a 1708 letter to Callender, Screven discussed the problem of religious persecution, writing, "New-England is guilty of many sins, I cannot but think that the sin of persecution is one, if not the chief, for which God is thus contending with them." Screven added that he would "pray God to grant a thorough reformation; then may you and we expect deliverance from all our troubles."[32] The troubles to which Screven referred must be attributed to the political turmoil in South Carolina between Dissenters and Anglicans.

The last known letter Screven wrote was dated August 6, 1708. His health was declining, and he sent his final instructions to Callender: "I pray God to be with your spirit, and strengthen you to the great work to which you are called, and that the little vine may be flourishing under your hand." Screven added, "I have been, of late, brought very low by sickness; but I bless the Lord I was helped to preach and administer the communion last Lord's day, but am still very weak; therefore can write but a little to you now."[33] He eventually found a replacement, a Reverend Sanford.[34] Francis Le Jau, a well-known missionary of the Society for the Propagation of the Gospel in Foreign Parts, recalled that in the summer of 1712 Sanford arrived in Charleston "to be a Teacher among the Anabaptists."[35] Commissary Gideon Johnston wrote the bishop of London in 1713, identifying Screven as a "Ship Carpenter" and "Anabaptist Teacher." According to Johnston, Sanford was a "Tallow Chandler, another Baptist teacher towards the Southward, both of them extremely ignorant, but this more seemingly moderate than the other."[36]

It is clear from surviving correspondence that Screven served the Charleston church in a part-time capacity after 1708. That year he and Bridgett sold their Somerton plantation to René Ravenel.[37] As late as 1713 Johnston identified

Screven as a minister in Charleston, so he must have remained somewhat active in church affairs, although Sanford was the head pastor by that time. It is certainly true that after 1710 Screven was much less involved with the Charleston church. By then he had moved sixty miles up the coast, where he would spend his final days.

THREE

The Settling of Georgetown

WILLIAM SCREVEN RETIRED to a remote location north of Charleston called Winyah or Winnea, part of a large and ill-defined Craven County. Winyah Bay would have been appealing to a shipwright and planter, and land was available and rich. While Screven was at a distinct disadvantage as a prominent Dissenter, he was a man of means and influence. He did not come to the New World as an indentured field hand but as an apprentice in a valuable and skilled trade he practiced successfully. He invested in land, buying and selling property in Maine and South Carolina. Before his final relocation Screven dispensed of both his Kittery and Somerton estates, sales which must have provided him with more than enough money to make considerable purchases in Winyah.[1]

Members of Screven's immediate family and church had been acquiring land in Craven County as early as 1704. At least six members of his congregation had secured approximately three thousand acres by this time. Screven's sons—Aaron, Robert, and Permanous—also preceded their father in obtaining land in the vicinity.[2] Screven himself may have relocated to this area around 1706 or 1708, but no records confirming his presence appear until 1709, when he purchased one hundred acres in Winyah.[3] When Screven and his flock settled there the region was largely unpopulated—sprinkled with natives, runaways, renegades, and squatters.[4] Nevertheless, Winyah Bay was a logical place for settlement after Charleston and Port Royal.

While towns were slow to develop, the easy land policies of the day meant that settlers, such as the Screvens, could establish plantations along the waterways.[5] On January 13, 1710, the traditional date for Screven's settlement at Winyah, he received a royal grant for two hundred acres of land in Craven County "paying yearly on every first day of December . . . one shilling for every hundred acres."[6] At the time no central office existed to monitor this process, and enforcement was lax. Before 1719 a settler was supposed to petition the governor to obtain a warrant for a survey. Once the survey was authorized, the surveyor general measured the land and drew a plat for the governor's or council's approval.[7] Governor Robert Gibbes put his seal on Screven's warrant on November 3, 1710. The tract was subsequently measured and laid out:

"Two hundred Acres of Land Situate and lying in Craven County on Sampeat Creek in Winyah River butting and bounding to the East on land not yet laid out, to the South on Sampeat Creek, to the West and North on land not yet laid out." The resulting plat was returned on May 9, 1711, and Governor Gibbes registered the grant on August 6, giving "William Screven a Plantation containing Two hundred acres of Land."[8] These procedures and the sheer volume of transactions gave rise to land disputes. Frequently the process of land acquisition was never fully complete, but generally a warrant and plat were sufficient evidence to prove ownership.[9]

Shortly after Screven acquired his first land grant in Craven County, he and his family were involved in a transaction that later became the center of a disagreement regarding the very origins of Georgetown, South Carolina. John Abraham Motte was an energetic land agent and developer in Craven County. Screven had encountered Motte as early as 1709, when he purchased one hundred acres of Motte's personal property.[10] Motte, a Huguenot, had been living on the British island of Antigua, where he met John Perrie (also spelled Perry). The latter hailed from Ireland and was very successful as a planter in the islands. A member of the Council for Antigua and provost marshall general of the Leeward Islands, Perrie had recently been awarded a large land grant in South Carolina from the lords proprietors.[11] On September 23, 1704, Perrie commissioned Motte to develop his new property.[12] Motte arrived on the ship *Success,* bringing with him twenty-five African slaves and ample provisions for an extended stay, amounting to an investment of £2,218 on Perrie's part. Motte was to work ten years, develop Perrie's plantations, and keep half the profits. It also appears from later records that Perrie agreed to pay Motte £4,000 for his services. By September 15, 1705, Motte had surveyed and laid out six tracts of land, three of which were designated for Perrie's siblings—Edward Perrie and Elizabeth Elliot. John Perrie's holdings comprised eight hundred acres located between "Sampeet Creek" and "Weenea River." Altogether, John, Edward, and Elizabeth controlled 3,300 contiguous acres in and around present-day Georgetown.[13]

Motte's attempt to carve out plantations in this primitive environment does not seem to have gone well. He, like most early settlers, was probably heavily in debt, short of cash, and, no doubt, eager to make a deal. In late 1710 he offered all the Perries' Winyah holdings to Screven. On December 1 and 2 the parties signed two contracts. In the first indenture Motte agreed to sell 2,500 acres to Screven for £250. Screven paid an initial £100, and Motte was to deliver a clear title from Edward Perrie and Elizabeth Elliot within six months. The most interesting aspect of the deal is the extent of the commitments Motte made to Screven. He vowed that should he fail to procure the proper deeds of conveyance, he would refund Screven's £100 and give him a long-term lease on his personal property in Charleston, which included a lot, a house, and other buildings. He meant long-term—a thousand years—and Screven and his heirs were obliged to pay "the yearly rent of one Pepper Corn if the same should be Lawfully Demanded."[14] On the following day Motte contracted to sell to John Perrie's three plantations totaling eight hundred acres. Here again, Screven pledged £250 and provided £100 as a down payment. In this case Motte had twelve months to deliver a good title, and he offered another thousand-year lease, this time to his property in Berkeley County. Screven also paid £50 for "all the Horses, Cattle, Sheep, Hogs and all the Plantation Tools" identified as Motte's property. Motte took the contracts to Charleston in May of 1711, where they were duly witnessed, sealed, delivered, and registered by the hand of Chief Justice Nicholas Trott.[15]

The paper trail disappears at this point. Shortly after closing the deal with Screven, Motte died. Just over three months before making the offers to Screven, Motte had written a simple will, noting that he was "sick and weak in body" and leaving all his possessions and property to his wife and two daughters.[16] To further confuse matters John Perrie had left Antigua for England and was doubtless unaware of Motte's dealings. Motte was certainly ignorant of events in England, where Perrie had consolidated his holdings with those of Edward Perrie and Elizabeth Elliot.[17] Under these conditions the contracts failed. Motte never delivered the official titles, and Screven never received his thousand-year leases or any other settlement.

After Motte's death his family was able to receive some satisfaction from Perrie. In 1712 Isaac Motte sued on behalf of John Abraham Motte's estate, claiming he was never paid the agreed four thousand pounds. The courts held Perrie liable and ordered that some of his South Carolina goods and chattel, not specified, be seized, and Motte's heirs received numerous slaves, tools, and livestock. These legal processes involved no transfer of real estate, and, as far as Perrie in England knew, he still owned the 3,300 acres.[18] At Winyah, Screven was busy cultivating those same acres. He built a house on the Sampit, ran his plantations, raised his children, and tended to his Baptist flock until his death on October 10, 1713.[19]

William Screven was an enormously energetic individual, and in the fifty-eight years since he had been called a "gifted brethren" in his native homeland, he had toiled tirelessly as a Baptist minister. He was dynamic, aggressive, and a perpetual thorn in the side of his adversaries. Another monument to Screven's memory is the enduring Baptist presence in Georgetown. It is from his January 13, 1710, grant of two hundred acres in Winyah, that the First Baptist Church of Georgetown celebrates its origin.

Given the many moves and misfortunes he endured, little of Screven's original writings have survived. Published after his death, one of his last letters was addressed to the Baptists of Charleston and may well have served as his final sermon. It is entitled "An Ornament for Church Members," and a portion of it reads, "And now for a close of all, (my dear brethren and sisters whom God hath made me, poor unworthy me, an instrument of gathering and settling in the faith and order to the Gospel). My request is, that you, as speedily as possible, supply yourselves with an able and faithful minister. Be sure you take care that the person be orthodox in the faith and of blameless life, and does own the confessions put forth by our brethren in London in 1689 etc."[20] Screven's death reverberated throughout the colonial Baptist community, and his legacy as the founding father of Baptists in the South would be remembered through the centuries.

When Screven died in 1713 he left all his belongings to his wife, Bridgett, who died on June 29, 1717. Neither William's nor Bridgett's wills has survived, but abstracts of land titles from the 1730s, called memorials, trace the ownership back through Bridgett to William.[21] According to a 1732 memorial, Bridgett willed 1,550 acres or "half of the land and plantation where she then dwelt at Winyah" to her son Elisha.[22] Elisha, the youngest of thirteen children, was just reaching manhood when his mother died, and he was destined to play a role in developing the area. This may have been a natural impulse, as Winyah had grown in the years following his parents' death. By the end of the 1720s Charleston was very much aware of the northward settlement, and in 1729 Governor Robert Johnson informed London that he desired to have a town laid out at Winyah, along with a port of entry, because of the growing number of colonists settling there.[23]

Given the prime location of the Screven land, it is not surprising that Elisha became involved in the town's development. In 1729, perhaps on account of the governor's interest, he devised a comprehensive plan for a community of 230 lots to be called George Town, a term that identified it with the ruling monarchs of England, the Hanoverians, and the recently established Prince George Winyah Parish and George Fort.[24] Elisha described his ambitious aims: "To promote and encourage the Settlement of Winyah . . . for a Township and Common Thereunto adjoining as well as for the Defense and Security of the Inhabitants of Winyah aforesaid as for advancing the Trade and Commerce of the part of the said Province and for the Building and Erecting of Churches and Publick Places for Divine Worship and for the Building and Erecting a school for the advancement of Learning and other pious and Charitable uses."[25] The town itself was to comprise 174.5 acres, which Elisha divided into blocks along five streets running parallel to the Sampit River and seven streets leading to Front Street. Elisha designated several lots for "places of worship," including an Anglican church, a Presbyterian meeting house, and lot 228 for a "place whereon to build a Meeting House for performance of Divine Worship by those of the Persuasion commonly called Antipedo Baptists and for a place for Christian burial." A grammar school was to be built on lot 225, a court and prison on lots 149 and 150, and a house of correction on lot 229. He also designated a site on Broad Street for a market. The land between Bay Street and the low-water mark was to remain vacant, giving residents access to the water. Elisha's plan required settlers to build brick or framed houses on their lots within eighteen months of sale. Houses were to measure a minimum of twenty-two by sixteen feet and be equipped with a double chimney. Elisha also laid out an additional one hundred acres, where each owner had a "right of common" to pasture one horse and one cow, but no oxen, sheep, goats, or pigs.

Lots were to be sold for £7.10, rising to £10 after five years and then £15 after an additional seven years. If buyers failed to comply with the conditions of sale, Elisha instructed the trustees to confiscate the property and fine the purchaser twenty shillings. Funds raised from property resale were to be put aside for a pilot and pilot boat for Winyah Bay and for potential lawsuits. Elisha reserved lots 33, 34, 65, 66, 185, 186, and 189 for himself and his heirs.[26] Sales of lots were well under way in 1732, when the *South Carolina Gazette* began carrying advertisements.[27] The building of homes had begun by 1734, although many owners still resided on their plantations. A visitor remarked in February of that year that "Georgetown is a very pleasant place. . . . The town is laid out very regular, but at present there are a great many more houses than inhabitants; but do believe it will not be long ere it is thoroughly settled, it being a place that has a very good prospect for trade."[28]

By that time Elisha was putting the finishing touches on his plan, which included turning the town's affairs over to trustees. On January 15, 1734, he signed a lengthy indenture, placing the town of 274.5 acres, including the 100-acre common, under the care of George Pawley, William Swinton, and Daniel LaRoche. Attached to the indenture was a town layout signed by Swinton, the royal surveyor.[29] Another step in the legal process of transferring the property required Elisha's wife, Hannah, to renounce her dower rights. Hannah Screven was the oldest daughter of Samuel Commander, Sr. By this time she and Elisha had been married for ten years.[30] On November 30, 1734, Elisha published in the *South Carolina Gazette* that Hannah would renounce her rights, "in order to prevent great Inconveniences and Charge to all those who have purchased Lotts in George Town Winyaw." Elisha requested that buyers redeed their titles to him before a meeting scheduled for January 1735, when he would "invest the Township of George Town aforesaid in the hands of Trustees." Those who had already purchased lots would receive legal titles after Hannah renounced her dower rights. There was also concern regarding the "many Persons [who] have made Choice of Lotts in the Town aforesaid, for which they have no Titles." They were to attend a special meeting in February and purchase legal titles or forfeit the property.[31] In February 1735 Hannah appeared before John Wallis, Meredith Hughes, and other appointed commissioners to swear that she had renounced her dower rights by her own will and not under the influence of her husband.[32] In the summer of 1735 the town trustees scheduled a meeting for September 1736 to present new titles to the lot owners.[33]

Because of developing events back in England, the final session Elisha and the town trustees had carefully planned never happened. John Perrie's daughter Mary inherited the Perrie family holdings in Winyah and Christ Church Parish after her father's death. In 1728 she married John Cleland of London, a member of the King's Council, and her prenuptial agreement stipulated that her South Carolina property be sold and invested in government securities or used to purchase land in England.[34] In carrying out the requirements of the agreement, the Clelands discovered that Elisha Screven not only occupied the land at Winyah, but had designs for a town as well. The Clelands left England for Charleston, arriving by the summer of 1735. Just as Elisha and his trustees were preparing a series of announcements in the *Gazette*, a new notice appeared: "Whereas the greatest Part of George Town Winyaw Stands upon Lands formerly granted to John Perrie Esq; and now belonging to his Daughter Mary, the Wife of Mr. John Cleland of Charles Town Merchant; To prevent future Inconveniences or Complaints, all persons concerned are hereby informed, that no lawful power or Authority hath hitherto been given for the Sale or Disposal of any part of the Said Lands; whereof they are desired to take this publick Notice. By order of Mr. Cleland & his Lady, July 10, 1735."[35] This complicated legal matter took several years to resolve. The Clelands cited the original grants from the lords proprietors and insisted that Elisha and his family had unlawfully "Possessed themselves of Certain Lands Near Georgetown . . . part of the Premises which belonged to the said John Perrie." Elisha asserted that his claim was legitimate by virtue of the Limitation Act, since he and his family had resided on the property longer than seven years. Negotiations dragged on for two years until the Clelands decided to avoid the "Charges & Expenses of a Law Suit" and made an offer to the Screvens. In the final settlement the Clelands used a portion of the profit from the sale of John Perrie's other plantation, Youghall, to buy out the Screvens' "pretended" claim.[36]

Covering all the legal ramifications involved two lengthy documents signed by both parties on June 13 and 14, 1737. This was the standard "lease and release" procedure, a common practice at the time, which first made the Clelands legal tenants of the property and then, on the following day, gave them outright ownership. In exchange the Screvens gave the Clelands a one-year lease for the token rent of one peppercorn. In the second document the Screvens granted a formal release of the 3,300 acres to the Clelands in exchange for £4,000. Since Elisha had already conveyed 274.5 acres to the trustees, the contract excluded the land "lying and being with the Town and Common of George Town in the parish of Prince George Wineau . . . laid out & granted by the said Elisha Screven." The agreement also excluded two hundred acres the Screvens had sold to John Forbes.[37]

On June 30, 1737, John and Mary Cleland devised a new contract with the town trustees and lot owners on account of the "Doubts and Disputes [that] have arisen touching the validity of the Title of the said Elisha Screven." Much of Elisha's vision for Georgetown was carried out, including lots for a market, court, prison, house of correction, grammar school, Anglican church, and Baptist and Presbyterian meeting houses. The Clelands also adhered to Elisha's rule prohibiting construction between Bay Street and the low-water mark, with the exception of small storehouses. The Clelands did add eighty-eight new lots to the town plan located along Bay Street to Church Street and between Wood Street and the recently named Cleland Street, along with five lots labeled A, B, C, D, and E. Lots 202 and 203 were set aside for a "glebe" or parsonage for an Anglican minister, and the Clelands retained twelve lots for themselves and their heirs. The price of each lot increased to £18, with the provision that each purchaser construct a house within three years of sale.[38] The 100 acres Elisha had designated for a commons were returned to the Clelands, who conveyed a different 130 acres to the trustees for the same purpose.[39] Shortly thereafter, Mary Cleland began the process of renouncing her dower rights, and soon all the paperwork was completed.[40] The final notice in the *South Carolina Gazette* appeared in the second week of August 1737:

> All Persons interested in any of the Lotts in George-Town Winyaw, with the Common thereto belonging, are hereby desired to take notice, that the Deeds and other Agreements concerning the same, are now actually executed between myself, Mr. Scriven and other the principle [*sic*] Inhabitants and Possessors of the said Lotts whereby all Parties concern'd are absolutely confirm'd in their Titles, provided they pay me or my Assigns 18£ Currency for each Lott on or before the first Day of July 1738. And in the mean Time execute the Deeds and Agreements prepared for that Purpose, and lying at my House in Charlestown, and at the House of Messrs. Laroche in George Town, where they may be peres'd and executed, at any time before the Said first Day of July, after which all such

as shall neglect to execute and pay as aforesaid are utterly excluded from any Benefit of the Confirmation.[41]

The Screvens lost the land they had owned since 1710, along with Elisha's town. Questions regarding the nature and fairness of the settlement continued throughout the years. Some sided with the Clelands, refusing to recognize the Screvens' claim to Georgetown. When David Ramsay published his popular *History of South Carolina* in 1808, he noted that the land upon which George-town was founded was granted to William Screven by "mistake" and rightfully belonged to Perrie's heirs.[42] Today there are those who say Elisha's role in devel-oping and planning the town has never been properly acknowledged.

It is difficult to know how Elisha felt about the matter. Perhaps he took some satisfaction that the Clelands honored his vision for the town, and the four-thousand-pound payoff was a handsome sum of working capital. With the exception of monetary compensation, all Elisha had to show for his ef-forts in Georgetown were the seven lots he originally assigned to himself. He eventually disposed of most of his property there, selling half his town lots to the well-known South Carolina merchant-planter and statesman Christopher Gadsden on July 2, 1756, for £2,500, including lot 65, where the Screven family home stood for more than two centuries.[43] He did take particular care in pre-serving a portion of lot 66 "for and as a burying ground My Father &c. being there buried."[44] The larger part of Elisha's heritage, however, was the continua-tion of his father's ministry on the Black Mingo.

FOUR

Equality or Nothing

BLACK MINGO CREEK is the largest tributary of Black River, which flows into Winyah Bay near Georgetown. The creek earned its name from the dark brown, tealike color of its water, the result of tannin from river foliage. Presumably Mingo was the Native American word for *black*. The village of Black Mingo, later known as Willtown, was located toward the center of Prince Frederick's Parish, and it became a crossroads between the backcountry and the affluent lowcountry.[1] For merchants the area served as a well-known trading post; for planters, fertile soil and water transportation fostered indigo and naval-stores production. The flow of traffic through Black Mingo provided customers.[2] Black Mingo residents tended to associate with Dissenters rather than with the established church, and the combination of relative religious toleration and prosperity attracted many Dissenters to the region.[3] One such individual was Elisha Screven, who acquired considerable property on the Black River and the Pee Dee.[4]

The Baptists and Presbyterians clustered in the area attended Black Mingo Meeting House, located just south of the village on a branch of the creek. That structure is considered the first dissenting church in both Craven and Williamsburg Counties.[5] Georgetown Baptists lay claim to this church since Black Mingo was then part of Winyah.[6] Little is known of the congregation since none of their records survived. William Boddie, in his early-twentieth-century work *History of Williamsburg County,* identified Elisha Screven as the central figure in its construction. According to Boddie, Elisha funded the project and preached the opening sermon.[7] A few other writers also recognize Elisha as a minister and the "director of both temporal and spiritual affairs in Winyaw."[8] In the records that have survived there is no mention of Elisha having been licensed or ordained to preach, and in his will he identified himself as a planter of Prince Frederick's Parish.[9] It is undeniable, however, that Elisha had an interest in the church. Oliver Hart, one of the most well-known Baptist figures in South Carolina's history, wrote a friend in the 1790s about the Screven family: "Speaking of these People reminds me of the Visits I used to pay to Black River. There was once a hopeful Prospect of a Baptist Church being raised there."[10] In another letter he addressed the same topic: "Once there was a hopeful Prospect for a Baptist Church at Black River; old Mr. Elisha Screven was anxious for it, and offered £50 Sterling per Annum, towards supporting a Minister."[11]

It was common for different denominations, such as Presbyterians and Baptists, to unite in building a place of worship. Since the Church of England was the established church, the government did not recognize Dissenter congregations and denied them funding.[12] Still, the construction of a meeting house was very important to Dissenters, who, according to one local minister, "were content to dwell themselves in shanties, not more comfortable than potatoe cellars, while their labors were more especially given to the erection of a house of worship."[13] The Baptist historian David Benedict described these structures as "rude and unsightly" and representative of the "inconveniences of new country life."[14]

The Black Mingo Dissenters may have been more fortunate than others. Boddie depicted their church as "an excellent brick structure, forty by sixty feet . . . erected in 1726."[15] While visiting Prince Frederick Church in the late 1720s, the Reverend Thomas Morritt of the Society for the Propagation of the Gospel in Foreign Parts remarked that the Dissenters had completed their building.[16] In 1733 William Swinton purchased property adjacent to the meeting house. In his will dated 1742 he left one hundred pounds to help build a new meeting house for the Dissenters.[17] That year, William Thompson, Jr., bequeathed four acres and one hundred pounds for the same purpose.[18] Whether or not a new building was constructed is unknown.[19] In 1756 the vestry of Prince Frederick's Parish listed two meeting houses in the region—Black Mingo and the Williamsburg Presbyterian Meeting House, established in 1736.[20] As late as 1848 Dr. J. R. Witherspoon, a former resident of Williamsburg, reminisced about a church below Black Mingo called the "Brick Church," erected prior to the church at Williamsburg.[21]

Elisha and his fellow Baptists must have played a role in this church for a very short time. From the 1730s forward there are no references to any Baptist members. In 1729 Reverend Morritt reported that the Black Mingo Meeting House had a "teacher from the Bermudas."[22] John Baxter, a Presbyterian minister, preached in the church during the early part of its existence.[23] It was not until 1744 that the congregation had a permanent minister, Samuel Hunter, who was also a Presbyterian. All of the ministers who served the church from that point were Presbyterians, and the Black Mingo Meeting House and three other congregations were incorporated as the Presbytery of Charleston in 1790.[24] The Presbyterian takeover was accelerated by the migration of the Scots-Irish to the Black River in 1732. Governor Robert Johnson's Township Plan, which included a provision to give each family fifty acres of land per member in addition to a town lot, attracted settlers to Williamsburg. The Scots-Irish, who were rigid Presbyterians, eventually dominated the population.[25] By 1824 the Black Mingo congregation had dissolved.[26] Local tradition claims that the British burned the church during the War of 1812, but that has never been substantiated.[27] The brick walls remained until the end of the nineteenth century, when they were taken down and the bricks used use elsewhere, but a few bricks and graves are still discernable.[28] There would not be another Baptist church in Black Mingo until Cleland Belin, a descendant of Elisha Screven, erected the Black Mingo Baptist Church in 1843.[29]

From what can be gleaned from Elisha Screven's will and surviving land records, he and his wife Hannah had a prosperous life. They raised eight children: Joseph, Elisha, Joshua, Samuel, Elizabeth, William, Hannah, and Benjamin. They also bought and sold thousands of acres in Craven County, their land holdings at least 5,500 acres by 1757. When Elisha died his heirs received more than £2,500, numerous slaves, a good deal of household silver, various bedroom suites, and the livestock and tools from his three plantations.[30]

South Carolina Baptists before the Revolution.
Created by Isaac Dusenbury.

By the time of Elisha's death on December 3, 1757, the Baptist element in Black Mingo had diminished considerably.[31] Boddie estimated that only a dozen remained, most of them Screven descendants, and by the outbreak of the Revolution the Presbyterians comprised 95 percent of the population.[32] Charles Woodmason, the well-known Anglican itinerant preacher, attested to the animosity that had developed among Dissenter groups, particularly Presbyterians and Baptists. In 1768 he recorded in his journal that "these Sects are eternally jarring among themselves—The Presbyterians hate the Baptists . . . But (as in England) they will unite altogether—in a body to distress or injure the Church establish'd."[33] The American Revolution presented Dissenters with such an opportunity.

The critical events that led South Carolina to break ties with Great Britain began in the 1770s in the Commons House of Assembly. There a power struggle brewed as many South Carolinians came to the conclusion that their policies were fundamentally at odds with those of Great Britain. Following England's implementation of harsh trade measures, South Carolinians realized that the British oppression occurring in Boston could easily happen on their soil and close the port at Charleston, crippling the economy. When the First Continental Congress convened in Philadelphia in the fall of 1774, South Carolina established its First Provincial Congress, later the General Assembly, to approve measures set forth by the Continental Congress. The Provincial Congress joined in the general boycott of British goods, permitted the seizure of weapons, issued currency, raised troops, and created the Council of Safety. After the battles of Lexington and Concord, however, it became apparent that a more aggressive course of action was necessary. If victory was to be achieved, South Carolina needed more men—including those in the Dissenter-ridden backcountry.[34]

Oliver Hart played an important role in leading the Baptists during the Revolution. A native of Pennsylvania and self-educated, Hart was licensed to preach by the Philadelphia Association in 1746 before becoming pastor of the First Baptist Church of Charleston in 1750, a position he held for thirty years. Hart was also the driving force in establishing the Charleston Baptist Association in 1751.[35] South Carolina officials recognized Hart's influence on Dissenters and requested that he serve on a three-member team to travel throughout the backcountry on behalf of the patriot cause. William Tennent, pastor of the Independent Church in Charleston, and William Henry Drayton, chairman of the Secret Committee in charge of gathering arms and ammunition, were the other two members.[36]

For fifty-nine days Hart, Tennent, and Drayton spoke wherever a crowd gathered. The reaction was mixed. While they experienced great success at

Tyger River and Lawson's Fork and many there agreed to join the Nonimportation Association, other stops proved challenging.[37] Hart wrote in his journal on August 12, "Upon the Whole there appears but little Reason, as yet, to hope that these People will be brought to have a suitable Regard to ye interest of America."[38] Despite initial difficulties, ultimately backcountry Dissenters proved to be an asset in winning the American Revolution.[39]

Enlisting in the campaign for political and economic liberty sparked Dissenter interest in achieving religious freedom and disestablishing the Anglican Church. On April 27, 1776, Dissenters held a meeting at the Baptist church in the High Hills of Santee to choose a representative to send to the General Assembly. Elhanan Winchester, pastor of the Welsh Neck Baptist Church, had proposed the interdenominational gathering, hoping the result would "obtain our liberties, and freedom from religious tyranny or ecclesiastical oppressions."[40] There, at one of the most important events in South Carolina's religious history, Dissenters put aside their differences and selected the Reverend William Tennent to lobby for equality in the new state constitution.[41]

On January 11, 1777, Tennent appeared before the General Assembly with a petition requesting "that there never shall be any Establishment of any one religious Denomination or Sect of Protestant Christians in the State by way of preference to another."[42] During Tennent's fiery speech he chastised lawmakers for allowing the Anglican Church to put "its hand into the pocket of nine denominations . . . to bestow upon one & support its dignity." Tennent observed that there were only twenty Anglican churches in South Carolina in comparison to seventy-nine Dissenter congregations, and he cautioned that "of all tyranny, religious tyranny is the worst, & men of true sentiment, will scorn civil, where they cannot enjoy religious liberty." Tennent demanded, "Let us all have equal privileges or nothing. Equality or Nothing!"[43] With the ongoing war with Great Britain (the Battle of Fort Moultrie occurred on June 28, 1776, shortly before the Declaration of Independence), some members were reluctant to add disestablishment to their already long list of political and economic demands. Despite protests, disestablishment passed unanimously.[44]

Before the new constitution became law, it was printed and circulated throughout the state for a year. On February 3, 1777, the Charleston Baptist Association held its annual meeting, and Elhanan Winchester boasted in the circular letter to members: "We heartily congratulate you on the Prospect of obtaining universal Religious Liberty in this State; an Event which must cause every generous Mind to rejoice."[45] Shortly thereafter, Oliver Hart wrote Richard Furman, at that time pastor of the High Hills Baptist Church, rejoicing in the "hopeful Prospect that we shall obtain religious Liberty, in its full Extent, in this State." Hart knew, however, that until the constitution was officially adopted, religious equality hung in the balance. In the same letter he warned that "it cannot fail if the Dissenters will be careful to attend the next Session of Assembly."[46] The General Assembly kept its word, and on March 19, 1778, the first permanent constitution guaranteed that no one church or religion would ever be given preference over another.[47]

The Dissenters may have won their battle in the General Assembly, but the Revolution was far from over. The British captured Charleston in the spring of 1780, and Lord Cornwallis soon after began his conquest of the state. According to Leah Townsend, of the 1,500 Baptist men eligible for military service, about 600 saw combat or donated supplies.[48] Her figures are probably accurate given the significant number of Baptist churches established in South Carolina by the Revolution. Morgan Edwards claimed that in 1772 there were twenty-four Baptist churches and forty-nine meeting houses in the province.[49] The two best-known South Carolina Baptists of the Revolution were undeniably Oliver Hart and Richard Furman. On March 30, 1776, Hart and Elhanan Winchester wrote Henry Laurens, on behalf of the Baptist congregations in South Carolina, to commend him for his recent appointment as vice president of the state and to offer their support, saying, "We hope to see hunted Liberty sit Regent on the Throne, and flourish more than ever, under the Administration of such worthy Patriots."[50] Hart and his family left Charleston in 1775 for Euhaw after a threatened attack by the British. From then on the prospect of imminent invasion kept him on the move until he escaped to Hopewell, New Jersey, in 1780 where he remained until his death in 1795.[51]

Richard Furman took Hart's place as head pastor of the First Baptist Church of Charleston. Born in New York, he spent the majority of his life in South Carolina, and, like Hart, was self-educated. Although raised in the Anglican Church, Furman converted to the Baptist faith in 1771 and was ordained three years later. He volunteered to fight in the Revolution, but he, too, was asked by the government to persuade Loyalists to join the Patriot cause. Furman experienced such great success that Cornwallis vowed to "make an example of so notorious a rebel" and is said to have offered a one-thousand-pound reward for his arrest.[52] This bounty was cause for concern, especially since Furman resided only twenty miles from Cornwallis's headquarters. He and his family moved to North Carolina near the Virginia line until hostilities waned in 1782. Upon his return Furman resumed his pastoral duties and was chosen as a delegate to the state constitutional convention in 1790.[53]

Hart and Furman were not the only Baptist preachers whose ministries suffered disruption during the Revolution. Evan Pugh, pastor of the Baptist church at Cashaway, surrendered to the British after Loyalists plundered his home. The Reverend Joseph Cook, from the Euhaw Baptist Church, lost all of his possessions while attempting to escape before the British advancement. The Reverend Joseph Reese left his congregation at Congaree and sought shelter in Fairforest.[54] Edmund Botsford was pastor of the New Savannah Baptist Church at the start of the Revolution. When the British captured Savannah in 1778 Botsford and his family moved to South Carolina; however, conditions were so dire he fled the state the following year.[55]

South Carolina was in shambles after the Revolution. Houses and farms had been looted and burned, fields abandoned, and thousands of slaves escaped or were taken by the British. The economy was devastated. The state had spent millions on the war effort, rice was in jeopardy after several bad harvests, and the demand for indigo was rapidly declining.[56] Georgetown, in particular, faced formidable losses. George C. Rogers, Jr., in his well-known *History of Georgetown County,* deemed the area, "the heart of militancy in the State," and from July 1780 to May 1781 British troops occupied Georgetown.[57] Many of Francis Marion's skirmishes took place in the vicinity, and much of the town was destroyed. Francisco de Miranda, having recently arrived in Georgetown in 1783, observed that "the population appears to be decent and there are some very good houses, although some of these are burnt and others completely in ruins as a result of the last war."[58] Five years later John Martin reported to his son in England that during the war "the Town was almost all Burnt by the British Troops."[59]

Churches in Georgetown paid a heavy price. One author noted that the British major James Wemyss had "burned a path through the heart of Georgetown District, destroying plantations and Presbyterian churches alike, the latter of which he deemed 'sedition shops.'"[60] One meeting house in Georgetown, shared by Baptists, Presbyterians, and Independents, was "partly pulled down during the war and rendered totally unfit for the purpose for which it was intended."[61] In the coming decades three men would be left with the task of revival: William Cuttino, John Waldo, and Edmund Botsford.

FIVE

A Work of Grace

AFTER THE REVOLUTION, Baptists and other denominations enjoyed the religious equality for which Oliver Hart and his fellow patriots had fought so fiercely. As Richard Furman wrote to a friend in England in 1791, "Our Liberty religious as well as civil is unrestrained, and those who have Ability and Worth of every Denomination are eligible to Places of civil Trust."[1] The difficulty in immediately exercising this freedom, however, was the sad state of affairs in Georgetown and elsewhere following the war. The effort to reorganize and rebuild churches was part of the long struggle to recovery. The British had turned Prince George Winyah Episcopal Church into a stable, which they later burned. One townsman recalled that the roof had been replaced and the church had "a Few Temperary Seats, but not half Finish'd."[2]

The brick meeting house used by Baptists, Presbyterians, and Independents was never completely rebuilt. The date of its founding is unknown, but it was probably constructed sometime in 1769 or shortly thereafter. The lot had been purchased and the building erected by subscription, a popular form of fundraising at the time. William Cuttino, Christopher Taylor, and Thomas Handlin owned the property, but the exact location remains a mystery.[3] The logical site for the meeting house was the end of Meeting Street at the water's edge. Elisha Screven's plan for Georgetown did not include such a street, but it appears in a 1797 map. Contemporary accounts place the church at the "very extremity of the Town," where it was subject to frequent flooding.[4] An attempt to repair the building was made after the war, but the amount of money raised was insufficient due to the funds being "misapplied" by one of the members. Nevertheless, William Cuttino began renovations.[5]

Cuttino was a descendant of an early Huguenot family, the Cothonneaus, who fled France shortly after the revocation of the Edict of Nantes, most of them immigrating to New York. Jérémie Cotonneau (Cothonneau) a cooper, arrived in South Carolina in 1687 with his wife and two children, Germain and Pierre. Pierre acquired a substantial amount of land in both Craven and Berkeley Counties and became a successful planter. His son, Jeremiah Cuttino, a gunsmith and member of the Georgetown Library Society, married Ann Judith

Bossard. William Cuttino, born November 30, 1747, was their only surviving child, and he came into possession of most of the land originally developed by his grandfather. William married Mary Elizabeth Coon about 1770. They had ten children, three of whom died in infancy. William is described in official documents as a "master carpenter," and two of the homes he built on Prince Street still stand.[6]

Baptized by Hart in Charleston in 1767, Cuttino moved to Georgetown two years later. During Hart's flight from the state after the fall of Charleston, he passed through Georgetown, stopping for a time with the Cuttino family. Hart recorded in his journal on April 28, 1780: "Rode to George Town and put up at Mr. William Cuttino & who with his wife and her mother received me with the greatest Cordiality and Esteem."[7] Cuttino was probably the driving force in establishing the brick meeting house. It is also likely that his energy and devotion led the small group of Baptists in Georgetown to constitute themselves permanently.

Richard Furman, Hart's successor as the principal Baptist leader of the state, took a special interest in Georgetown. At Cuttino's request, Furman and other Baptist ministers, including Edmund Botsford, visited frequently. Furman was a particular favorite of the congregation, and he often spent several weeks a year ministering there.[8] On June 29, 1788, Furman wrote his sister concerning the "great Door opened for preaching the Gospel in George Town, and the Solicitation for my visiting them urgent." Furman also remarked that he "opened the new Place of Worship while there," referring to the latest renovations by Cuttino.[9] In July, Furman sent this report to Hart in New Jersey:

> It may not be improper, however, to mention that there seems to be a Work of Grace begun in Georgetown, I have been twice there this spring; at the last Visit I baptized Mrs. Cuttino and her oldest Son, and administered the Lord's Supper to Twelve Communicants; the Administration of the Ordinances carried great Conviction, and was attended to with much Solemnity. I received Six more Applications for Baptism before I left the Place, together with many Requests to visit them again; and as they have now a New Place of Worship in tolerable Order, I am not without Hopes God is about to raise up a Church in that Place.[10]

Hart responded that he was "pleased to hear of the Addition to your Church, and that Religion wears so favorable an Aspect at George Town," and he felt encouraged that "Jesus Christ will ere long have a baptized Church there."[11] In the coming years Furman continued to speak of the "favorable Appearances in George Town" and about the increasing congregation.[12] Three years later, in 1791, Furman informed Samuel Pearce in London that in "George Town a

Seaport there is a Branch of the Church under my Care which will probably be soon Constituted. A Work of Grace has prevailed there for some years and the Prospect is still favorable."[13]

By the early 1790s Furman and Cuttino were actively seeking a pastor for Georgetown. They first approached Henry Smalley, a graduate of the College of New Jersey (now Princeton University) who had been licensed to preach by the Piscataway Maine Baptist Church. At the time Smalley was acting as a supply pastor to the Cohansey Baptist Church of New Jersey and, according to Hart, was "an agreeable, promising young Man" with "an Inclination to go to the southard."[14] Smalley declined Hart's offer since Georgetown was "reputed a sickly Country" and instead accepted a position as the full-time pastor of the Cohansey church, where he remained until his death in 1839.[15] Colonel Thomas Screven, William Screven's great-grandson and trustee of the First Baptist Church of Charleston, was also approached, but he declined "on account of the Character it bears for being sickly." Furman considered the church's preference for a "young Man without a Family" to be an obstacle in their efforts to find a pastor, and he "sent a Message to Mr. Cuttino on the Subject requesting his Sentiments on it."[16]

In the end Hart and Furman turned to John Waldo, a graduate of Rhode Island College (now Brown University) who had recently been licensed to preach. Furman had written James Manning, president of the college, to inquire after a pastor for Georgetown. Manning responded in February 1791 that Waldo was the "only graduate, of our Denomination, who promised for the Ministry Soon," and he assured Furman that Waldo was a "worthy young man, of solid parts, indubitable piety, and an amiable Character, and a tolerable good Scholar." Manning, however, was uncertain that "his qualifications would answer for Georgetown, should he listen to their invitation." He advised Furman that Waldo had "a degree of hesitancy in his speech," which he feared would "militate with his popularity as a preacher." He also warned that "his manners are plain, & carry in them a degree of that stiffness." Nevertheless, Manning suggested that if Waldo chose to make a southern tour, he stop in Georgetown and "let the people see & hear for themselves, as I may venture to assure them, I presume, that they will see & hear the worst of him at the first."[17]

In the fall of 1792 Furman received word that Waldo intended to accept his offer at Georgetown. That October, Furman commented in a letter to his sister, "We now expect a Minister for George Town: Mr. Waldo recommended by Dr. Manning has informed me by letter, he intends being out in November."[18] Waldo arrived in Charleston from New York shortly thereafter and began his trial period as a preacher. Upon hearing Waldo's first sermon, Furman remarked: "Mr. Waldo is arrived for George Town. He seems to be a sober

Good man; but I fear will not altogether answer our Hope as a Preacher, his delivery is but indifferent."[19] Waldo left Charleston for Georgetown that December and reported to Furman: "I feel some more encouragement than I did when I left home that I may be accepted with this people. But I feel a need of divine support & desire the prayers of my christian friends."[20]

Despite Waldo's efforts he was not well received by the congregation, and he notified Botsford concerning the church's attitude toward him. Botsford described the contents of this letter to Furman in April 1793: "I received a line from Mr. Waldo who informed me of the sentiments of the Church respecting himself, he seems much at a loss what to do."[21] In May, Hart wrote Furman to inquire about the recent events in Georgetown: "Should be glad to know why the Preaching of Mr. Waldo did not suit the George Town People, and whether He has yet left them? I never saw that Gentlemen, but am apprehensive He is an Hopkintonion; or, what we call a New Divinity Man."[22] The New Divinity, or Hopkinsianism named for Samuel Hopkins, was an interpretation of Calvinism initiated by Jonathan Edwards that was very popular in New England during the eighteenth century. Followers of the New Divinity shifted toward the radical side of Calvinism, believing that God predestined some to eternal damnation and that all should be willing to be damned. Hopkins also preached the end of time, predicting Armageddon to occur around the beginning of the twenty-first century.[23] Hart denounced these doctrines and was pleased that the Baptists in Georgetown rejected Waldo as their pastor: "I must conclude that Mr. Waldo has imbibed the New Divinity System. . . . Am glad the Geo. Town People have been better taught than to embrace such Sentiments or to approve of such Preaching."[24] By September, Waldo had resigned, and Furman informed Hart that Waldo was "not employed as a Preacher" but had opened a Latin school where he "has very good Success in that Line, and gives great Satisfaction."[25] Waldo remained in Georgetown as an active member of the church.

Waldo's resignation left Furman and Cuttino with the task of finding another pastor. In 1793 Furman wrote John Rippon, a prominent Baptist minister in England, to request aid and advice. Rippon responded: "Your inquiry, concerning a Baptist minister for Georgetown, arrived at a time when one of our junior ministers is disposed to cross the Atlantic, and you have . . . described him in every respect except his name." The man to whom Rippon referred was William Staughton, a graduate of Bristol Baptist College and a licensed pastor of the Birmingham church. Rippon assured Furman that Staughton was "above par" and that he would "answer to the character he has hitherto borne, of an unblameable man, and an acceptable, evangelical, and popular minister of our Lord Jesus Christ."[26] The Reverend John Hinton of Oxford described

Staughton as "a young man of strict integrity, ardent piety, and of ministerial abilities, highly acceptable in England" and claimed his labors were "highly pleasing, even to the last Sabbath of his stay in England, to whom, also, his design in coming to America is fully known, and his character fully approved."[27] Thomas Dunscombe, also of Oxford, said of Staughton: "His piety is sterling, his dispositions amiable, his education good, his manners pleasing, his preaching talents popular and of the superior kind, and he has moreover an inclination to go to America."[28] Staughton accepted Furman's offer and set sail for Charleston in 1793.

The young preacher left England for reasons other than seeking a ministerial position abroad. Accompanying him on his voyage was Maria Hanson, a recent divorcée. When Furman requested that Staughton's church properly dismiss him, members refused because they viewed Staughton's relationship with Hanson in an "adulterous light." The Reverend Samuel Pearce explained: "I must do our People the justice to Say that they appeared quite free from all prejudice or disaffection towards Mr. S. yet they said they could not accede."[29] Before sending Staughton to Georgetown, Furman married Staughton to Hanson and wrote John Waldo to explain the situation. Although Waldo was no longer serving as pastor, he continued to work closely with Furman and Cuttino. Waldo shared the letter with key members of the congregation, and they agreed to "Mr. Staughton's making us a visit & giving us an opportunity of having a trial of his gifts among us." They considered Staughton's personal circumstances "unfortunate . . . to none more so than himself and lady."[30]

Staughton's reputation as a minister made him very appealing to the Charleston Baptists, many of whom strongly insisted he stay there as associate pastor. The congregation's desire to keep Staughton caused a temporary schism in the church that deeply troubled Furman. John Hinton wrote Furman in 1794 regarding this situation: "The conduct of some of our friends appears to have been highly incautious. Charleston is a tempting situation [and] popularity is enchanting."[31] Furman worried the debate in Charleston would be an "obstacle" to Staughton's going to Georgetown. While Staughton was in Georgetown on his trial visit, Furman confided to his mother: "It is not yet known how it may determine; but it seems pretty certain we are at the Eve of an eventful period."[32]

The question of Staughton's position was resolved in Georgetown's favor. When Waldo received word that Staughton had accepted the offer, he wrote Furman: "I am truly pleased with the prospect of Mr. Staughton's settling with us in the ministry & hope God may render him a blessing in the place. The circumstances of the place are very favorable at present for an able & faithful minister to Settle with us."[33] Staughton was quite popular in Georgetown, and as one author noted, "all classes and professions in the community contributed to his support."[34] Staughton too was pleased with his new congregation, writing to a friend: "Our reception was equal to our expectations, and the conduct of the friends, since our arrival, evinces fully their solicitude to contribute to our happiness."[35] Staughton wasted no time, and within a year of his move to Georgetown he led the church in joining the Charleston Baptist Association. According to the association minutes of 1794, Georgetown "originated from the Charleston church, and was constituted in June last." Staughton and Cuttino represented the congregation, then comprising thirty-six members, at the association meeting that November.[36]

Staughton's tenure in Georgetown lasted only seventeen months. He and his wife deemed the coastal climate unhealthy, and they were opposed to slavery. The Georgetown church pleaded with him to stay and offered to double his salary, but he declined.[37] Edmund Botsford was in the lowcountry on the eve of Staughton's departure in 1795 and recorded his observations in a letter to Furman: "Religion at a low ebb, as is the case everywhere in my knowledge. Mr. Staughton intends to remove, so that our friends will probably be left destitute, I am sorry for them as they are a worthy People." Botsford noted that the church had been experiencing trials and that Staughton was increasingly discontent: "I am truly sorry to perceive the distance which is kept up between the Minister & the people. . . . What a pitty that so amiable a Man, such a good preacher, such an agreeable companion which everyone allows Mr. S. to be, should be so unhappy."[38] Staughton moved to New York in 1795, taking with him a letter of recommendation from Richard Furman, who said of him that "Mr. Staughton's conduct has justified the recommendations given him by his European friends, and procured him the love and respect of his acquaintances in general, who esteem him as a man of piety, and a gospel minister of eminent abilities."[39]

Staughton went on to become one of the best-known and respected Baptist ministers of his day. He served as pastor of the First Baptist Church of Philadelphia and the Sansom Street Baptist Church, in addition to being chosen the first president of Columbian College (now George Washington University).[40] The Reverend Samuel Lynd, Staughton's early biographer, noted that throughout Staughton's life he remembered the kindness displayed to him by the Georgetown congregation and townspeople: "Their liberal contributions for his comfort, received from the church and the inhabitants, were recollected through life, by him, with the most sincere and lively gratitude."[41]

Staughton's resignation did not discourage Furman and Waldo's determination to find a permanent minister for Georgetown. Waldo assumed temporary pastoral responsibilities while he and Furman searched for a replacement.

In the meantime Waldo remained in close contact with Furman and was active in the Charleston Baptist Association, serving as clerk to the association and secretary to the general committee in 1795. Church membership remained steady at thirty-six, and the congregation continued to make its annual contribution to the association.[42]

At the end of a year-long search Furman turned to Edmund Botsford, a stalwart among South Carolina Baptist preachers and pastor of the Welsh Neck Baptist Church in the Cheraws, a large area up the Pee Dee River from Georgetown. Botsford had followed Georgetown closely through the years and was quite familiar with Furman, Waldo, and Staughton. A close friend since the war, Furman kept him abreast of the latest church news, including that of Georgetown.[43] When Furman first approached Botsford about taking on the pastorate at Georgetown, Botsford declined, responding that "I am more & more satisfied my work is done in this place and the Lord only knows how I am to be disposed of; . . . I am however really sorry that I cannot oblige my dear friend, for such I esteem Brother Furman. . . . I do not feel how I can leave them."[44] It took a plea from William Cuttino to convince Botsford to make the move. On July 18, 1796, Botsford wrote Furman: "In consequence of a letter from Mr. Cuttino I informed him of the resolution I had taken of leaving this place & the steps I had taken relative to it."[45] The official appointment came three months later: "I had acquainted my friends of my intention to leave the Cheraws, & in question to a letter of theirs, had given them some intimations they might expect me to George Town while I was in Town the C[hurch] gave me a call, & it appeared to me to be the voice of the Town in general for me to settle there, I have therefore concluded to go."[46]

With twenty-five years in the field, Botsford was already an established preacher. Born in England on November 1, 1745, he grew up in poverty and was orphaned at age seven. As a young man he enlisted in the British army during the Seven Years' War. Leaving England for Charleston on November 18, 1765, Botsford underwent a conversion experience while at sea. In Charleston a friend suggested he seek the spiritual guidance of Oliver Hart. In his memoirs Botsford reminisced about this occurrence: "This was the best news I had heard in America, for I had entertained the notion, that if I could hear the gospel, there would be a possibility of my being saved."[47] That August, Botsford visited the First Baptist Church of Charleston, and on March 13, 1767, he was baptized by Hart and joined the church. Botsford considered Hart to be a father figure and thought "more of Mr. Hart, the Minister, than any person in the world." Botsford often referred to him as Father Hart.[48]

Botsford felt called to the ministry, and after being freed from a harsh apprenticeship, he committed himself to that career. Hart encouraged Botsford to begin by seeking an education, and for two years he studied under Hart and David Williams. Botsford received financial support from the Religious Society of Charleston, instituted by Hart to educate prospective Baptist ministers. When he completed his studies, Botsford was licensed to preach in February 1771, and he subsequently moved to Euhaw to assist Francis Pelot. Another branch of the church was located at Tuckasee King, Georgia, outside Savannah. The congregation was without a minister and requested Botsford's services for one year.[49] The Charleston church was so impressed with Botsford that Hart ordained him on March 14, 1773.[50]

When the British took Savannah in the spring of 1779, Botsford fled with his family to South Carolina, where they found shelter with Arthur Simkins near Edgefield, and Botsford accepted a position as chaplain for General Andrew Williamson's brigade. While Botsford was serving in the military, the Welsh Neck congregation asked him to be their supply pastor.[51] His time at Welsh Neck was cut short when the British seized Charleston in 1780, forcing him to leave his family and escape, with Hart, to the north. Botsford was later reunited with his wife and children, and the family remained in Virginia until Charleston's liberation in December 1782. Upon his return to South Carolina, he commented: "The war had made sad havoc on friends and property; and as for religion, it was almost forgotten."[52] Botsford remained at Welsh Neck until he accepted the call from Georgetown in 1796.[53]

Botsford faced many difficulties in Georgetown—a small flock and an inadequate place of worship. In 1797 he lamented: "I perceive little signs of the increase of the church."[54] From the records it appears that Botsford was correct. From 1796 to 1800 there were few additions to the congregation.[55] Church finances, however, remained fairly stable. In 1798 Botsford wrote to Furman: "Our Church have this year made out pretty well in payment."[56] Most years the church was able to maintain its annual donation to the Charleston Association.[57]

Another tribute to the church's progress was its legal incorporation in 1801. The previous year, the congregation had submitted a petition to the General Assembly requesting incorporation as the Antipado-Baptist Church of the Town of George Town, with the right to "have, hold, prosper and enjoy such privileges and powers as have been heretofore granted to religious Societies of other Sects and Denominations."[58] The petition was signed by Edmund Botsford, William Cuttino, Sr., John Waldo, Ezra Pugh, Jeremiah Cuttino, John Evans, William H. Lide, William Cuttino, Jr., Savage Smith, William Grant, Thomas Blackwell, Michael Blackwell, James Mackray, William B. Johnson, and William Murray.[59] On November 29, 1800, the committee reported that "the prayer thereof should be granted and that leave be given to bring in a bill for that purpose."[60]

The Antipedo Baptist Church in Georgetown, built in 1845.
This photograph was taken about 1900 shortly before the church was
sold and torn down. Courtesy of Georgetown County Library.

For reasons that remain unclear, the congregation resubmitted the petition in 1801. Neither Thomas Blackwell nor Ezra Pugh signed the second petition, but new names appeared: John Bossard, Cornelius DuPre, John Davis,
Samuel Blackwell, James Lane, John P. Dunnan, William Dunnan, and William Walker.[61] On November 27 the committee once again gave the petition
its stamp of approval.[62] On December 19 the act of incorporation passed both
houses of the General Assembly, making the church "a body corporate, in deed
and in law." The act, with a life of ten years, gave authority to have "perpetual
succession of officers and members, and a common seal, with power to change,
alter and make new the same."[63]

Incorporation was a significant achievement for the church, but Botsford's top priority was building a place of worship. As early as 1792, Furman began making arrangements for a new facility. That year he wrote Hart about a Mr. Hammit who possessed "great Popularity in Charleston and in Building a Place of Worship here 78 by 52" and had "formed his Plan for building another in George Town."[64] Hammit visited Georgetown frequently, but in 1798 the congregation was still meeting in the old and unfinished brick church, which had almost completely deteriorated.[65] In July, Botsford lamented: "We have had such heavy rains which entirely deprived us of our place of worship One Lords day & with difficulty a few of us could attend, two or three. The house was entirely surrounded with water; we have now drained it off."[66] Botsford described the conditions to Furman as "dangerous to health to attend worship in it, owing to the moist situation." He recalled that "in the wett season the last summer it was so compleatley surrounded with water we could not attend worship in it. We cannot conveniently bury our dead there." In 1798 Botsford began making an effort to build on the church's lot on Church Street, originally designated for that purpose by Elisha Screven. Botsford was pleased that William Cuttino appeared to "take with it" and was confident that he would "contribute largely toward it." The likelihood of finishing the project amid difficult economic times, however, was slim, and Botsford admitted, "How it will be accomplished I cannot tell."[67]

On February 25, 1800, members of the church subscribed funds for the "purpose of erecting [a] Baptist Meeting house on the lot known in the plan of Georgetown No. 228," while promising to pay William Cuttino by the following February.[68] Progress was slow but steady, and in early 1802 Botsford reported that "framing" was under way.[69] Setbacks occurred, and at times Botsford grew disheartened, confiding to a friend later that year that "I much question if I shall live to preach in that church."[70] In 1803 Botsford informed Furman that "our place of worship is now raising."[71] By the following year Cuttino's construction was advanced sufficiently to allow the congregation to begin holding worship. In 1805 the doors were in place and the pews painted. Benjamin Hanks of Connecticut contracted to "supply such a bell as may be wanted at 36 Cents per pound."[72] The Baptist historian David Benedict, who visited Georgetown during Botsford's pastorate, recorded this description of the building: "This church has a handsome and commodious wooden meeting-house, which was well finished in 1804. It stands on a lot of one acre. . . . This house, which is about 60 feet long, is situated on a delightful eminence, directly opposite the market-house, and commands a view of the whole town from the front of it, and of very extensive rice fields from its rear."[73]

The church had come a long way in the decades leading to the construction of the new chapel and its incorporation as the Antipedo Baptist Church. Through the efforts of strong leaders—William Cuttino, Richard Furman, John Waldo, Savage Smith, Edmund Botsford, and others—the congregation had survived the war and had started to rebuild. The church was unequipped, however, to face the challenges of the next thirty years. With a numerically small white membership, Botsford would face many battles alone, having only the advice of his distant friends and fellow ministers to guide him. He would never see an increase of white individuals attending service, and that number would steadily decline during his tenure at Georgetown. Instead, Botsford reached out to the body of people making up the vast majority of his congregation—slaves.

SIX

The Antipedo Baptist Church

IN THE TWENTY YEARS since the Revolution, the Antipedo Baptist Church of Georgetown had achieved several significant goals. The active congregation had found a full-time minister in Edmund Botsford, a man widely recognized in the Baptist community. Another landmark in the church's history was its incorporation, which coincided with the construction of a new chapel at a time when no other denomination in Georgetown, save the Episcopalians, had their own place of worship. Francis Asbury, the founder of American Methodism, visited Georgetown frequently, posting observations in his journal. In January 1804 he wrote, "The Baptists have built an elegant church, planned for a steeple and organ: they take the rich; and the commonality and the slaves fall to us." Asbury was unimpressed with Georgetown in general and deemed it "a poor place for religion." He complained, "I feel the want of religion here: indeed, the gross immoralities of the place are obvious to every passenger in the street."[1]

Great thought and preparation went into the design of Baptist chapels. Baptists were very cautious in the construction of their edifices since anything elaborate was associated with the Anglican Church. David Benedict, who frequented Georgetown, was concerned about this trend: "The danger at present is, that at some points they may go to the other extreme, and go as much too far in future, in splendor and profuseness, as they did of old in parsimony and plainness."[2] Asbury's laudatory comments were probably unfounded given the church's limited budget and Botsford's dedication to the "plain simple stile of many of the dissenting congregations, who are more solicitous for the power of religion, than for outward show & form." True to Baptist tradition, Botsford disliked anything resembling Anglicanism, particularly the "pompous vestments of the clergy, & the splendour of their places of worship."[3]

We know little of the Baptists' handsome and commodious wooden meeting house, but from Botsford's manuscripts and the records of surrounding churches we get a glimpse of the chapel's interior. Most meeting houses constructed during the 1800s in South Carolina had two doors with two aisles leading toward the pulpit.[4] The design of the pulpit itself ranged from simple to ornate. Richard Furman's was rather elaborate. Made of mahogany imported from the West Indies, it rose above the congregation and was surrounded by spiral stairs. There was no split chancel nor was there a sounding board.[5] When preaching in the open air, Botsford often used stumps and logs. His biographer recalled an incident when, in the heat of a sermon, Botsford fell through a barrel.[6] As minister, Botsford may have used the presider's chair, and other church leaders sat on the platform as well. William B. Johnson, who studied under Botsford, remembered that during one sermon Botsford turned to his brethren to emphasize a point.[7]

Pews were the most recognizable feature of the Baptist meeting house. There were two different styles: three-sided or box pews with congregants facing one another and slip pews facing the pulpit. Pew rent was a major source of income for most Baptist churches.[8] In May 1804 the church announced in the *Georgetown Gazette* that on "the first of June next, twenty-eight Pews will be finished. Persons wishing to engage Pews in the said Church, will make application to . . . the subscribers."[9] The Georgetown church rented pews yearly for $30, with payments made quarterly. Those in arrears were prohibited from voting in church affairs and had to forfeit their pews after a year's duration. Congregants desiring to give up their pews could do so on the first of January, with advance notice submitted by the annual meeting. Funds raised from pew rent went to pay Botsford's salary and for repairs to the meeting house. In 1805 the church set his income at $800 per year, to be increased to $900 if pew rent totaled $1,100, and to $1,000 if it reached $1,200. The church's budget never met those goals. The year 1808 was the most financially devastating, with Botsford earning a mere $200. By 1810 the church owed Botsford a staggering $2,000, and from then on he was paid annual pew rent, no matter how little the amount.[10] Botsford struggled as a result of the church's inability to pay him a decent wage, and he lamented to a family member that he was unable to "get hardly any thing as a minister." Still, he was determined "to go no more in debt."[11]

The services themselves were much different from Baptist services of today. It was not until 1800 that music became a major aspect of worship. Since instrumentation was associated with the Anglican Church, music in early Baptist churches was most often a cappella. Nevertheless, Botsford, Furman, and other Regular Baptists, as they were then known, considered music a central aspect of a worship service. Francis Asbury noted that Georgetown intended to have an organ.[12] According to David Benedict, congregational singing was the most common form of music found in Baptist churches. In this setting the leader stood in front of the pulpit and led the congregation in singing hymns. All able members also stood, as sitting was considered irreverent.[13] Although Botsford never mentioned there being a choir at Georgetown, given that many other Regular Baptist churches in South Carolina had choirs by this time, it is likely that Georgetown followed suit. The First Baptist Church of Charleston had its first choir around the turn of the century.[14] Choirs were designed to support congregational singing, not to perform "special music."[15] Botsford had high standards for singing, even going so far as to criticize Richard Furman for his lack of vocal ability, to which Furman responded that "the Charge if I understand it is: that I sing; that I am a poor Singer, and that People think, I think, I am a good Singer, and am vain about it."[16] Botsford felt that a hymn should be delivered with the utmost sincerity, and Charles Mallary cited an incident in which Botsford became emotional while flipping through a hymnbook.[17] Botsford also sold hymnals throughout Georgetown.[18]

He may have been an advocate of music, but Botsford did not allow kneeling or bowing at any point during a service, even during communion: "The New testament does not give us any information . . . or command for kneeling at the administration of the Lord's supper."[19] Charleston used a common cup and communion table, but there are no references to this practice in other South Carolina Baptist churches. Most likely, deacons carried the wine to the congregation.[20] Laying on of hands and foot washing had become virtually extinct in the churches of the Charleston Association by this time. Botsford made no mention of either practice.[21]

The most important act of worship was baptism. While large churches, such as the one in Charleston, had interior baptisteries, most congregations had exterior pools or held baptisms in local creeks and rivers.[22] It is clear that Georgetown had some sort of makeshift baptistery located near the meeting house. During a dry season Botsford wrote Furman: "Pray how is the Baptistery to be supplied with water. The crops on Pee dee are very much damaged."[23] It appears that Botsford preferred the river, since in 1804 he baptized his wife and her sister in the Sampit "in the presence of a very large number of spectators, who behaved with decency and seriousness."[24] Years later Botsford described a peculiar incident to his friend William Inglesby: "I very much question if ever you saw such a baptistery as was contrived yesterday. Knowing it would be dead low water about the time for baptizing, we examined the river up and down to find a place that would answer, but none could be found. Mr. M. and Mr. C. got a Cheraw flat, 4 feet deep, hauled it up between two wharves, the upper end aground, bored 2 or 3 holes in the bottom, and let in the water. We got water of a proper depth and baptized in the flat."[25]

Botsford opposed the sponsorship of baptismal candidates, explaining in his essay "Reflection Fifth" that "it is not once mentioned in the New Testament the use of the cross in baptism; nor of sponsors, as godfathers & godmothers. Nor do we read of particular persons being confirmed, in order to take on themselves the vows made by their godfathers & godmothers at the time of their baptism."[26] The most important part of baptism to Botsford was the genuine piety of the person being baptized. Regular Baptists, including Botsford, insisted on thoroughly examining candidates prior to baptism and opposed the baptism of young children.[27]

The seriousness with which Botsford viewed baptism and the other aspects of his ministry explains his skepticism regarding the Second Great Revival. In the eighteenth century several waves of religious enthusiasm swept through the nation. The first came in the 1740s with the Great Awakening, championed by George Whitefield. Shortly thereafter, Oliver Hart formed the Charleston Association in an attempt to unite South Carolina Baptist churches, and in the meantime many churches were formed in the Backcountry. Religion took a downturn during the Revolution, however, and by the turn of the century church membership was at a standstill.[28] In 1799 the Charleston Association noted in its circular letter the "languishing state of religion in the southern parts of these United States."[29] By 1800 the revival they had prayed for finally arrived. The movement began in Kentucky in 1797 and made its way to the coast. One author described it as "the first revival common to the whole South, and the first in which all denominations shared simultaneously."[30]

The most recognizable feature of the revival was the camp meeting. Visitors came from all over to witness a "general meeting," where pastors from different denominations united to preach the gospel to the masses. Botsford described an experience he had in North Carolina:

> I have preached, as was supposed, to between four and five thousand. The meeting continues two or three days. There are frequently ten or a dozen ministers present, most of whom pray, preach, or exhort, as they find freedom. After public service, those who live near the place of meeting, whether members or not, ask every person who comes from far to go home with them; and generally, the greater the number who accept the invitations, the better they are pleased, especially if a minister can be prevailed upon to be one of the guests. When you come to the house, they entertain you with the best they have, both horses and men; and as soon as you have all dined, to preaching, praying, singing, exhorting, etc. Near midnight you retire to rest: by sun-rise in the morning to prayers, then breakfast and to public worship again, but not before our company is requested the next night, if the meeting continues. This is the common practice in Georgia, South and North Carolina, and in Virginia, in what we call the back parts of the country.[31]

What troubled Botsford was the nature of the meetings, particularly the bodily gyrations and emotional outbursts that overcame people with the observance of general communion. Botsford was relieved to attend one meeting where there was "no irregularity, no disorder, no clapping of hands, no raving, nor stamping," and claimed that "if every camp meeting was conducted with as much care I should be very fond of them."[32] Furman was also cautious of the revival movement and, according to Botsford, did "not fully approve of encampments, on account of ye bad use made by some of night meeting etc— nor does he approve of general communion—nor of ye conduct of those who make so much noise." Regular Baptists were leery of sharing communion with other denominations and, as a result, customarily held gatherings with their own congregations. In a letter to John Roberts, Botsford explained his position against Methodism: "I am sorry the Methodists are such a noisy people, I wish to have as little connexion with them as possible." Botsford disapproved of their "tenets" and their "vociferous manner of conducting worship, in which they seem to glory." He could not bring himself to share communion with them and feared their conduct would "long check ye real work."[33]

Botsford may have disapproved of the "irregularities" of camp meetings, but he longed for a revival in Georgetown. He relayed to a friend in 1802, "I wish we had something to move us in this place. I confess it would please me best to see and be ye instrument of a work, still, calm, yet powerful—like it was in New England—however, a rushing mighty wind, rather than such a miserable wretched languid state in which we still continue." Even after the chapel was occupied in 1804, Botsford's work showed no signs of improvement, and he was discouraged by the "little success in my ministry, in this place, that it has produced much uneasiness of mind. It seems as though I should live to bury all the members of my church. . . . Several times I have had hopes of a revival, but have been disappointed." By this time Botsford was sixty years old and had been in the ministry thirty-three years. During those three decades he baptized 286 people, preached 4,500 sermons, and traveled 70,000 miles, earning the nickname the "flying preacher." He had also been married four times and had twelve children, only five of whom were still living in 1804. Botsford was never able to reconcile the loss of his children. "I suppose that I idolized them," he wrote Sarah Evans in Georgetown, "hence God has been depriving me of them."[34]

Despite personal setbacks and the declining state of Botsford's ministry, church business moved forward. After incorporation the church adopted a procedure for conducting regular business affairs. The structure provided a president, treasurer, two wardens, and a secretary for overseeing "congregational concerns." An unusual aspect was the presence of wardens, a role generally associated with the Episcopal Church. Georgetown was the only Baptist congregation in South Carolina to use wardens, who were responsible for collecting pew rent and managing church property.[35] In January 1805 the leaders met at John Waldo's house, where Savage Smith was chosen president, William Cuttino treasurer, John Waldo and William Murray wardens, and Jeremiah Cuttino secretary.[36]

One of their initial acts as a corporate body was to devise bylaws to govern the congregation, provide standards for choosing officers, and outline the duties and responsibilities of the pastor, deacons, officers, and church members. The pastor and two deacons were to "conduct the spiritual concerns of the church."[37] The pastor was the highest office in the church, with the authority to preach the gospel and administer baptism and communion anywhere in the world, although his home church was to remain top priority. Deacons were chosen from the congregation and given authority over any matters not directly relegated to the pastor, such as discipline, finance, and mediation. Both pastors and deacons underwent an ordination ceremony. All church offices were limited to males, although women could act as witnesses.[38] Business meetings were usually held monthly on Saturdays, with prayer, preaching, and singing sometimes prefacing church business.[39] Those who were not members could attend business meetings, but had no voice in church affairs.[40]

Although Georgetown was part of the Charleston Association, the congregation was still an autonomous body. According to the association, each church had the "keys, or power of government, within itself, having Christ for its head, and his law for its rule." Since Georgetown was self-governing, it had the authority to grant and deny membership. Individuals applying for church membership were admitted after making a satisfactory profession of faith. Prospective members not from the community were expected to provide a letter of dismissal from their previous church. If a member committed an offense within the church, it was presented before the congregation. When the transgression was public, the case also became public.[41] Common misdemeanors within the church included drinking, gambling, dancing, shooting matches, and similar offenses. Excommunication was the highest degree of punishment but was rarely implemented. Instead, as Leah Townsend points out, "In the main, the disciplinary measures of the churches were only the expression of public indignation against cruelty, injustice, and immorality."[42]

One of the most formidable obstacles facing the leaders at Georgetown was not discipline but disposing of the old brick church. As early as 1798 Edmund Botsford asked Richard Furman for advice. The matter was complicated since legally the Baptists had an equal partnership with two other denominations. Botsford asked Furman, "Could not some plan be formed for us to get our third from the present building & lot on which it stands?"[43] In February 1805 William Grant, William Murray, and Thomas Chapman were appointed to investigate the possibility of a sale. The church still owed William Cuttino more than £53 for renovations he had started in 1786, in addition to £258 for the new building on Church Street. Since the Presbyterians and Independents had no plans to "form themselves into Societies so as to use the said house for the purpose intended," the Baptists opted to sell the facility at public auction rather than see it "entirely wasted by their negligence." From the sale they intended to "provide some means by which the demand of Mr. Cuttino can be satisfied out of the property on which his labor was bestowed." They considered this decision to represent "complete justice to all persons" and promised to be liable "for such shares of the balance as the Presbyterians and Independents may shew a right to." Another issue was that only William Cuttino, one of the original three owners, was still living. In the end the committee recommended, and the church approved, that the house and lot be advertised for sale. By the following year Archibald Taylor had purchased the property and begun making payments. Some fifteen years later the Cuttino family had never been completely reimbursed.[44]

Shortly after the old brick church was sold, William Cuttino died at age fifty-nine. He had been the main force in establishing the Baptist church in Georgetown and had remained active in church affairs until his untimely death.[45] According to the *Charleston Courier,* Cuttino passed away after a "long and painful sickness," leaving behind a widow and seven children.[46] Botsford was deeply troubled by the death of Cuttino. While visiting Rhode Island, he wrote Evans in Georgetown: "The account of the death of my old and tried friend Mr. Cuttino, has had such effect on my spirits, that I can scarcely bear up under it, though I expected it. . . . When I think of returning to Georgetown, where there is so little appearance of religion, and shall miss my dear old friend Cuttino, I assure you I can scarcely refrain from bursting into tears."[47] The little appearance of religion in Georgetown of which Botsford spoke referred to his inability to reach out to white residents in the community. He wrote Furman in 1803, "I am now in my seventh year in GeoTown & have not baptized one white person."[48] It was not until the following year that Botsford finally baptized two white individuals.[49] He was pleased at the "very considerable attention among the Negroes who attend worship at our church" but regretted the lack of "attention among the white people." He had hoped that bringing slaves into the church would "attract the notice of the whites," but this plan failed.[50]

Botsford's outreach to slaves had always been a main component of his ministry. While preaching in Charleston in 1785, Furman remarked to Oliver Hart, "Mr. Botsford preached a great deal . . . and appeared to be blest, he Baptized some Negroes."[51] Botsford was satisfied that "numbers of blacks come to see me," even though white membership lagged.[52] In a 1790 letter to John Rippon he described the nature of his ministry to his black brethren: "I am very fond of teaching them: have preached to 300 of them at a time, and not one white present but myself. They sing delightfully; and those who are truly religious, in general far exceed the whites in love to each other, and in most other duties. Many of them can read, and are remarkably fond of hymns. We have several in our church who go to the plantations, and preach to their own colour on Lord's-day evenings, and at other times when we have no service in the meeting-house."[53] Botsford had no reservations about preaching to a church with a black majority. In fact, during his tenure at Welsh Neck he integrated the separate black church with the white congregation.[54]

Botsford's slave ministry proved indispensable in Georgetown, where the white congregation died off and slave membership steadily increased. In 1808 Botsford reported that the "poor blacks appear very attentive . . . great numbers still attend." Within three years the white congregation was at a standstill: "I say my labor seems in vain, except to the poor blacks; they indeed hear. I have had no less than ten or twelve of them lately in my study, telling me good news: some will get tickets for baptism, some will not."[55] By 1812 Botsford's ministry among African Americans was thriving, and he informed Furman that the "Lord seems at work among the poor black people. Many attend Worship & appear to be very attentive. Last Sabbath morning I baptized 18 . . . several of these gave in their experience some time past, and some of them who had leave, could not attend at our last baptizing."[56]

Black Baptists were members of the congregation but could not participate in official church affairs. Yet they were quite active. Botsford was happy to have three or four "leading characters in the church [who] are in good esteem by their owners & the world at large" and considered them "a great help, so far as concerns the black people."[57] The black leaders to whom Botsford referred were considered deacons within the slave community. In most South Carolina Baptist churches at least one black member was given authority over a portion of his fellow slaves and assisted the pastor in ministering to slave communicants. An African American deacon's responsibilities included giving communion, receiving complaints, performing marriages, and preaching at funerals. Some slaves went beyond these duties and served as pastors. If a black communicant desired to preach, he was licensed by the church upon approval of his qualifications by a majority of the congregation. On a few occasions black preachers addressed the congregation as a whole. Black individuals obtained church membership in the same fashion as white persons—upon confession of faith or by letter.[58]

The ceremony of a black baptism at the river was an impressive and widely attended event. Dozens of white persons came to watch Botsford baptize slaves. In 1811 he baptized "14 Negroes on the ferry landing" and had never "seen more white people present," nor such a "large . . . Congregation at that place before."[59] Five years later he recalled a similar incident: "I baptized 17 poor black sheep yesterday in the presence of a very numerous assembly."[60] In his first twelve years he baptized almost four hundred individuals, very few of them white.[61] Occasionally black and white persons were baptized together. In 1817 Furman informed Botsford that "we had but one white Person baptized, but there were 8 Negroes."[62] Thomas Fuller of Beaufort recorded the following incident in his journal in 1803: "I was baptized in the river with several negroes who had been received the afternoon before. This act has caused some estrangement between my friends and myself. Nevertheless, I shall ever have cause to rejoice that the blessed Lord my God led me in this way."[63]

White persons and slaves may have been baptized together, but they did not share pews in the church. Churches customarily built galleries above the white congregation, where slaves sat during the service.[64] Other churches constructed slave "sheds" either in place of or in addition to the gallery. Botsford's former church, Welsh Neck, built a shed—described as a "large addition on one side of the whole length of the building for the use of the negroes." According to the church record, "it was divided from the larger part by a low wall about as high as the banks of the pews with an aisle extending from their side entrance to an open door into the main auditorium."[65] The Ebenezer church near Florence had both a gallery and a slave shed.[66] David Benedict failed to note whether or not the Georgetown meeting house had a designated area for slaves, but at times the crowds were so large they could not fit in the chapel: "Yesterday was a day to be remembered, our large meeting-house was crowded, and a number of blacks without the doors."[67] Most likely a second service was held after the white congregants left. Later Georgetown constructed a separate facility, a "lecture room," for slaves. Slaves still had duties to perform and could not remain completely segregated from their masters during a service. The elderly white members often had special needs requiring a nearby attendant, and there was also the matter of children who were supervised by slaves. Georgetown native Peter Horry allowed his slaves to attend church not necessarily for their benefit but to assist him in getting around.[68]

Discipline was perhaps the most complicated aspect of race relations within the church, since settling slave matters called for a practical rather than a literal translation of the Bible. One question that plagued church leaders was the separation of husband and wife through sale. Could a slave remarry without being adulterous? Most churches approved of remarriage on the grounds that slaves were given no choice. The presence of polygamy, slave breeding, and miscegenation was disturbing to white congregants, who could not reach a general consensus on these acts but judged each case individually. Other offenses included running away, lying, murder or accessory to murder, drunkenness, fighting, disobedience, witchcraft, and stealing.[69]

While white congregants had formerly been opposed to slave membership in the church, by the turn of the nineteenth century their attitude had become more lenient. When David Benedict enquired about the nature of slavery in South Carolina, Botsford responded: "There are but few plantations in South-Carolina, which have not an opportunity of attending worship, either among themselves or at some publick place."[70] A significant difficulty for slaves wishing to attend services was state law restricting their mobility. Slaves could not travel without tickets—written permission from masters. White residents feared that the free movement of slaves could lead to insurrection, as evidenced by the 1739 Stono Rebellion, and so masters exercised caution in the number of tickets issued and for what purposes. Slaves usually received tickets to visit family members on neighboring plantations or to run errands for their masters. Issuing a pass to a slave did not always guarantee his or her safety. Slave patrols, companies of white people with authority to punish slaves for disruptive behavior, monitored the passes. One Carolina slave recalled that if a slave offended the patrol "even by so innocent a matter as dressing tidily to go to a place of worship," he would be seized, beaten, and his pass shredded.[71]

The 1740 Negro Law emphasized the importance of keeping slaves from congregating, particularly on Sundays.[72] In 1800 the state ruled it unlawful for "any number of slaves, free negroes, mulattoes or mestizoes, even in company with white persons, to meet together and assemble for the purpose of mental instruction or religious worship, either before the rising of the sun or after the going down of the same."[73] The Charleston Association petitioned against this law in 1801 and 1802 on the grounds that it infringed "on the Religious Rights and Privileges of Churches and Citizens of this State" to offer religious instruction to slaves as part of their "ministerial Duty."[74] The state repealed the law in 1803, and all religious assemblages meeting before 9:00 P.M. with a majority of white persons present could do so without risking arrest. The law that no slave could seek freedom through Christianity or baptism remained intact.[75]

Although masters and slaves held membership in other denominations, Baptists had several advantages over their peers. While the Episcopal Church remained the church of the planter class, the ritualistic and esoteric nature of its services was generally unappealing to slaves. Added to this was the scarcity of Episcopal ministers and churches.[76] Initially, the Methodists and Baptists took an antislavery stance, but after the Revolution both gradually receded from this policy. In 1795 South Carolina Methodists preachers convened in Charleston to discuss excluding slaveholders from the denomination. This concerned Francis Asbury, who feared the decision would hinder them from being able "to supply this State with preachers."[77] South Carolina native William Capers, one of the founders of the Methodists in Georgetown, helped shift the denomination to a proslavery position. A slaveholder himself, Capers became the spokesman for Southern Methodists.[78] The Baptists had taken their stand against slavery a few years earlier in Virginia, but this proved fruitless.[79]

The trademark of the Methodists and Baptists was the itinerant minister, who travelled from plantation to plantation holding services. Botsford preferred ministering to slaves, and on one occasion remarked to a friend, "If I was a young man, and possessed of only as much zeal as I once possessed, I should be very fond to go preaching and talking from one plantation to another, and be wholly a preacher to negroes. I can suit my talk to them, and enter into their views of things, and doubt not, with the blessing of God, I should be of considerable service."[80] Botsford visited many plantations in the lowcountry, preaching to thousands during his tenure at Georgetown.

Early black membership figures are difficult to estimate since most churches did not report separate figures for white and black persons until about 1830. David Benedict, who wrote his *General History of the Baptist Denomination in America and Other Parts of the World,* estimated that in Virginia, the Carolinas, Georgia, Kentucky, and Tennessee there were 90,000 Baptists, of which about half were black.[81] In South Carolina the churches of the lowcountry had the highest number of black congregants, and the ratio of black persons to white in the Charleston Association was two to one. Georgetown had a membership that wavered around thirty-five for the first fifteen years of the church's existence. After 1810 membership steadily increased, and by 1825 it skyrocketed to 304 attendees. Speaking of John Waldo's role in the Georgetown church, the association made a shocking statement: "For years he stood almost alone in the church, his venerable Pastor, the late Rev. Edmund Botsford, and himself, being the only white male members." Georgetown submitted its first set of white and black membership figures in 1831: 430 black members and 34 white.[82]

Botsford became a slaveholder before the Revolution. When he fled with Oliver Hart to the North, his wife followed him with "a cart, two horses, the negro man, and such necessary articles as she could conveniently carry."[83] In 1789 Botsford told Furman he had two slaves though "one not my own."[84] According to the 1800 census, Botsford owned thirteen slaves. That number dropped to six in 1810 and to three in 1820, the year after his death, when his wife Hannah inherited them. Botsford was not a prominent slaveholder by any means, but the Georgetown church came by its black membership honestly with the leading members owning from fifty to two hundred slaves each. The Cuttinos were a fairly prominent slaveholding family. In 1800 William Cuttino owned almost fifty slaves and Ann Cuttino eighty. Savage Smith, one of the more active leaders in the church and Georgetown's intendant (or mayor), owned more than slaves in 1808. Another member, John Bossard, owned about a hundred slaves. Most of the men who petitioned for the church's incorporation in 1801 were slaveholders.[85]

Botsford supported the South's proslavery ideology, but he continued to doubt the morality of slavery. With a black majority in his congregation and himself a slaveholder, Botsford had no choice but to reconcile his ministry with the growing abolitionist movement. When the ties between Great Britain and the colonies were severed, efforts to maintain the institution moved to the forefront of the political scene. Although many Southerners did not see the hypocrisy in fighting for liberty for themselves while enslaving others, the Revolution undeniably altered the attitudes of their northern counterparts. Adding to the budding sentiment at home regarding the immorality of slavery were signs of an emerging abolitionist movement on a global scale, with France, Great Britain, and some other countries abolishing slavery before the start of the new century.[86] It was against this backdrop that ministers such as Botsford and Furman defended slavery as a "positive good" in an attempt to protect the reputation of their denomination. With a congregation comprised almost solely of slaves, Botsford would continue to fight this battle throughout his career.

SEVEN

Botsford's Dilemma

ALTHOUGH EDMUND BOTSFORD had not been exposed to slavery as a child, his relocation to South Carolina introduced him to a society whose laws and social customs revolved around slavery. It was at the First Baptist Church of Charleston that Botsford initially witnessed the presence of slaves in the church. Oliver Hart, his highly respected mentor and pastor at Charleston, had several slaves. David Williams, Botsford's tutor, owned two plantations and more than seventy slaves.[1] Botsford observed his role models' interaction with slaves both in the church and at home, and it was through these experiences that he learned to accept the institution. David Benedict's *General History of the Baptist Denomination in America and Other Parts of the World,* relays Botsford's sentiment:

> I have now been in this country upwards of forty-six years, as I arrived
> in Charleston from England in 1766, then something more than twenty
> years of age, and had never heard much respecting the negroes, or had
> seen more than four or five. I had every prejudice I could have against
> slavery. I must confess to this day, I am no advocate for it. But it does
> not appear to me in the same light it did on my first arrival. It is true,
> the slaves have no hope of freedom, and it is also true, they have no
> proper idea of the nature of freedom. Many in their own country were
> slaves, and many who were not, were miserable. Several with whom I
> have conversed, have really preferred their present state in this country
> to their own country, though in that they were free. It is more than prob-
> able, however, were the slave-trade abolished, their own country would
> be more desirable.[2]

Botsford justified owning slaves on the grounds of necessity: "Providence has cast my lot where slavery is introduced and practiced. . . . Servants I want; it is lawful for me to have them; but hired ones I cannot obtain, and therefore I have purchased some: I use them as servants; I feed them; clothe them, in- struct them, etc."[3] He felt slavery was often misrepresented and that Northern- ers "who had not travelled have very wrong Ideas of the situation & of our

Negroes." He thought it better to be "a slave to a good Master than a foot Soldier in the British Service for life."[4]

Botsford may have struggled in accepting slavery, but he was also influenced by Richard Furman, who spent most of his life in South Carolina. In 1823, on behalf of the South Carolina Baptist Convention, Furman wrote *Exposition of the Views of the Baptists Relative to the Coloured Population,* in which he cited both the Old and New Testament to justify black slavery. "The right of holding slaves is clearly established by the Holy Scriptures," Furman asserted. "Had the holding of slaves been a moral evil, it cannot be supposed, that the inspired Apostles . . . would have tolerated it, for a moment, in the Christian Church." Furman opposed cruel treatment and the denial of religion to slaves: "Much tyranny has been exercised by individuals, as masters over their slaves, and . . . the religious interests of the latter have been too much neglected. . . . But the fullest proof of these facts, will not also prove, that the holding men in subjection, as slaves, is a moral evil, and inconsistent with Christianity." Furman called for slavery "tempered with humanity and justice" until a time arrived when the "Africans in our country might be found qualified to enjoy freedom."[5] In the meantime he called upon his brethren to "purchase as many as they can of these poor people with an honest intention to render them as happy as circumstances will admit."[6] In his unpublished "Essay on Slavery," Botsford recognized that the "punishment inflicted on the Negro is often severe. . . . After all, this kind of slavery in its best state is a very great evil." Generally speaking, however, Botsford felt that South Carolina slavery was "misrepresented" and that life as a slave could be enjoyed with "more satisfaction than millions in the world." Botsford made these suppositions based on his impression that African Americans did not "view freedom in the same light as most considerate white men do." According to Botsford, slaves enjoyed life more than the lower classes in England who "work harder, & are not so well fed & cloathed as a field slave in Carolina, who has a good master & is himself honest and industrous."[7]

In 1808 Botsford published *Sambo and Toney: A Dialogue between Two Servants.* Having written in what Botsford termed "Negro style," he explained his concept to Furman:

> Myself and a friend or two have been much puzzled respecting the language it should be written in. However finally, since receiving your letter have concluded to print it in much the same style as that part you saw. Sambo, Toney, his wife & Titus are made to speak something more in the Negro style. Davy who is represented an old professor, & one who can read & having conversed frequently with ministers, his style much as

the piece you saw. I am not without hopes the piece may be of some use. . . . I think, if I know my heart my views are the benefit of that class of our poor deprived fellow creatures who are too little attended too [*sic*] by all of us.[8]

In the story a recent convert, Sambo, reaches out to his old friend, Toney, who refuses to partake in the "praying and singing, exhorting and preaching all around us, and some on our plantation." Toney felt that he was "as good as them that make such a noise" and that the "minister never preach to we black people." Sambo assured him that the Bible "speak to every body alike, white people, black people, rich man, poor man, old man, and young man." Sambo then shared the details of his conversion with Toney, how he left behind his vices and started a new life as a devout Christian, which led to better relations with his master. Although Toney felt his sins were relatively minor, Sambo urged him to "think upon your poor soul before it is too late—before you drop into hell." Toney intended to live a long life and "to 'joy all the pleasure I can." Sambo and Toney departed, and Toney had a dream that he was very sick and on the verge of death. The unexpected passing of a dear friend and a serious discussion with a black class leader named Davy, who was an "old Christian" and had been "fighting the good fight for a long time," inspired Toney to have a change of heart. Toney's conversion also resulted in his wife Fanny joining the church. The story ends with Sambo visiting Toney, Fanny, and Davy, to discuss resisting temptation in their spiritual journeys.[9]

Botsford's work had several important implications. First and foremost, he suggested that slaves and their masters had a moral responsibility to each other. *Sambo and Toney* encouraged white people to allow their slaves to seek membership in the church, but, most important, Botsford's pamphlet convinced slaveholders that Christianity could serve as a form of social control. Botsford inserted carefully constructed statements into his characters' dialogue in order to relay this point. Toney told Sambo that when he converted, he fell down before his master and begged for forgiveness: "Oh, my master, I've been a bad servant; I've been cursing and lying and stealing, and doing every bad thing; I hope you'll forgive me; I trust I shall never do the like again." His master pardoned him, which made Toney "love him more than ever." Thus portrayed, Christianity worked to the advantage of white people by producing hard-working and obedient slaves. Only a wicked man, according to Botsford's character Davy, would "use his servants worse for being faithful and honest."[10] In the end Botsford hoped his narrative would be distributed "among the Negroes" and benefit "that class of our poor deprived fellow creatures who are too little attended too by all of us."[11]

Sambo and Toney sold widely throughout the North and South. Botsford ordered an initial one thousand copies, which he intended to sell at five cents each, never anticipating making a profit, but desirous of recovering the printing costs.[12] In 1809 he reported to Furman that he had "pretty good success with Sambo & Toney" and requested an additional three hundred copies to fill orders. He had received no interest from Charleston, however, and intended to target Georgia, where "there are a great many Negroes in and about Savannah."[13] An additional five hundred copies were reprinted in Norfolk, Virginia, that same year, and pastors in Hartford, Connecticut, also planned to reprint it.[14] By 1814 *Sambo and Toney* was selling well in Charleston, and Botsford boasted to Furman that a sea captain had seen a copy in London.[15] Botsford's work continues to be cited by slavery historians, who consider *Sambo and Toney* a perfect example of the rise of paternalism in the South.

Botsford's outreach to slaves continued to be a key part of his ministry, but another important role was mentoring prospective Baptist preachers. William B. Johnson, who became the first president of the Southern Baptist Convention, was one of Botsford's protégés and frequent correspondents. When Johnson entered the ministry Botsford advised him to "study hard; preach often; pray much; converse some; be watchful over your flock; never omit the least duty connected with your office. Rise early, but not sit up too late; prize every moment, and let it not pass in absolute idleness." Botsford reminded Johnson of the scrutiny he would endure as a minister: "Remember, my son, the eyes that will be on you; the characters that will either secretly or openly oppose you; your own weaknesses; your soul, body, and family trials; also remember, you have a remedy at hand for all; the Bible." Botsford was particularly concerned about preparation and delivery, and he insisted that a sermon never be read: "The introduction should be pertinent to the subject, not to fit any sermon, not too far-fetched, not long, spoken deliberately, with a voice just to reach the farthest person in the house, so as with ease he can hear. If you divide, be sure, your divisions be clear, and easy to be understood; and now look well to your audience, to see if they take in your meaning. . . . Now, in one word, to fit you for all this, your subject, and that in every part, must, to us who hear you, seem to come from your heart." John Roberts, pastor at the High Hills of Santee church, was reprimanded by Botsford on one occasion for his lack of speaking ability: "I insist you shall try to speak better. Don't tell me about your mediocrity of talents; you are not to put, either yourself, your people, or me, off with such stuff. Roberts, God has done great things for you, and will you not improve the talents?" Botsford expected every sermon to be delivered with the utmost sincerity. "Let every member of your church see that their welfare lies near your heart," he told Johnson. "Often inquire into their state." To accomplish this goal Botsford suggested ministering to the congregation not as "elect or non-elect," but as sinners, and to "invite them, even the vilest to the marriage feast, and assure them no qualification is necessary to introduce them to the notice of Christ, if they feel themselves sinners."[16] This de-emphasis of predestination reflects a change in Baptist thinking—the missionary impulse trumped Calvinism. By this time Furman and Botsford were identified as Regular Baptists to distinguish them from newer sects, such as the New Light, Separates, and Free Will Baptists.

The advice Botsford offered these men was reflective of his own experiences as a minister. He read scripture daily and spent ample time in prayer and meditation. He often attended the services of his fellow ministers, even those belonging to other denominations. Botsford was what he termed a "Bible minister," spending time studying and comparing the scriptures before writing out his sermons. He was fastidious in using notes when delivering a sermon but vehemently opposed to reading anything verbatim. "It surely never was the design of our Master," claimed Botsford "that his servants should read the Gospel, when he said, 'go preach.'" His objective was to engage the church through animation and illustrations and not bore them with formality. Botsford's primary concern was the welfare of the congregation regardless of race or status. He encouraged unanimity and ministered to anyone who was a "stranger to religion."[17]

Botsford's dedication to studying the Bible and being well-versed in scripture was rooted in his support of the movement for an educated clergy. In 1755 Oliver Hart had formed the Religious Society in Charleston to aid prospective ministers. A young man desiring to pursue a career in the ministry served under the tutelage of an older pastor, who granted him access to his books and acted as his instructor. Trainees were first licensed to preach and ordained when proven capable of serving a church. Botsford was one of the first to enroll in and complete Hart's program, but the organization ceased to exist in 1780. Regular Baptists such as Botsford and Furman were at the forefront of this movement. Rhode Island College conferred on Furman an honorary master's degree in 1792, and he was honored twice with a doctor of divinity—one from Rhode Island and the other from South Carolina College (now the University of South Carolina).[18] Just before his death Botsford received an honorary master of liberal arts from Rhode Island.[19] In 1791 Richard Furman informed the Reverend George W. Pearce in Birmingham, England, that "a great part of our ministers as well as members are illiterate," which he deemed a "great hindrance" to the denomination.[20] Botsford held a similar view, commenting to Furman, "If I was a despotic King I should make a shocking work in the Church of God, for I should be very strenuous to have all my preachers, at least speak good plain English correctly."[21] Furman helped establish the General Committee of the Charleston Association to remedy this problem. Under the supervision of the committee, a yearly charity sermon was to be preached in each of the churches of the association and a collection taken up and placed in an education fund for the training of men called to the ministry.[22] Botsford supported Furman's efforts to revive ministerial education in South Carolina, and beginning in 1800 Georgetown gave regularly to the fund.[23]

While Botsford was fervently trying to increase the membership in the Georgetown church, his health steadily declined. About 1800 he began complaining of a stinging sensation in his eye, the details of which Aaron Marvin described to Charles Mallary:

> Mr. Botsford's principal complaint was in the nerves, on one side of the head, called Tic Dolouroux. It usually came on in paroxysms of unequal duration, sometimes lasting several minutes, at others not more than half a minute; at which times, the blood would rush to the head sudden as thought, and inflame the countenance, till it would almost seem bursting through the pores. At such times, he was fixed as a statue. In whatever position he was in, when it seized him, he remained until it passed off; and then the blood would recede, the nerves and fibres relax, the countenance grow paler and paler; and he would slowly and cautiously resume his occupation, as though he feared its recurrence. Frequently, for weeks at a time, did it recur in quick succession, so that he could not, without difficulty, eat, or drink or speak. A particular contraction of the lip in any of these acts, appeared to bring it on.[24]

In 1806 Botsford sailed for New York, searching for a cure and hoping that a change in climate would bring relief, but his ailment only worsened. He tried many remedies, including blisters and bleeding, until surgery became his only option, with a Dr. Simons of Charleston performing the operation. Peter Horry noted in his journal in the fall of 1812 that "Reverend Mr. Botsworth of the Baptist Church is Gone to Charles Ton to have a Second Attropfia on his Eye. He Suffers Greatly, his Affliction nearly Equals my own which however is not So long Standing as mine."[25] The surgery was only a temporary fix, and Botsford continued to struggle. His illness incapacitated him, and as a result the church was frequently without a minister. He forced himself to preach whenever possible, writing to William Johnson that "every motion of my mouth produces a prickle in the eye. Yesterday I preached in the greatest torment I ever did; but I feel determined while I can speak to preach."[26] In the spring of 1813 he predicted that he would "never more preach, except occasionally," the entire right side of his head being "affected."[27] He was happy to mount the pulpit in 1818, but considered his preaching of "little account at best, and less now than ever."[28] Botsford's only source of relief came from laudanum.[29] The church suffered from his absence, but Botsford never lost hope that the "Work of Grace [will] revive and flourish in George Town."[30]

Writing served as a source of relief while Botsford coped with his condition. Since preaching was painful, he desired to be of use at "second hand, or in an indirect way; no matter if not a soul on earth knew it, so that it proved itself in the sight of God."[31] Most of his pieces are inspirational, although a few concern politics and historical figures. After *Sambo and Toney* Botsford's next major publication was *A Spiritual Voyage,* which he wrote about 1814. He attempted to emulate Paul Bunyan's style in *The Pilgrim's Progress,* a book he used as a model in many of his writings. Botsford regarded Bunyan's novel as "one of the best books for a minister, and also for a common Christian, of any ever published."[32] Referring to himself as an "everlasting scribbler," Botsford worried his work would never gain recognition due to his "round-about way of writing" and awkward way of expressing himself.[33] He considered his "itch for writing" unfortunate, since he doubted "that any one sentence that I ever wrote, except some very short ones, is rightly constructed." Botsford often sent manuscripts to close friends for review. He requested that William Johnson "write in a concise manner your most candid opinion; then show it to others as prudence may direct, and as candidly note their observations of every kind. . . . I do not wish to have any thing published, that would expose the Baptists to ridicule."[34] Botsford was particularly interested in Furman's thoughts concerning *Sambo and Toney:* "I am much obliged to you for your friendly observations on the piece written for the use of the Negroes."[35] Furman found the task of advising Botsford daunting at times and worried that Botsford relied "too much on my Judgment."[36] Most of Botsford's works are undated and unpublished and can be found in his papers at Furman University.

As Botsford's illness progressed, he called upon his fellow Baptist ministers to preach in Georgetown in order to keep the church open. In 1812 "Brother Cook," perhaps the son of the Reverend Joseph Cook, preached on his behalf.[37] Furman noted in 1814 that a Mr. Hand was at Georgetown. While noting the "oddities attending his manner of preaching, and behavior," Furman trusted that he was a "good man, and that his preaching is owned of God."[38] The year 1817 saw another minister, a Mr. Ellis, enter the "sunken church."[39] Furman described him as a "humble, candid, pious Man" and was confident that his "labours will be blessed among your People." Furman desired that "supplies . . . be obtained in such a Manner, as to keep the Place of Worship open, as much as possible."[40] In 1818 Lee Compere, a missionary to Jamaica and a noted Baptist minister, began preaching.[41] "I hope he will prove a blessing to us, especially if we can curb his hasty & somewhat abrupt turn," Botsford wrote Furman.[42] Compere continued to preach throughout that year, but the church could not afford to support both him and Botsford.[43] As the year came to a close Botsford saw no prospects of finding a full-time minister: "If some cleaver single Man could be procured, it would be the plan so we think, but God does not, therefore we must content ourselves. To me it appears awful to see the Church declining & no additions & no prospects of a preacher."[44]

Botsford spent his last year in agony while the church searched for his replacement. He often wondered why God continued to spare him, and he lived in "daily expectation of my last change." Botsford's "sweetest hours" were in bed, where he was "generally easy and often sleepless for many hours."[45] By July he had resigned himself to death, and he wrote Furman: "It may be an idle conjecture; but it is my earnest prayer to God, that he will send a person whom he will honor in building up the almost extinct church."[46] Botsford was deeply distraught by the state of the congregation. As his close friend and church leader Aaron Marvin said, "It grieved him to the heart to see the languishing state of the Church, consequent as he supposed, upon his illness; as the house was shut up months at a time during fourteen years, and the members had died off greatly." Botsford remained in contact with his congregation by writing letters to them, hoping to communicate "something useful to those who lie near my heart."[47] On Christmas Day 1819 Botsford died in Georgetown at age seventy-four, leaving behind a wife, four daughters, and a grieving church.

Few South Carolina Baptist ministers can match Edmund Botsford's legacy. To his family he was a devoted husband and father. As a friend he was a candid and honest adviser who desired to see his brethren grow in Christ. With grace he steered his church through many challenges, never losing hope that God would make a great work at the Georgetown church and that the fruits of his labor would not be wasted. The Baptist community, as well as the nation, mourned the loss of Botsford, and newspapers throughout the country announced his death. The *Southern Evangelical Intelligencer* said of him that "he was a pious, faithful minister of Christ, and highly respected for his correct, exemplary conduct."[48] The Charleston Association honored him thusly:

> That this Association contemplate with mixed emotions of regret and
> pleasure, the death of the Rev. Edmund Botsford, A.M. late Pastor of
> the Church in Georgetown, standing in their immediate communion—
> regret for the departure of so excellent and faithful a servant of God from
> the Church militant, where aid in the cause of God is so much needed,
> in which through the blessings of God, who owned him for his servant in
> the gospel, his services were rendered imminently useful—pleasure, and

even joy, from the consideration that he has passed through the painful scenes of heavy affliction, which he sustained for a course of years in the latter part of his life; that he supported with purity and dignity his christian profession, and ministerial character to the end, and . . . died in faith and in peace, triumphing in his Redeemer's complete salvation; and that his brethren who loved him, and must ever acknowledge his worth, have reason to believe, that he is now crowned with glory and immortality in the heavens, enjoying the ineffable pleasures which are comprehended in the beatified vision, and full enjoyment of God and the Lamb to eternity.[49]

The most celebrated memorial to Botsford was a piece written by Richard Furman entitled *The Crown of Life Promised to the Truly Faithful,* which he presented to the Georgetown congregation shortly after Botsford's death.[50] One author compared Furman and Botsford's relationship to that of Jonathan and David.[51] The two had a deep and abiding appreciation for each other, a respect that continued to grow stronger during their forty-year friendship. In 1789 Botsford told Furman, "I really have a more sincere regard for you than I ever had in my life, as a minister of Christ, as a master of a family, as a Christian gentleman."[52] Furman had an equal admiration of Botsford: "But if I should say, that among my numerous Correspondents who often compel me, in a manner, to write . . . there is one whose Correspondence affords me the greatest Satisfaction, and that this Correspondent is Mr. Botsford, I should not err from the Truth."[53] Furman's address poetically outlined Botsford's life and accomplishments, but, most important, it focused on Botsford's blameless character as "a man of the most excellent spirit; candid, humble, friendly, affectionate and faithful. . . . You saw in him an Israelite indeed, in whom was no guile." Furman spoke to the congregation not merely as a friend of Botsford but as one of the original founders of the church as well. For four decades Furman had held a vested interest in Georgetown. He, along with William Cuttino and John Waldo, had worked diligently to keep the congregation alive while trying desperately to find a permanent minister. Over the years he had offered Botsford his candid opinion on the many struggles facing the church. That day he spoke to them as someone who had shared in their joy and in their sorrow:

> Beloved brethren, members of this church—I can never be indifferent
> to your interests, while I remember that, unworthy as I am, it pleased
> God to make my imperfect ministry the means of calling you, originally,
> by his grace, and of establishing you in a church state. I must therefore

necessarily feel for you, in no common degree, on this mournful occasion: especially, when, in your deceased pastor, I have lost my most particular friend on earth. . . . The loss you have sustained is felt far beyond your bounds: and particularly by the churches of our immediate connexion, for your late excellent pastor, was extensively known, and greatly beloved. As far as the church militant is concerned [we] may truly say, "a pillar in the temple of God has fallen."[54]

Furman survived Botsford by six years, dying in the fall of 1825, just before the State Baptist Convention in Camden.[55]

Upon Botsford's death the church was again without a pastor. Peter Cuttino, Aaron Marvin, and John Waldo continued to represent the church at the annual meetings of the Charleston Baptist Association.[56] In the summer of 1820 Joseph Cook reassured Furman that "George Town has been greatly blest. The fruits of the Vineyard, will, no doubt, appear for years to come."[57] The reports Georgetown sent to the association, however, reflected a different scene, and for years one minister after another resigned the position. In 1822 J. C. Harrison served, but he left the following year. Two years later Cyrus Pitt Grosvenor, a leading abolitionist Baptist minister, took the charge at Georgetown only to leave before the next association meeting in 1825.[58] On that occasion the association ruled that churches without a sufficient number of male members and an ordained minister should dissolve and connect with another church, which put Georgetown in peril of shutting its doors. The association allowed Georgetown to remain open, probably due to its status as one of the oldest churches in the association.[59]

In 1826 the church endured yet another loss in the death of John Waldo. One of the first licentiates commissioned by Furman to serve the Georgetown congregation, Waldo served as pastor in the church for a brief period only. He pursued a career as an intellectual and opened a Latin school, which had twenty-nine scholars in 1809, and co-owned a general store in Georgetown. He was also a member of the Winyah Indigo Society, for which he may have been a master at one time, and the Georgetown Library Society.[60] Waldo was an eccentric individual, one of the reasons Georgetown dismissed him as a pastor. Botsford considered him a "good Man & a good friend" but also someone who moved "out of the common way."[61] While residing at North Island in the summer of 1812, Peter Horry recorded that Waldo was the "most Gaughky man on the Island," although he did not deny Waldo's talents as a "Great Scholar & good School Master."[62] Teaching occupied most of Waldo's time, but his most recognized contributions were his acclaimed books *A Latin Grammar, Rudiments of English Grammar,* and *The Dictionary Spelling Book.* The

Georgetown Gazette deemed them as having "uncommon merit" and antici-
pated his English grammar becoming a "standard work."[63] Still, he remained
an active church member and leader. Waldo attended association meetings,
served as a licentiate and warden, and opened his home to visiting ministers.[64]
Having survived what Botsford called a "mortifying stroke" in 1816, he lived
another decade before passing in his sixty-fourth year.[65]

Peter Ludlow, former pastor of the Second Baptist Church in Providence,
Rhode Island, became their minister in 1826.[66] Through Ludlow's efforts the
church received perpetual incorporation in 1827. With this came a name change
from Antipedo Baptist Church to Baptist Church of Christ in Georgetown.[67]
Ludlow had moved on by 1829. According to the association minutes of that
year only one service took place in nearly eighteen months, although the congregation continued to meet in a lecture room and "attended to such exercises
as were within their power." Twenty communicants were ready for baptism,
and the church "secured the labors of br. A. B. Smith, late of the Newton
Theological Seminary; whom they expect shortly to see ordained and settled as
pastor." Smith served for a year but left to complete his studies at Newton. In
the meantime the congregation was supplied by D. C. Bolles, another Newton
student. Among the African American communicants there was an "increased
attention to religion." Several had been baptized and a number awaited "the
next administration of the Ordinances."[68] In the coming decades the congregation continued to struggle to find a pastor. An insufficient salary, the notorious "sickly" weather in Georgetown, and low white membership ensured that
Botsford's dream of revival would not be realized for decades.

EIGHT

The Antebellum Church

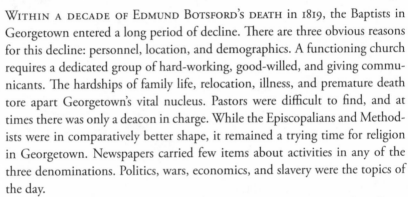

Wɪᴛʜɪɴ ᴀ ᴅᴇᴄᴀᴅᴇ ᴏꜰ Eᴅᴍᴜɴᴅ Bᴏᴛsꜰᴏʀᴅ's ᴅᴇᴀᴛʜ in 1819, the Baptists in Georgetown entered a long period of decline. There are three obvious reasons for this decline: personnel, location, and demographics. A functioning church requires a dedicated group of hard-working, good-willed, and giving communicants. The hardships of family life, relocation, illness, and premature death tore apart Georgetown's vital nucleus. Pastors were difficult to find, and at times there was only a deacon in charge. While the Episcopalians and Methodists were in comparatively better shape, it remained a trying time for religion in Georgetown. Newspapers carried few items about activities in any of the three denominations. Politics, wars, economics, and slavery were the topics of the day.

Equally unfortunate was the Georgetown environment—quite literally, in the sense that for most of its history this low area was regarded as extremely unhealthy, especially in the summer. The great rice barons were gone much of the time, and from June to October the small middle class left for either the upcountry, North Island, or, later, Pawleys Island. Winyah Bay attracted a steady traffic of coastal schooners and steamers, as well as flatboats and side-wheelers from the interior. While the port bustled, the social climate deteriorated. One plantation owner, writing in 1835, regretted the lack of culture and genteel society in Georgetown, which "presents so many melancholy memorials of premature decay." The reason for Georgetown's predicament, he said, was not the economy nor the climate, but "Absenteism."[1]

Nineteenth-century racial demographics for the South Carolina lowcountry are striking, especially in Georgetown District. In 1830 Georgetown's population consisted of 2,145 white persons and 17,798 slaves. The slave population represented 89.24 percent, the highest it would reach in the antebellum period. In 1850 slaves still made up 88.41 percent.[2] African Americans were admitted into churches, and the ratios there were similarly skewed. Throughout the antebellum period, lowcountry Baptists experienced a rapidly increasing black membership. The peak years were just before the Civil War, and the last specific data from Georgetown is for 1857, when there were 28 white individuals and

1,044 black persons in the congregation.[3] Only a minuscule fraction of the Georgetown black population was free.

In 1831 Georgetown Baptists felt "signally blessed by the Lord" under the leadership of D. C. Bolles. In the first five months he baptized 157 people, bringing the total membership to 34 white and 430 black congregants. Unfortunately, Bolles suffered from "the prejudices of our brethren at the North to a southern climate" and he declined the offer of a permanent pastorate.[4] The church hoped to have a replacement by fall the following year, but that prospect proved unavailable. The Baptists found themselves "in a destitute and afflicted condition" and could only hope for "visits of mercy" from Charleston ministers.[5] The Charleston Baptist Association sent Basil Manly, James C. Furman, and James du Pre to assess the church's condition. The three Baptists reported that the only preaching available was occasional supply. In addition, Georgetown's beloved deacon, Peter Cuttino, died, "a heavy loss to the Church and community."[6] Despite this setback, the congregation continued to meet every Sunday and maintained a Sabbath School and a Ladies' Society. In March 1833 Basil Manly arranged for James Clement Furman, the son of Richard Furman, to spend the month preaching in Georgetown by appointment of the association. "Now this is one of the things that must be done," Manly instructed the younger Furman. "Do not fail, my brother, for rest assured it will be a visit of mercy to a sinking church."[7]

The association appointed a second committee in 1834 to "assist the Georgetown Church in their discipline" and to hold a protracted meeting there. The church was closed most of the year, except for two months when Stephen P. Hill of Maryland preached and three Sundays when a Reverend Reaves of North Carolina visited. A letter to Charleston, signed by "many members" and the "church corporation," described the "confusion and discord" and begged for guidance.[8] The following year saw no improvement, with very little preaching where "the field of usefulness, especially among the colored people, is great."[9]

The church experienced some stability in 1836 with the pastorate of Charles Middleton Breaker and visits by the missionary William Nolen from Charleston.[10] An energetic man, Breaker would be in and out of the picture for many years, but his tenure in Georgetown lasted only twelve months.[11] The congregation failed to convince Nolen to stay, and Georgetown remained without a pastor and could only "mourn over their desolation, and solicit the prayers of God's people."[12] The church was unable to send any report to the Charleston Baptist Association in 1839 and the following year could only acknowledge their appreciation of several visits by Charleston missionaries.[13] By 1841 the white membership had shrunk to 16 and the black participation had dropped from 552 to 469.[14] Early 1841 did see one sign of improvement, with a bequest from the late Mrs. Elizabeth F. Blyth. How much she willed is unknown, but it was enough for the deacon to publish an acknowledgment of her "kind benefaction."[15]

The Baptists' prayers for a resident minister were answered in early 1842, when Willis W. Childers accepted the call and preached his first sermon on February 6. Finally Baptists could read in the newspaper that "service may be experienced regularly every Sabbath. Seats provided for strangers."[16] In May, Childers was ordained in Georgetown, with Breaker, then pastor at Camden, officiating. The order of service began with Breaker's sermon on a minister's duties and responsibilities. Next, the association missionary T. Mason examined the candidate on "his religious experience, call to ministry, and doctrinal views." After prayer by Breaker and his charge to the pastor and church, Childers received the right hand of fellowship "by the Presbytery and Church."[17] Soon after his ordination he was busy baptizing slaves, and he and the deacons were talking about building "a new lecture room."[18]

Two years later Childers convinced the congregation to build a new church. The drive to raise funds for the facility at Highmarket and Queen began early in 1844 with a public appeal. Childers, in a published statement, argued that the present structure was in need of major work and that it was "at the remote end of town [and] is consequently inconvenient to many—particularly at night." He promised the congregation that this would be his only solicitation, and he proposed "a neatly finished Chapel" that would be an "improvement to our town and a standing monument of the liberality of the contributors." Fearing that supporters were planning a small building for evening meetings only, he insisted that "the Chapel is designed to be used regularly and permanently as a place of worship not simply as a Lecture Room."[19] *Lecture room* was a Baptist term used to describe a temporary facility constructed for the purpose of holding worship services while the church raised funds for a chapel. The construction of a lecture room was sometimes preferred over building a chapel, as it was a less expensive endeavor. The church edifice was usually erected adjoining the old lecture room.[20] The room was a separate unit used primarily for the instruction of slaves. Its date of construction is unknown, and references to it do not occur until 1827, but it appears to have been in use for some time before.

On January 12, 1845, the final service in the old church, some forty years of age, was a special event. There the members gathered to "hear the messages from heaven pronounced from this old time-worn pulpit, to occupy for the last time the seats which their fathers . . . occupied before them, and to pronounce . . . the last sad adieu to the house of their ancestors and the scene of their own innocent childhood."[21] As much as Childers knew the move had to be made, he consoled the elder members in their loss of the place where the "pews, the sacred desk, the walls and every post and pillar and every crevice, should have spoken . . . to tell the mingled joyful and mournful story."[22]

While the new facility was under construction, Childers promised that regular services would be held in the lecture room. The church corporation's contract with Daniel Goldfinch, "whose skill as a mechanic, is known to the community," called for dimensions of 55 by 35, including an 8-foot "tetrastyle portico" and a "cupalo" reaching nearly 50 feet. The desired look was "Grecian, or Greek prostyle temple." The pastor continued with other details:

> The entrance of the building will be a large door, in front under the portico, six feet wide extending upwards within a few inches of the ceiling. In the front end two large windows five feet wide extending upward to the height of the door. In the rear end, two windows of the same size and height. In each side three windows of the same size and height. Each window furnished with a neat pair of Venetian blinds. The interior to be neatly furnished in style corresponding. Galleries on three sides, and the form-front deep sunken anel-work between each column and anati. Each side gallery supported by four turned Grecian columns 12 inches at the base end and the end by two of the same style and size, and double antis at the meeting angles and single anti where the side gallery juts the wall on the right and left of the pulpit. The pulpit simply Grecian after recessed from the wall, and the steps formed in the recess. Seats open pews, one row under each side of the gallery, and one row in the nave divided by a partition in the centre—all capped. Two side aisles, and a transept immediately in front of the pulpit. The whole building, as to its appearance, to convey to the mind the idea of plainness, neatness, and solidity, and as its use, the idea of utility, comfort and convenience. Hence all foreign aid of ornament will be carefully omitted leaving nothing but the simple style of the order.[23]

On Saturday, March 29, 1845, the whole town gathered for the laying of the cornerstone. A major attraction was the first procession put on by a new secret society, Georgetown's Hayne Lodge Number 11 of the Independent Order of Odd Fellows. Accompanied by a band and a colorful array of officers in full regalia, Marshall Commander led the order through "several of the principal streets" and called a halt "in front of the foundation at No. 139, Highmarket Street." After an ode and hymns, the pastor offered a prayer and "immediately proceeded to make the deposites." A spokesman for the Odd Fellows delivered an address, and "the Tablet was then laid." Childers spoke, and one of the order's two chaplains "addressed the Pastor and the I.O.O.F. commendatory of the order." The chaplain pronounced the benediction, and the Fellows marched out to retrace their route. Overall, "the exercises of the day passed off agreeably and pleasantly to the gratification of many."[24] The new church was ready for dedication in eight months, with a special Sunday service on November 30. The ceremony took place that morning, followed by services in the afternoon and evening by visiting ministers.[25]

Meanwhile, there was activity in the old Black Mingo area. About 1810 a young refugee from Georgetown, Cleland Belin, fleeing an unhappy relationship with his stepmother, went to live with his uncle, John Screven. Belin became a Baptist and a rich and powerful merchant, boat builder, and shipper. At Black Mingo was a new economic center, Willtown, and Belin's stores and wharves thrived at the key location of rivers, bridges, and roads. On his considerable property Belin built two great monuments—his house and his church. His magnificent home was the regional center where the militia mustered and well-known important guests stayed. One visitor, Governor William Henry Gist, said that with the benefit of a formal education, Belin would have become "the most powerful man in South Carolina." His fourteen-bedroom mansion featured numerous books and collectibles from around the world. Especially notable was his large collection of grandfather fairy clocks, with their timing offset so that somewhere the fairies were always dancing.[26]

A stickler for detail, Belin had expert craftsmen build a remarkable church that became a legend and stood for 150 years. Announcing its completion, a Georgetown editor explained that "this building was put up at the private expense of Cleland Belin Esquire as he seemed to judge that a place of worship was called for at that place. We hope he may live to see the altar in it crowded with acceptable communicants, and that his purse may never need the dollars he has expended on the edifice."[27] On the last Saturday and Sunday of November 1843 James C. Furman preached and led the dedication ceremonies. Rectangular in shape, built of wood, and set on brick pillars, the church had many notable architectural aspects, including "the round headed window and door openings with intersecting tracery; the two-story, unfluted corner pilasters; the wide beaded entablature; the deep, boxed pediments; and the slave gallery supported by elongated columns." Passages of scripture painted on the friezes showed a strong Regular Baptist influence. One quotation read, "The angels shall come forth, and sear the wicked from among the just, and cast them into the furnace of fire; there shall be wailing and gnashing of teeth." Another piece warned "God knows thy thoughts. Verily, verily I say unto thee: except a man be born of water, and of the spirit, he cannot enter into the Kingdom of God." A brief history written in 1943 has it that Belin, when in his role as senior deacon, wore a black silk gown and was "regarded by the people with almost superstitious awe."[28]

Nationally, the most important news for Baptists came in 1845 with the split over slavery and the creation of the Southern Baptist Convention. The man who led this secession, William B. Johnson, was another giant in Baptist history, but his unique relationship to Georgetown is seldom mentioned. Born on Johns Island in 1782, he soon moved with his family to Georgetown. There young William grew up listening to the sermons of William Staughton and Edmund Botsford, in addition to studying under John Waldo. Connected to the many Baptist educational movements in South Carolina, Johnson always required Waldo's *Latin Grammar*. He was the only individual ever to serve as both president of the Triennial Convention and the Southern Baptist Convention. Johnson was baptized by Botsford and licensed to preach in Beaufort in 1805. He died in 1862 and is buried in Anderson, South Carolina, where he is honored as the founder of Anderson College.[29]

In 1846 the Georgetown church was once again experiencing growth, with white membership reaching its antebellum peak at 31, in addition to 824 African American members.[30] Childers spent less than a year in the new house of worship, leaving sometime in 1846. He was followed by James W. Hill for a brief period and in 1847 by A. B. Smith.[31] There is no record of any preaching in 1848. The following year Henry Cuttino and D. U. Smith attended the association's annual meeting and described their dire situation: "This Church has but few white members, and has had neither a pastor nor occasional supply for the past year, and their meetinghouse has been closed." Only the lecture room was available, and there some members met on Sundays to hold prayer meetings and give "religious instruction to the colored people."[32] In 1850 church clerk Henry Cuttino submitted membership figures showing 24 white and 770 black members. The association report on missionary work summarized the situation: "From the Georgetown Church, one of the oldest in this body, we have still more gloomy tidings. Our hearts bleed as we read the letter of our brethren at this place." The church was closed and "more melancholy by the removal of five efficient members." Cuttino said his heart sickened when he looked back and remembered a time "when this Church was the only one that was regularly opened in Georgetown . . . and now it is the only one that is regularly closed. . . . We can only say, unless the Lord appear for us shortly, and revive his work of grace . . . there will be none to communicate to your body the extinguish mint of this branch of his Zion."[33]

Even if the church could secure a pastor, it had no means to support one. Its only hope was aid from the association's home mission board. That agency, however, simply could not meet the demand. Georgetown was not alone in its suffering. Consider this 1851 general report on missionary work: "The board have received pressing calls for immediate aid from Georgetown, Camden, Fellowship, Black River, and others, all more or less destitute of the preached word." For that large section, only the services of H. W. Mahoney were available, and for a mere two months. Mahoney preached in Georgetown a few times, and another visit was made by James H. Cuthbert, who preached there a week, baptizing thirty black individuals and one white. C. M. Breaker also made a return appearance and baptized ten black persons.[34]

Finally, in 1852 A. D. Cohen, then pastor of Morris Street Baptist Church in Charleston, began supplying Georgetown for part of the year courtesy of the mission board. He sent the association an encouraging report: "I have baptized 82 souls; preached 36 sermons; delivered 14 lectures to the colored people; held 23 prayer meetings; visited each family at least once a month, and administered the communion three times." He found "a wide field of usefulness" in Georgetown and "thousands unprovided for in the immediate vicinity, who are anxious to hear the Gospel preached, and accessible to a Baptist Minister stationed at Georgetown." The mission board hoped to provide Georgetown with "an efficient Minister for at least half of the year." The only obstacle was a lack of financial means.[35]

As a result of such pleas, contributions to the association's mission work doubled in 1853, and the board was able to distribute $1,450 across the lowcountry and into the midlands. Morris Street, still under A. D. Cohen's care, received the largest sum, $350, with the church adding another $150. Georgetown's award, the second highest for a single church, was $200. The rest of the money went to staff two large mission circuits, with the exception of $50 each given to Bethlehem and Fellowship. Georgetown Baptists were able to convince L. M. Cohen to join them, and the association appointed him missionary to the church in January 1853.

Ordained in March, Cohen worked with "energy and zeal . . . , and with remarkable success prosecuted his labors." In a short time he gathered "a respectable congregation," baptized seventy-two people, and established a Sunday school of fifty pupils. Like so many before him, he "delighted in the humble work of preaching to the colored people," and many plantation slaves "learned to look up to and esteem him as their 'loved teacher.'" Unfortunately, Cohen died after only a few months as pastor. At the association meeting in the fall, a Reverend Cuthbert spoke about Georgetown's "afflicted condition," and, upon a motion, led the meeting in prayer on behalf of the town's Baptists. The summary of Georgetown's report of that year communicated "the mournful intelligence of the death of its beloved pastor, Bro. L. M. Cohen. . . . They beg the prayers of God's children for them in their destitute and conflicted condition."

For its part, the mission board asked, "Who will take the place of this faithful servant of Jesus Christ? Who will respond, 'here I am, send me' to this bereaved and stricken Church?"[36]

No one answered that call in 1854. Although Georgetown received another two hundred dollars in mission funds, it went unused. The association's assessment was grim: "During the past year, they have not heard a single gospel sermon save on a few occasions when the Charleston pastors have visited them. They are still without a pastor, and beseech us earnestly to send them the word. If a man can be found, this old and valuable Church with its 600 colored members must be aided."[37] The six hundred figure for black members is low; that membership was closer to nine hundred.

In 1855 the association's two-hundred-dollar allotment went unspent again, and the church remained unsuccessful in obtaining a pastor. Late in that year, however, Georgetown was able to convince one of its own, the Reverend David W. Cuttino, Jr., to join them the first of 1856, and the association upped its support to three hundred dollars.[38] Born in Georgetown on November 17, 1819, Cuttino was five years old when his physician father died. His mother moved to Columbia, where he grew up and was baptized by Dr. James Lawrence Reynolds. Ordained at Moriah Church in Sumter County in 1853, Cuttino was already active in Charleston Baptist Association affairs by the time he answered the call to Georgetown.[39] With funding dependent on the association, Cuttino's appointment was on a yearly basis, but Georgetown was extremely grateful, writing in its annual letter that "without your donation, in all probability the church would have remained closed." They hoped for a time "when it will be unnecessary to ask your assistance."[40]

In his first year Cuttino added forty black members and generated "deep interest" from young people in "the prosperity of the Church." The new preacher left Georgetown for three months during the summer "owing to the sickly season" and traveled inland as a missionary for the association. Despite the sad news that their hard-working deacon Henry Cuttino died, 1856 saw a definite rise in the spirits of the growing congregation. Indeed, the church felt confident enough to invite the association to hold its next meeting there, a request that would not be granted for many years.[41] Pastor Cuttino was ably assisted by his fifteen-year-old son, David William Cuttino III. Baptized by his father in Georgetown, he taught in the Sunday school and led the singing.[42]

Except for the summers, Cuttino's schedule in Georgetown included morning and evening services on Sunday, with religious instruction for black persons on Sunday afternoons. He also held a special service for black church-goers each Wednesday evening. In addition to his visitation requirements in Georgetown, he enjoyed holding services on plantations, particularly one some twenty-one miles up the Waccamaw River. "Persons come there from two to fifteen miles," he reported, "to hear the word of God preached and to witness the ordinance of baptism." The plantation owner was highly pleased with Cuttino's work, and was considering building a meeting house. Cuttino's summer missionary work was cut short by the death of his wife, and he struggled to manage his young family while being ill himself. He did, however, spend some time in Clarendon District, preaching at Manning, Moriah, Fellowship, and Zoar. Including Georgetown and up the Waccamaw, Cuttino baptized sixty-five people, one of whom was white.[43]

After the death of his "amiable companion," it is understandable that the young widower (Cuttino was thirty-nine at the time) grew uncomfortable in Georgetown. White membership remained stagnant, but he was having success as a missionary elsewhere. He continued to visit the Waccamaw station and had a regular appointment fifteen miles from town at Carraway's School House. He went there every third Thursday, and on his way stopped to preach to the slaves at D. H. Smith's plantation. The congregation was all white at Carraway, and he reported encouraging news: "Our little School House cannot hold any more. The building of a meeting house for the accommodation of the people is spoken of." In 1859 he calculated that his work as a missionary amounted to "tracts distributed, 756; traveled 1347 miles; family visits, 325; sermons preached, 60; lectures, 15; baptized, 42; say 19 whites, and 23 blacks." In Georgetown he had baptized only six black persons and two white individuals. Some of his most exciting work came in Clarendon District, where he and his missionary colleagues, John L. Rollins and H. W. Mahoney, revived and energized several churches. Three of these—Manning, Home Branch, and Bush Arbor—called Cuttino as pastor. He accepted, with his resignation at Georgetown effective at the end of 1859. Subsequent association minutes list Cuttino's three-point charge as Manning, Home Branch, and Taw Caw.[44] His career as a prominent Baptist lasted until his death on May 29, 1886. For years he served as moderator of the Charleston Baptist Association, and was highly regarded for his work in the temperance and Sunday-school crusades.[45]

Cuttino's experiences also provide a window into the role of African American leadership within the church.[46] There are a few clues from the press and from the church's reports to Charleston. From these it is clear that Georgetown referred to its "large colored population" far more times than any other church.[47] It is also true that the Charleston Baptist Association minutes contain no references to any ordinations of black preachers and deacons. The role of black congregants was entirely unofficial, and they were certainly not involved in the church's decisions as a corporate body. In addition to Cuttino's work with black leaders, there is a fascinating moment when Georgetown's

First Baptist Church of Georgetown Church Membership 1831–1889

Year	Black Members	White Members	Year	Black Members	White Members
1831	430	34	1849	792	26
1832	430	34	1850	770	24
1833	449	27	1851	786	23
1834	449	27	1852	352	28
1835	469	24	1853	898	27
1836	497	24	1854	898	27
1837	493	23	1855	961	23
1838	514	22	1856	984	28
1840	552	17	1857	1,044	28
1841	469	16	1871	1	9
1842	608	16	1872	0	23
1843	706	20	1873	0	22
1844	721	19	1874	0	22
1845	741	29	1875	0	22
1846	798	31	1876	0	22
1847	806	29	1888	0	13
1848	808	28	1889	0	27

Source: Compiled from Charleston Baptist Association minutes.

black Baptists were particularly well organized. In 1854, before the association's meeting, a group of black congregants traveled to Charleston to seek aid for the church. The chairman of the home mission board gave them an audience and was impressed with their "earnest countenances on behalf of their Brethren." They pleaded, "Do not let our children die without Jesus Christ." To that, the board could only ask, "Brethren, shall they die? The question is for us to decide."[48]

Many Georgetown Baptists were slaveholders, although it is clear from the extensive number of slaves in the church that most of the black congregants' white masters attended church elsewhere. Charles Breaker, former pastor of the church, owned only five slaves in 1840. According to the 1860 census, David W. Cuttino, then in Clarendon District, owned a dozen slaves and C. M. Breaker five. Deacon Henry Cuttino owned sixty-five slaves in 1840, but that number dropped to fifteen in the following decade. The Cuttino family owned quite a few slaves, with each male member possessing about twenty. Cleland Belin in neighboring Williamsburg had ten slaves as of 1860, but that was the most he had owned in twenty years. Georgetown Baptists had at least a few prominent slaveholders. Active members John Bossard and Thomas F. Goddard owned 75 and 180 slaves respectively. These men were probably exceptions to the rule, with most wealthy white slaveholders remaining in the Episcopal Church.[49]

In 1841 an African American preacher from the Baptist church in Georgetown caused a great debate between the Methodists and Baptists. He, too, is unidentified, although throughout the discourse the fact that there was a black preacher is never questioned and was accepted as a matter of course.[50] Quite surprisingly, it was the white Baptists who rushed to his defense. The Sampit Methodists, just outside Georgetown, had been supplied by missionary Paul A. M. Williams, and what he found there disturbed him. In his view the black Baptist preacher was baptizing slaves far too quickly on the promise that the act of immersion granted salvation and freedom from sin. When Williams finished his tour, he filed, on January 20, 1841, a report with William Capers, head of the Methodist mission effort in South Carolina, and that document was published in the *Southern Christian Advocate* and the local newspaper. What angered Baptists and other community members was the letter's unseemly comments about Baptist beliefs. Writing under the name "Candor," a self-professed member of no denomination claimed that "the Revd. Gentleman in said letter has at least made insinuations, if not assertions, in reference to the doctrines and teachings of the Baptists, which should either be proved or unsaid." Another writer signed himself "A Bona-Fide Baptist" and charged that Williams had "cast reflection upon the Baptist denomination, in ascribing to the colored portion of it, the belief that baptism is regeneration." Williams was surprised that his report "excited a great deal of astonishment and dissatisfaction among a certain class of this community." He was quick to point out that his critics were writing under "fictitious signatures," while his work and name were "held out to the view of every one." Williams claimed to mean no offense but insisted he personally knew slaves who believed that "baptism by immersion is the means of a present, full, and eternal salvation; and that after you have been baptized, it is impossible to sin or fall from grace."

Bona-Fide provided a lengthy account of the great caution Baptists took about baptizing freely, insisting that a time of regeneration is required. To that the Methodist noted, "To my certain knowledge persons have been admitted to the communion of the Baptist Church (I do not say in Georgetown) who were never regenerated." He insisted that the majority of "ignorant and superstitious rice field negroes" were convinced that it was "only necessary to be immersed and they are then sure of a seat in Heaven."[51] In the end Williams had nothing to fear from the Baptists—he is honored in the historical marker at Sampit Methodist.

As the antebellum period came to a close, the church was again in dire straits, and its situation would only grow worse with the advent of war. Perhaps the biggest achievement within this period, aside from the new building, now long gone, was the nurturing of African American lay leaders, whether preachers, exhorters, deacons, elders, or watchmen.[52] While we have no mention of any of these men being officially ordained by Georgetown Baptists, their presence and role are undeniable. Similarly, we have no accounts of Georgetown African American Baptist funerals or weddings, although it seems certain that black lay leaders handled these affairs. The best examples of slave religion in Georgetown District come from the wealthy Episcopalians who were plantation owners. Robert F. W. Allston had "a place of worship" for his slaves that was "open to all denominations of Christians." He added that under his rules "the Methodists and Baptists have pray-meetings at given houses, each twice a week, besides Sunday, when they meet, and pray and sing together. These meetings are exclusively for the negroes on my plantation. I have had this custom for 15 years, and it works well."[53] John H. Tucker, also on the Waccamaw, noted that working with his slaves were "one Episcopalian, two Methodists, and occasionally, one Baptist." The Episcopalian Alexander Glennie visited twice a month on Sunday mornings. On his Pee Dee plantation Tucker employed a Methodist minister. He required his slaves to attend the services, and an unexcused absence was punished by a cut in rations.[54] William Fripp, a Baptist from St. Helena, reported that in addition to Sunday services, black individuals "meet two or three times a week in the prayer-house on their own plantations and unite in singing, praying and reading the work of God." He reported that he had an effective method for black children: "Every evening they are assembled by an old black man, who is a Christian and can read. He teaches them the catechism as put out by our Methodist bretheren, and with great success."[55]

David Cuttino left the Georgetown church in 1859 with the largest membership in its history, a functioning Sunday school of fourteen scholars and four teachers, and a budget that allowed a donation of forty-eight dollars to the mission efforts of the association. In 1860, without a preacher, the church would soon close during the Civil War and for some time thereafter. The association received neither word nor monetary contributions from Georgetown for more than a decade. Not until 1872 was the all-white congregation of twenty-three able to scrape together $2.50 as a donation. Real stability would not be reached for another two decades.[56]

NINE

Recovery

THE WAR HIT GEORGETOWN EARLY, when the bay came under Federal siege and gunboats patrolled the rivers. The town and plantations were largely deserted as white people fled inland. Some went as far away as Greenville and some as near as Conwayboro, taking many of their slaves with them.[1] Everything went to support the war, including the bell of the Baptist church. By conflict's end Georgetown District was truly a world turned upside down. With a new state constitution in place, even the name of the place changed to Georgetown County.[2] Some of the refugees never returned, and after the war there was a scramble for "abandoned lands."[3] Seven years after the war conditions along the South Carolina coast remained terrible. In 1872 the Baptist home mission board reported that, with the exception of Charleston, "the whole range of coastal country, from Georgetown to Savannah River, presents a picture of destitution truly deplorable—churches burned or deserted, a population demoralized or broken-spirited, and everywhere poverty under circumstances the most trying and discouraging."[4]

The postwar political revolution in Georgetown, where African Americans had some authority, lasted longer than in any other South Carolina county. Not until the race riot of 1900 did the attempt at "fusion" end. In addition, the economy was very slow to recover. The rice culture began a steady decline, but not solely because slavery had ended and not entirely due to world market changes. Weather conditions tended to be adverse, and the great hurricane of 1893 was certainly a death knell. Then there was the coming of the "rice birds," with their dreaded arrival announced each year in the press and their devastation remarkable. They were Bobolinks, small in size but in numbers extremely destructive.[5] Within a couple of years after the turn of the twentieth century, the rice culture was completely dead. Today there are thousands of acres of abandoned rice fields, and, while wild rice grows abundantly and the area is a sporting delight, the rice industry, like indigo production, is a thing of the past, remembered only in the names of restaurants and housing developments.

The Baptist church in Georgetown, built back in 1845 and last pastored by David W. Cuttino, stood empty—its congregation decimated by the unhappy

Edward Cuttino pictured here as a young Confederate soldier shortly after
his father, D. W. Cuttino, concluded his pastorate of the Baptist church in
Georgetown. Edward Cuttino served from 1894 until his death in 1896.
Courtesy of Georgetown First Baptist Church.

course of events. In 1870 only five members remained, a strong image of the
depth of the calamity for Georgetown, a once great church now nearly extinct.[6]
There is another image, however, that highlights even more sharply a religious
world on its head. The development of African American churches took off
upon emancipation, and such speed suggests that religious freedom was among
the first rights exercised, and strenuously, by former slaves.[7]

The study of this transformation in Georgetown centers around Bethesda
Missionary Baptist, which grew directly out of the antebellum church. While
it has been suggested that some white persons resisted the creation of African
American–controlled churches, in Georgetown the conversion seems to have
been congenial and consensual.[8] Shortly after emancipation, African American

Baptists organized Bethesda under the leadership of the Reverend Edward G. Rhue. In the spring of 1867 they paid $150 for a lot on Wood Street. Lacking any building, they continued to meet in the old lecture room until they rolled it on logs to their new property.[9] To this day the pews in the balcony at Bethesda are from the lecture room, dating at least to the 1840s. In 1867 Bethesda was a founding member of South Carolina's first black Baptist Association, Gethsemane, with a Sunday school of fifty students.[10] The Bethel African Methodist Episcopal Church likewise grew out of the prewar Methodist Church in Georgetown. For many years thereafter, there were five churches in Georgetown—the Episcopal, Methodist, and Baptist, in addition to Bethel and Bethesda.

In the case of Georgetown the old Baptist church retained at least one African American member until 1871.[11] This was not atypical. Joel Williamson found that in 1874 there were 1,614 African Americans still in white-controlled churches.[12] Of the fifty churches in the Charleston Baptist Association in 1871, thirteen had black members. Ten were in single digits, but Pine Grove reported ten black members, Mt. Pleasant thirty-five, and St. James forty. St. James was alone in the association with a majority of blacks—forty out of seventy-five.[13] The best-known case of this inversion in the Charleston Association is Morris Street Baptist Church in Charleston.[14]

While African Americans were enjoying their right as Baptists to be autonomous and independent, the white establishment believed the new churches needed assistance. The concern was that many of their black brethren were meeting in crude shelters and, more important, without trained ministers. The efforts on the part of white Baptists began in 1866, when the state convention appointed a committee, including James C. Furman and Basil Manly, Jr., to facilitate "the religious instruction of the colored population."[15] In 1877 two "colored brethren" were seated at the South Carolina Baptist Convention as messengers from the newly formed black Baptist state organization.[16]

By 1889 white Baptists were funding black ministers and organizing black churches, working with C. E. Becker, president of Benedict Institute.[17] In 1891, for instance, white Baptists employed nine African American preachers throughout the state. The conflict between the growing white-supremacy movement and the Baptist obligation to mission work is obvious in the state home mission reports. In 1889 African Americans were termed "ignorant, superstitious, immoral, yet they are patient, inclined to be religious, and have shown a capacity of great development. . . . If the gospel can make a negro in the heart of Africa Christ-like, it can do it in South Carolina." In 1891 the issue was restated: "The Negroes are here in considerable force, and so far as we know, are here to stay. We say they are superstitious, grossly immoral, and proverbially dishonest. Then it becomes the more binding on us to elevate them. . . . We Must evangelize the Negroes." This attempt at religious fusion failed, however, and the black convention in 1902 resolved against any cooperation with white Baptists. The latter concluded: "We do not believe that this is a sentiment of the masses of our colored brethren, but so long as it is the sentiment of their leaders, we are powerless to do any work among them."[18] The case in Georgetown is quite interesting. In 1904, when the Charleston Association met in Georgetown, Hugh Oliver introduced the Reverend R. B. Salters and the Reverend A. B. Wright, pastors of African American Baptist Churches in Georgetown and Williamsburg County. The association invited them to speak and "hardily responded in admirable addresses, advocating the cause of the colored Baptist[s] of South Carolina; in which they expressed their purpose of co-operating with the white Baptists in future. These speakers were well-received and the brethren thanked for their fraternal utterances."[19]

The venerable church of the Cuttinos and related families sat silent until 1871, when communication was restored with the association. The situation was essentially the same as in 1860: missionary desperately desired. This first sign of life included a commitment to contribute to a pastor's salary and a request for a prompt visit from association leaders. Membership for 1871 consisted of one African American and nine white persons.[20] The visiting committee came in late December "to survey the ground and ascertain what we could do for the ancient Church there." The team judged Georgetown favorable territory and reported that pledges in the amount of two hundred dollars had been made by the citizens for the year 1872. Generally they saw good prospects for the "reopening of the Church." That effort did produce results, and A. I. Hartley, from Warrenton, Georgia, took the missionary appointment in early 1872. With aid from the mission board the church delighted in "having preaching three times every week since March."[21]

Hartley's early success grew "large and attentive" congregations, but he discovered "a systematic effort to prejudice the community against Baptists"; in fact, with the church closed some members "had attached themselves to Pedo-Baptists." He began lecturing on the basic tenets of "close communion and baptism," and within a few weeks he had baptized eight, including three Methodists, and had received others by letter. Hartley summarized his work as "sermons preached 147; baptized, eight; received by letter, six; restored, one." The church wanted Hartley to continue, but he was "prayerfully considering . . . the want of progress." Soon he took, as his "path of duty," the call from Antioch Church in Orangeburg County, leaving Georgetown around the first of April.[22] There was no Baptist minister in Georgetown for the remainder of 1873.

These pews in the balcony of Bethesda Missionary Baptist Church came
from the Antebellum Lecture Room of the Antipedo Baptist Church.
Photo by Isaac Dusenbury.

There is some confusion in the records about how long the church was ac-
tually closed. The minutes for 1872 put the number of years without a preacher
at fifteen. The visiting committee from Charleston late in 1871 has it that the
church during "the last thirteen or fourteen years suffered greatly for want of
a supply of the preached word." The correct number seems to be eleven, with
the church closed from 1860 through 1870. The lack of any written records
for those years supports the idea of an absolute closure. The Baptist presence,
however, never completely died out. Preachers were in short supply during
and after the war, working as chaplains and colporteurs distributing tracts and
Bibles. Alternatively, there may well have been times when a sojourning minister was pressed into the pulpit. It is also hard to believe that those years elapsed
without a single prayer meeting, and it is possible that the term *closed* referred
only to a lack of ministers and not to a complete closure, with no functions at
all.[23] While it remains a disturbing puzzle, the significant outcome is that the
church may have been closed for years, but it never became extinct. Officially
the Baptists claimed nine members in 1871, while the investigating committee

found "seven white communicants" and received three more by letter. When Hartley arrived he counted eight members.[24]

With the departure of Hartley, the church found itself once again without a pastor and quickly became one of the "weak and destitute churches" the Baptist hierarchy hoped to aid. There was no Sunday school, and in 1875 the contribution to the association amounted to a mere $1.10.[25] A brief moment of near recovery came in early 1877, when Hugh Forsyth Oliver arrived as a missionary to Georgetown and a church up the Black River in Williamsburg County. In town he saw "peculiar local difficulties to contend with," and at Black River the church was "nearly dead." Oliver, a graduate of the state Baptist Theological Seminary, claimed to have walked six hundred miles and preached one hundred times that year. He worked Georgetown semimonthly with Sunday services at eleven, three-thirty, and seven.[26]

Oliver married into the influential Cuttino-Smith family, but despite his ties to and genuine affection for Georgetown, he found it impossible to resolve those local peculiarities. Precisely what they were is unknown, and they may have had less to do with internal church matters (although there are hints) than with the old complaint that Georgetown was hard ground for religion to take root. The state convention's assessment of Oliver's ability to succeed was bleak: "There does not seem to be any hopefulness as to the building up of a self-sustaining church at Georgetown." The opposite was true at Black River, where Oliver had been much more successful.[27] Soon he added Belin's church at Black Mingo to give him a three-point charge.[28] That was the end of his Georgetown pastorate, and Oliver moved on to other missionary posts. In 1879 he was preaching in Edgefield, and in 1883 he returned twice and preached in Georgetown.[29]

Perhaps the association's prediction was self-fulfilling and the difficulties were insurmountable. For whatever reason, the church once against found itself in a decade-long state of near closure. From 1878 to 1887 the church failed to make any report, and when communication resumed the following year, Georgetown had thirteen members and no Sunday school. Other than visits by Oliver, there is very little mention of the Baptists in the press during the 1880s. A Reverend Samuel M. Richardson preached there in the spring of 1882, and David W. Cuttino held services at least three times in the summer of 1885.[30] The state mission board in 1886 reported that between Georgetown and the Northeastern Railroad there were "six-hundred square miles . . . almost entirely destitute of the gospel. In Georgetown we have a house of worship and a parsonage, and yet no Baptist preaching."[31] In many respects the church's struggle to recover paralleled that of Georgetown and other towns in the South. The key was the coming of the railroad and telegraph in 1883. At that same time the port returned to life and social improvements were made, particularly the organization of the Palmetto Club, also in 1883. Politically the town became an incorporated city in 1892, led by a mayor instead of an intendant.[32]

The Georgetown Baptists witnessed substantial growth from 1884 to 1888. The heroine in the story is Mary A. Butts, a devout Baptist who took the initiative of contacting Dr. T. M. Bailey of the state home mission board. When he visited Georgetown in 1884 what he saw was not pleasant. The old church building was in a state of disrepair. At night the constellations could be seen through the roof, and it was, in a word, "uninhabitable."[33] To solve this problem Bailey made arrangements for the Baptists to use the Methodist Church.[34] At that time the church consisted of fifteen members. Their use of the Methodist facility seems to have been limited, and the only known preaching came three times during the summer of 1885 when William Cuttino Smith visited.[35]

Mary Butts's contributions did not end there. She would be the mainstay of the church for the rest of her long and full life. Her biggest service, however, came in convincing her husband to remodel the old church. Oliver J. Butts was a mechanical engineer and respected in the area. Before serving in the war he built the Keithfield rice mill, and after the war constructed the mill in Georgetown. He also designed the cupola for Prince George Winyah Parish Church. Butts was not an official member of the Baptist church, but he donated the required funds and probably designed and directed the restoration of the building. In 1886 "an excellent brother" told one of Bailey's missionaries that he stood ready "to lay down on the church lot, free of cost, all the lumber necessary to repair the church building if your board will establish regular preaching there."[36] The benefactor, no doubt, was Oliver Butts. Renovations at Highmarket and Queen began in the spring of 1887, when, as the *Georgetown Enquirer* noted, the church "will be put in good order, and our Baptist friends hope to be able to open its doors and have regular services once or twice a month."[37] When the job was completed in the spring of 1888 Butts joined the church.[38] Also helping in the restoration was Robert W. Mustard, a longtime engineer of the fire department and "an upright and consistent member of the Baptist church."[39] In 1888 the church could report to the association that, although it commenced the year "under unfavorable prospects," by the fall it rejoiced "in seeing the work of the lord progressing."[40]

Working out of Greenville, Dr. Bailey continued to be a vital part of this regeneration, preaching in Georgetown for four nights running in March 1888.[41] He also arranged for a new missionary, L. T. Carroll, who accepted a dual appointment at Georgetown and at Sampit Station on a salary of three hundred dollars.[42] Preaching in town occurred on the second and fourth Sundays, with a total membership of twenty-seven. Carroll had high hopes at

Sampit, where a small church stood. He figured that he had traveled one thousand miles, preached ninety-five sermons, baptized fifteen, organized one Sunday school, and collected $30.76 for mission work.[43] At Georgetown, Carroll was assisted by other visiting missionaries, and during the year he received five new members by baptism and letter. Oliver returned twice, once to participate in a protracted service in the spring of 1888.[44] When Carroll's assignment at Georgetown ended, a newspaper editor reported that his leaving was regretted "by his flock, as well as numerous friends here. The good will and esteem of everyone will follow this devoted disciple of the Lord and Master."[45]

While waiting for a new missionary, the Baptists invited visiting evangelist W. S. Monteith, a Columbia lawyer and ordained Methodist minister, to their pulpit. He had preached in Georgetown before "in the open air, on Sunday afternoons, near the Market," but his services in 1890 were held in the evening in the Baptist church "and were attended by large and respectful audiences." Dr. Bailey returned to Georgetown on March 16, 1890, accompanied by William M. Gordon from Spencer, North Carolina. Gordon began preaching twice a month at a salary of two hundred dollars.[46] By his calculations he preached thirty-two sermons, made sixty visits, performed ten Sunday-school addresses, organized one prayer meeting, increased membership to thirty-four, and raised forty dollars for missions. Georgetown estimated that it would take four hundred dollars for a full-time pastor, and they pledged to provide three hundred dollars themselves. The church did have a functioning Sunday school, with Mustard as superintendent and a student body of forty.[47] That spring, Gordon put on a revival led by the Reverend C. C. Brown of Sumter, followed by another in October under T. E. Jasper of Blackville. One of Gordon's innovations during the revivals involved holding separate services for men and women. That spring he had a service at four in the afternoon for ladies only. In the fall revival he spoke at the courthouse exclusively to men: "The reverend gentleman called a spade a spade and did not mince matters at all in dealing with some of the serious sins of our community. Quite a crowd listened to him." Gordon's term ended, and he preached his last sermon in Georgetown in March 1891. "His numerous friends here," noted the *Georgetown Times*, "part with him with regret."[48]

A significant indication of progress is that when Gordon left he was replaced within the month. Never again, for any extended period, would the Baptists be destitute of the preached word. Moreover, the position was no longer a two- or three-point charge. Now they proudly proclaimed "regular services in the church every Sabbath at the usual hours, morning and evening." The new pastor, J. S. McLemore of Kentucky, arrived in town on April 11. The appearance of this "eloquent young divine" signaled the beginning of a robust recovery. His arrival prompted a local editor to recount the years long ago when the church had "a large and wealthy congregation," but "the war (among other sad things) broke up this church." Now it was regularly open every Sunday, and with Pastor McLemore making "a fine impression" and having "secured the friendship and love of all," the editor expressed "the sincere wish of all that their present stand may be maintained."[49]

What was the spark that caused such an explosion of activity? It may have been as simple as a complaint about the condition of the old Antipedo Baptist Cemetery on Church Street. In early 1887 the editor of the *Times* noted that the graveyard was "in terrible condition; the weeds and brambles are in such abundance that it is almost impossible to discern a tombstone, much less peruse its inscription."[50] The *Georgetown Enquirer* agreed and observed that "every burying place in the town and vicinity" was in "dilapidated condition. . . . Even a stranger might blush for very shame at their woeful and neglected appearance."[51] The Baptists had their cemetery sufficiently cleared in the spring of 1890 for the ladies of the church to adorn the graves of the Confederate dead. Unfortunately, the improved graveyard, properly fenced and gated, became an inviting place to pen livestock. There were several instances when the lock was broken and cattle enclosed. The church publicly warned the trespassers to cease and desist or face "the full penalty of the law. It is sacrilegious to thus invade the sanctity of the dead and we hope there will be no further complaints on this score."[52]

Improving the church was part and parcel of a larger movement, a New South optimism expressed by local boosters everywhere. A neat cemetery was one thing, but the real symbol of progress was Butts's remodeling the church edifice itself. The rebuilding is evident in the increasing value of church property. Church assets were a new category in the association minutes. In 1890 the Georgetown structure was valued at $1,300; in 1891 that figure jumped to $3,500 and then reached $4,000 in 1895.[53]

The efforts of the Mustards, Butts, and others in the late 1880s produced a restored and modernized building. As the newspaper pointed out in June of 1891, "the Baptist church is always well lighted at night; in fact, it is the best lighted church in the town."[54] Another noticeable improvement came in the music department, which boasted a cornet, as well as an organ and a piano. The finishing touch was the addition of a bell to replace the one donated to the war effort.[55] The new facility, and the momentum generated by it, allowed the expansion of programs and services. The first reported Children's Day came in June of 1891, when a dozen boys and girls recited verses, sang songs, and read scripture. The church was "magnificently dressed, evergreens and flowers being used in profusion." The first modern wedding of record drew a large crowd. "The church was nicely decorated with flowers and wreaths and presented a fine appearance." McLemore's fall 1891 revival, featuring a Reverend Ratcliffe of Kentucky, was a big success, producing many baptisms—it took two nights to dunk them all.[56] Encouraged, he planned to have "special meetings" in the fall. While still requiring aid from Charleston and Greenville, the church was relatively prosperous. The Sunday school had grown to thirty-nine pupils and six officers and teachers, and they met every Sunday. Prayer meetings also became more regularized under McLemore; he held twenty.[57]

In 1892 the church was on a rising tide. Bailey preached twice early that year, and the pastor of Citadel Square in Charleston spoke three times in late March.[58] The biggest event given by the church came in the spring of 1892 with the largest Children's Day ever. The *Georgetown Times* reported with enthusiasm: "The Children's Day at the Baptist Church: A Beautiful Service—Crowded House—Complete Success." Mary Butts was the chief organizer with the help of Pastor McLemore. Mrs. White "presided at the organ," and Mr. Leland, the music director, was "a genius—at least where music is concerned." Mr. Croft and Mr. Sparks performed on their cornets. In addition to prayer and scripture reading, the program featured nineteen different components involving the children. What "particularly pleased" the *Times* editor was "the presence of so many members of different religious denominations."[59]

Back before the war, when the church was thriving under David W. Cuttino, it requested, unsuccessfully, that the Charleston Baptist Association hold its annual November meeting in Georgetown. In 1891 Georgetown renewed its invitation. This time it was accepted, and what an occasion it was—both in real and symbolic terms, a major milestone had been reached. The event began at ten o'clock Thursday on November 3, 1892, and lasted for three days, with preaching every morning and evening. The Reverend W. J. Snider of Santee was elected moderator and W. G. Wells of Sumter was elected clerk. T. M. Bailey was there, along with A. J. S. Thomas, editor of the *Baptist Courier,* and J. L. Voss of the Connie Maxwell Orphanage. Hugh Oliver preached the final sermon on Sunday night, and the event concluded with everyone singing "God Be with You Till We Meet Again." Wells wrote a lengthy thank you letter to the pastor and the citizens of Georgetown: "Our stay in your city has been a most pleasant one, with not one occurrence to mar the pleasure of the meeting or of a single individual."[60] The minutes expressed thanks to the church and community who "opened their hearts and homes to our delegates and visitors."[61]

Another pleasurable event for the town was the pastor's wedding on December 1, 1892. The church was crowded "almost to suffocation" that

Wednesday night to see the Reverend J. S. McLemore marry Miss Minnie Skinner. "Everyone agrees that it was a beautiful ceremony," the newspaper reported,

> the church being handsomely decorated and the happy young couple being united while standing under an arch of roses and evergreens, while Mrs. S. E. White rendered the wedding march as they entered the church. Rev. M. W. Gordon read the marriage service and made it a complete success. The popular young people departed for Aiken the next morning, where they are now in attendance at the Baptist Convention. Quite a number of their friends and invited guests assembled at the residence of Mr. and Mrs. O. J. Butts after the services at the church, where congratulations and good wishes were given and exchanged.[62]

Social events in general were increasing in Georgetown, and Mary Butts was right in the thick of it, raising money for the church. Sometimes the ladies of different denominations worked on shares. One popular fundraiser was the "dime reading." The price of admission is obvious, but the program, while it contained some recitations, was really a community talent show offering "young people an evening of rare fun and amusement." Organized by Mary Butts and Mrs. W. W. Taylor of the Methodist church and held at the Winyah Indigo Society hall, the June 27, 1893, reading was a success, with good attendance, refreshments, and "a neat little sum raised." The response was enthusiastic, with the *Georgetown Times* calling for more "delightful hours of pleasure . . . during these dull summer evenings." The following year, in December, Mary Butts put on a reading at her large home on Front Street, "a very entertaining evening." The crowd overflowed into the yard, "and the proceeds of the entertainment [were] very gratifying." Such was typical, the editor said, of "the entertainments given under the auspices of this good lady." Later she moved her venue to the Standard Theatre, and in April 1895 produced "the most successful entertainment of the season." The gate alone raised $83.75, plus the profit on concessions.[63]

Another popular event was an Apron Party. Mary Butts put one on at her home on a Friday evening in February 1894. Admission was ten cents for the benefit of the parsonage. Again, there were recitations, vocal and instrumental music, and food, but the new part of the evening was the apron requirement. The young ladies brought unhemmed aprons, and the men drew names to learn whose to hem. First, they had to thread the needle and then do the sewing: "Some used their left hand, some sewed backwards, all without thimbles, and it did not seem to appear to them that they even needed one." E. M. Doar took the prize, "a handsome card receiver," while Herman Shenk got the "booby," a clay pipe. Lester Johnson, complaining that his material was "too full of holes . . . it was scrim," received honorable mention.[64]

In April and May of 1894 the Reverend J. B. Shelton of Corsicana, Texas, held a protracted revival in Georgetown. He had gone to seminary with Pastor McLemore, who called him "one of the most eloquent young men in the South."[65] At the revival's conclusion Shelton and the pastor left on the train for the Southern Baptist Convention in Dallas, Texas. McLemore was able to go because the church and the community had passed the hat for him. He called it "one of the greatest pleasures ever afforded me . . . doubly sweet . . . since it comes not alone from my own church but the city at large."[66] Unfortunately for the church and the town, McLemore's mother, who resided in Kentucky, was gravely ill. In June 1894 he preached his last sermon and left for home with his wife and infant child. Before the summer was out, the church had a new pastor with a familiar name.

Edward H. Cuttino was the son of David W. Cuttino, pastor at Georgetown before the war. His father baptized him there. Unfortunately, his time in Georgetown and on earth was brief. While moving into the repaired parsonage, he broke his leg when a piano fell. Already a sufferer of consumption, the weakened pastor was often unable to preach. He brought in a series of ministers and tried to keep up visiting "on an invalid's bicycle . . . a spontaneous gift of his bretheren at the convention." He died on February 24, 1896; "A Long, Useful And Beautiful Life Comes To An End."[67] His remains were sent to his beloved Ebenezer Church in Florence County. "The people to whom he ministered were very poor, and our brother lived and labored on the meager salary of the missionary. . . . Through rain and swamp and malaria and heat, he urged on his work at the sacrifice of comfort and health."[68]

With Cuttino gone, McLemore returned in March 1896 and was followed by a series of visiting preachers, one of whom was Charles A. Jones of Columbia. He accepted the call from Georgetown in June 1896. Jones, however, did not stay long because of his health. He left in October to go to the Mullins church in Marion County.[69] Jones was replaced by E. D. Wells in 1897. Wells took charge on April 1, and at that time the church had fifty-five members, a seating capacity in the sanctuary of 350, a parsonage and lot valued at $1,200, and the church itself valued at $2,000. The clerk was J. M. Nettles, and B. M. Shackleford was superintendent of Sunday school.[70] During Wells's tenure the church established a Baptist Young People's Union (BYPU), and programs for the youth increased. In the fall of 1897 the BYPU entertained at Mark Moses' Standard Opera House: "Besides music, recreations, dialogues, and refreshments, there will be a mid-winter picnic basket."[71] With these efforts enough money was raised to paint the Baptist parsonage, "which adds greatly

Front Street, Georgetown, about 1900.
Courtesy of Georgetown County Museum.

to Highmarket Street."[72] The good work under Wells continued until he left in the spring of 1901 to serve in Hasellville, Chester County.

When the long and painful century ended, the church was very near sustainability, though still considered a "mission" dependent on association and state support. The ninety-seven members enjoyed preaching every Sunday, and spring and fall revivals were held regularly and with great success. There were thirty-five students in the Sunday school, including five officers and teachers. In 1900 Oliver Butts died, honored as one of Georgetown's giants. Mary Butts, however, had many years left. She would be there to raise the money, to lead the Women's Missionary Society, and to drive her surrey around town to pick up her Sunday-school students.[73]

TEN

Growing Pains

THE TWENTIETH CENTURY OPENED BRIGHTLY for Georgetown when it realized the New South dream of attracting northern capitalists to invest in development. The industry was timber, and in January 1900 the Atlantic Coast Lumber Company constructed its first mill and began cutting the vast pine forests around Georgetown. Acquiring land and timber rights on a massive scale, the company bought the Georgetown and Western Railroad and built a new depot and two round houses. Calling itself "the greatest lumber plant in the world," the company erected a new town on the west side around its impressive headquarters and hotel. Even the great financier J. P. Morgan came in his private train to inspect the facilities.[1] Another important development was the introduction of bright-leaf, flue-cured tobacco throughout the Pee Dee region. Indigo was gone, rice was gone, but in the interior tobacco thrived.[2] Reporting on all of this was the intrepid editor of the *Georgetown Times,* Josiah Doar. Most issues of the *Times* after the mid-1890s have survived and provide a fascinating window into cultural history. A Methodist himself, Doar gave ample coverage to other faiths. He regularly announced and described important Jewish holidays, and he gave considerable print to African American social and religious events.[3]

Jobs brought people, and church membership everywhere increased. Georgetown Baptists reported rising demands on the pastor and the church "owing to increase of population."[4] In addition to the Methodists, Episcopalians, and Baptists, the Presbyterians, after a long absence, organized their own church. Roman Catholics dedicated the Church of Saint Mary of Ransom in 1902, and three years later the historic Jewish community in Georgetown formalized a congregation.[5] By that time there were five white churches and five black churches within the corporate limits of Georgetown.[6] With Pastor Wells leaving in the spring of 1901, the church relied on visiting preachers for several months. In October they extended a call to a Reverend Mackey, who preached there for a few weeks before returning to Charleston. "Personally," opined the *Times,* "we found this gentleman very agreeable and courteous, and he made many friends here during his short stay."[7] The Baptists hoped to sell the church

Georgetown celebrates Centennial Day, 1905.
Courtesy of Georgetown County Museum.

and build a new one on upper Highmarket Street as soon as they could find a lot. Mark Moses was the proposed buyer of the church and parsonage for five thousand dollars and he planned to erect a synagogue on the site. The *Times* was moved to predict that "Georgetown will soon be known as the 'city of churches.'"[8] That sale never materialized, and it would be more than a decade before the Baptists would be able to build.

In November 1902, after a brief stint by B. M. Forsman, a permanent minister arrived. J. W. Powell preached his trial sermon on the second of the month and was installed on December 7. The *Georgetown Times* found him "an interesting and forcible talker and is head and shoulders above any preacher this denomination has had here in our time."[9] Under Powell the church grew dramatically, and the prospects were, as one editor said, "very bright for the Baptists to be one of the largest and strongest denominations in the city."[10] Since the sale of the old church had not gone through, the deacons decided to repair and enlarge the existing structure. The contract to "put it in modern shape" was for $1,500.[11] While the repairs were being made, the church met in the Steele Opera House.[12]

Mary Butts and her cohorts continued with their social activities, and now they were organized as the Ladies' Aid Society. One of their earliest successes was an auction at the opera house that cleared one hundred dollars.[13] In May the ladies had a "measuring party" at the parsonage.[14] Also in May, Miss Mamie Majette put on a "sock party," another "grand success" for the benefit of the church. A new event was a singing Christmas tree, which was held on Christmas night. The church was "packed with people who enjoyed seeing the children receive their gifts from old Santa."[15] Similarly, the church began conducting special Easter services. Prior to this time, unlike the Methodists and Episcopalians, the Baptists' Easter and Christmas celebrations had been very somber. The Christmas event in 1904 was particularly unusual. Behind the pulpit and over the baptismal pool was "a splendid imitation of a small brick house of about 10 x 10, twelve feet high." When Santa appeared on the rooftop, the "children went wild with delight."[16]

In his first year Powell increased membership by 10 percent to 110. The Sunday school had twenty-seven students and the Women's Missionary Society, headed by Mary Butts, had twelve members. In its report the church noted that "under the efficient pastorate of Bro. Powell the church has taken on new life . . . and $2,500 has been expended in renovating and refurbishing a house of worship, and the purchase of an organ."[17] Prior to becoming a preacher, Powell had practiced law for seven years, after which he attended the Baptist Theological Seminary in Louisville. The young pastor was also an avid member of the Knights of Pythias, a popular white fraternal society in the New South, and Georgetown had two chapters with more than two hundred members.[18] Powell arranged for member of his order to come to church in a group, where his special sermon on Pythianism was "an eloquent discourse." To supplement his income Powell was an agent representing the Roberts Marble Company out of Georgia.[19]

His enormous energy, for he was "a man who was never idle," took its toll. The good pastor was gone after a short but painful illness. The Knights of Pythias escorted his body to the train station for burial in his hometown, Rocky Mount, North Carolina.[20] The church's report to Charleston was most appreciative: "In his death, the Georgetown Baptist Church loses a faithful shepherd, the Charleston Baptist Association, a zealous worker, and our community a Godly citizen. . . . He encountered very discouraging obstacles; but bringing into play his inexhaustible store of tact and willpower, he, almost immediately, began to bring order out of chaos. Under his leadership the membership of our church was doubled, and repairs to the amount of $2,000.00 were made on the church edifice. Our church, completely revived, stands today, as a living monument to his memory."[21] Powell died in late August 1904, and by October the church had a new pastor, G. G. O'Neill of Mooresville, North Carolina. O'Neill had a series of successful revivals, but in early 1907 he departed Georgetown. Why he left is unclear, since there are no references in the press and the church minutes did not survive. Evidently his pastorate was unsuccessful since membership decreased to 84. O'Neill moved to Shelby, North Carolina.[22]

The new preacher in Georgetown was W. L. R. Cahall of Greenwood, South Carolina.[23] By that summer the Baptists were serious about constructing a new church, having just paid one thousand dollars for two lots on the corner of Highmarket and Cleland.[24] At the end of 1907 Cahall was about to leave Georgetown, but a "numerously signed petition" convinced him to stay.[25] Something happened during the following two years to mar the relationship between pastor and congregation, and in early January 1909 Cahall resigned.[26] The issue involved domestic difficulties that resulted in the preacher and his wife separating. When Cahall applied for his letter of dismissal so he could join another church, members were deeply concerned and debated the issue for two months. The problem was "certain rumors in circulation over town regarding Rev. Cahall's character."[27] The deacons were considering erasing the preacher and his wife's names from the church roll "because of their living separated from each other as man and wife and being out of fellowship with the Church." Cahall was at that meeting and said he could "prove scriptural grounds for not living with his wife." A compromise was reached by which the preacher was given a proper letter of dismissal, with the caveat "there being nothing proven against his moral or Christian character."[28]

In late 1909 the church issued a call to J. Hartwell Edwards of Ridge Spring, South Carolina, but he declined. The church then called C. H. Turner from Fairfax, South Carolina, at a salary of eight hundred dollars.[29] Turner became pastor in January 1910, and soon earned a reputation as a powerful preacher. The press gave this synopsis: "The pastor of the Baptist Church, we learn, 'went for' sin and wickedness in his evening services on Sunday last. It is reported that he advocated civic righteousness in strong terms, as he should, and in the course of his sermon referred to the loose women, blind tigers, gambling, drinking, etc., infesting our community, as he claimed, but he charged that the policemen could not see these things; they were too busy trying to catch a 10 cent chicken if it got over the fence."[30] Progress under Turner included the addition of electric lights with a "middle chandelier with 32 candle bulbs." Another first was hiring a sexton to keep the church swept out and to build fires during the winters.[31] Fundraising remained a consistent problem with repairing the parsonage, improving the church, servicing the debt on the new lot, and paying the preacher's salary. About the only bills paid on time were the utilities and the insurance premium, while the preacher stood last in line.[32] As of September 30, 1910, the church had paid the following amounts:

Pastor's Salary	$ 492.60
Sunday-school Expenses . .	$ 50.00
State Missions	$ 120.20
Home Missions	$ 15.61
Foreign Missions	$ 19.60
Other Objects	$ 311.88
Orphanage	$ 3.07
Ministerial Education	$ 37.63
Ministerial Relief	$ 8.35
Minutes and Clerk	$ 2.25
Total	$1,061.19[33]

H. L. Orvin served as church clerk and Sunday-school superintendent, aided by the secretary, H. H. Higgins. The school used conventional Southern Baptist literature and boasted 65 pupils and 6 teachers. For the year Turner achieved an increase of 48 members, bringing the total to 144.[34]

While church discipline had loosened considerably over the last two hundred years, the Baptists, compared to other denominations, were still fairly conservative and did not hesitate to chastise their members. For example, in early 1910 Hassie Gault wrote the church from Mississippi. She had been properly dismissed from Georgetown but had not joined another church. She admitted that she had been dancing, and she sought the church's pardon for her sin. The deacons demanded that she submit a written "promise of a discontinuance of dancing" before they considered her request. She was placed on probation for six months and afterward granted a new letter for the church in Mississippi.[35] Another discipline case arose seven years later regarding the "manner in which some members are reported to be living." The deacons summoned several to answer charges before the congregation, and one had his name deleted from the roll.[36]

Turner was so popular that his one-year contract was extended indefinitely.[37] In the summer of 1911 he went to seminary in Chicago and afterward took a vacation at his wife's home in western Georgia. During his travels he reviewed his situation. Certainly financial problems were a concern for him—the church was two months behind in his salary and still owed eighty-three dollars on money borrowed to pay him earlier. He offered his resignation in November, and, although the church asked him to stay, he departed at the first of 1912 for Louisville, Kentucky.[38]

His replacement, Hasford B. Jones, arrived shortly thereafter and got off to a fast start "doing a wonderfully good work for his church, as will be seen by the large crowds attending all the services."[39] Dramatically increasing membership, Jones consistently listed the topics of his Sunday sermons in the newspaper, something no other minister in Georgetown did. Known for his preaching, Jones had one sermon in particular covered at length in the press. In "Is Human Life Held Too Cheap?" he addressed homicide and suicide and also broached directly the issue of "lynch law and mob rule." That sermon, according to the *Georgetown Times,* "should be re-echoed in every pulpit in South Carolina and supported by every newspaper in the state."[40] Also under Jones, in addition to the Baptist Young People's Union, separate classes were organized for young adult men and women, Baraca and Philathea respectively. Baraca (from the Hebrew word for blessing) and Philathea (lover of truth) were interdenominational Bible study classes. At Georgetown, the Baraca class, in addition to the Ladies' Aid Society, was crucial to the development of the church. The Sunday school itself was organized into grades, starting with the Sunbeams and including classes for older members. Just as in the public schools, the achievement of "graded classes" was a definite mark of progress for any church.[41] At Christmas the congregation gave a special thanks to the preacher and his family, a "pounding": "The members and congregation of the Baptist church gave their pastor, Rev. Hasford B. Jones an exceedingly pleasant surprise on Thursday evening last, when they all met at the parsonage and gave him a tremendous pounding. Besides everything one could wish for in the way of edibles, the young men of the church gave their pastor a "pound of money." Of course, it goes without saying, that Mr. Jones and his good wife appreciate such thoughtfulness on the part of their friends."[42]

Another significant development in the history of the church was severing its long standing ties with the Charleston Baptist Association and joining the Southeast Association, organized in 1886. The deacons discussed leaving Charleston in early 1911, but the decision was not made until Jones arrived the following year.[43] Once again the lack of minutes hampers understanding the motivation for the move. Georgetown had been associated with Charleston since the beginning and surely the separation was a moment for reflection. Changing associations is generally a matter of routine, but it does require a formal request for dismissal, and presumably the 1912 records would have noted the historic occasion. It may, however, have been an obvious decision based on existing circumstances—Southeast Association churches were all in the Pee Dee area, some of them old and out of the Welsh Neck Association and others new efforts. Jones himself may have been the pivotal factor, having pastored in the Southeast and currently serving on its executive board. The center of the association was Lake City First Baptist, organized in 1829. Old Belin's was also in the Southeast, having joined in 1886. The area of Black Mingo, also known as Willtown, was in rapid decline after the war and out of Old Belin's

Georgetown Baptist Church, built in 1914.
Courtesy of Georgetown County Library.

grew Nesmith down on the railroad and also an association member.[44] Another Georgetown County church in the association was Mt. Tabor, organized in 1832 and a member since 1890.[45] All in all it made good sense for Georgetown to join the young association, where it automatically became the oldest church and one of the largest.

Pastor Jones's greatest contribution came in building a new house of worship at the corner of Highmarket and Cleland, fulfilling a longtime prayer. In the fall of 1912 the Baptists reportedly issued a contract with C. E. Harris of Greeleyville, South Carolina, in the amount of $13,560.[46] That effort stalled, however, and it was not until the following year that the church was in better financial shape. In March and April 1913 Jones held a twenty-one-day revival with preaching twice a day and thirty-six new members added. It took a number of starts and stops before the final arrangements were perfected, but in the end, the contract went to L. A. Bellonby of Charlotte, North Carolina. This time the deal did go through, and the structure, according to the *Georgetown Times,* "will be an ornament to the city and a monument to the pastor . . . who has labored night and day for his church and people."[47] Bricks started arriving in early 1913, and a drawing of the projected building was on display at the People's Bank.[48] It took a year, however, to publish the plans:

> The new church is to be one of the handsomest and most commodious religious edifices in any city of the size of Georgetown in this state or

section, and it is to have features that will make it a strictly modern and convenient house of worship. Six hundred and fifty opera chairs will be placed, 500 in the auditorium and 150 in the balcony. With chairs in the aisles the seating capacity of the church will be about 800. The decorative scheme will be chaste and simple, yet beautiful. The windows are to be of art glass. The plans provide space for a large pipe organ, which the ladies of the congregation propose to install directly after the church has been completed. The cost of the edifice will be in the neighborhood of $17,000.[49]

How could this dream have become a reality? Until recently the church was unable to pay eight hundred dollars a year for a preacher, and that included a two-hundred-dollar, and sometimes three-hundred-dollar, supplement from the mission board. While Mary Butts and her ladies, along with the Baraca class, were working hard, their sums were in the hundreds, not thousands. The answer was Jones's careful cultivation of the Baptist state mission board. Since the Civil War home mission work had been coordinated at the state level, headed by Georgetown's old friend T. M. Bailey. The year 1909 was crucial for the church. Pleading for Georgetown, the Charleston Baptist Association said of Bailey, "we feel that it is useless to urge our Secretary of State Missions in the interest of Georgetown, as his heart is already there."[50] Jones cultivated other key state officials as well, inviting them to preach. His work was rewarded with a six-thousand-dollar grant, and the church borrowed the rest of the required amount. Under the terms of the award the structure had to be called a "Sunday School Building" and the sanctuary referred to as an "auditorium."[51] Groundbreaking took place in the spring of 1914, and the event drew "quite a large audience, composed not only of Baptists but as well of adherents of other religions, including the Jewish." The ceremony on that Monday morning was simple: prayers, a short address, and the use of a spade. While the new church was being built, the old pews were moved to the second floor of the Steele Opera House for services.[52] At the same time the church acquired the lot and residence next to the new church for use as a parsonage.[53]

At the groundbreaking in the fall of 1914, the pastor's wife placed the first brick, and Jones, "the moving spirit in the raising of what will be one of the most striking religious edifices in the city," laid the second. The next honor went to Mary Butts, "one of the older and most energetic members of the congregation working for the consummation of the earnest desire of all Georgetown Baptists for a sanctuary worthy of the cause." Others involved in laying bricks were Mr. and Mrs. F. B. Joynes, Mr. P. R. Robbins, Mr. and Mrs. J. W. Wilson, Mrs. Rivenbark, Mrs. D. C. Morgan, Mrs. R. G. Johnson, Mr. R. Z.

Robinett, Mrs. J. T. Savage, Mr. Harris, Mrs. Mallette, Miss Mallette, Mrs. W. E. Doar, Mr. Griggs, and Mr. J. O. Hathcock.[54] The property at Highmarket and Queen, the old church and parsonage, had been sold to J. M. Ringel, who tore down the sanctuary and renovated the pastorium for rental. In late 1914 Jones and his wife occupied the new parsonage. The congregation continued to meet in the opera house, but it was too difficult to heat during the winter, so they moved to the Peerless Theatre. Not long afterward, the Presbyterians offered the use of their facility.[55]

The installation of the tin roof was the work of Vernon O. McLeod, an African American and longtime Democrat. Bad weather had delayed his work and when he finished, "so overjoyed was he that he decided to celebrate the event by getting married to Julia Moise." When he placed that last sheet of tin on January 28, 1915, he and Julia went next door to the Baptist parsonage, where Jones married them and "both seemed very contented and happy at the conclusion of Mr. Jones' admonition."[56] The dedication came on Sunday, March 28, 1915, and featured some of the "greatest of the Baptists ministers of the state: Dr. W. T. Derieux, Dr. J. J. Gentry, Dr. W. J. Langston, of Columbia, Dr. John S. Sowers, of Florence, and Dr. Rufus Ford, of Marion."[57] Special recognition was given to building-committee chairman R. Z. Robinett and deacon F. B. Joynes for their contributions. The successful event raised the extraordinary sum of $840 in fifteen minutes, and by the end of the day the total reached $1,010.[58]

Georgetown Times editor Josiah Doar was a great supporter of Pastor Hasford B. Jones, upon whom "too much praise cannot be bestowed."[59] Something, however, had gone terribly awry in the church. Three months after the dedication, Pastor Jones was gone. The problems began in the previous summer, when rumors flooded Georgetown regarding Jones's involvement with a young lady at Sampit. The deacons acted immediately to investigate and concluded that their pastor was innocent of any wrongdoing. Nevertheless, the matter was so grave that they took the unusual step of publishing a document entitled"Statement to the Public":

> Having learned of certain derogatory reports against the character of
> Rev. H. B. Jones having been widely circulated in connection with the
> recent serious illness of a young lady of this county, we, the undersigned
> deacons and members of The Georgetown Baptist Church, hereby state
> that we have personally investigated said reports having seen the father
> of the young lady in question personally, who says that the reports are a
> fabrication of falsehoods and lies, emanating from irresponsible parties
> caused from a spirit [of] jealousy, envy and hatred to try [to] injure, not

only the character of Rev. Mr. Jones, but also that of the family of the young lady in question; all of which he most emphatically denies and declares to be lies. He further states that he and his family hold Rev. Jones in the highest esteem, believing him to be a perfect gentlemen incapable of being guilty of the conduct ascribed to him, and there is absolutely no foundation in fact for said reports. With these facts in our possession we hereby warn all parties who have been circulating these reports to desist immediately and if we hear of any further tatling accountable in an action at law for [several words illegible] for libel slander. F. B. Joynes, E. G. Carpenter, P. R. Robbins, P. H. Pow, B. E. McLeod, H. L. Orvin.[60]

While the deacons may have been satisfied, evidently other members were not. A significant number stopped coming and stopped giving. By the end of the year the church faced two crises: the financial crunch and "matters pertaining to neglect of pastor to perform his duty." He was accused of "not working in strict harmony with the church thereby causing members to stay away from services."[61] Specifically, the deacons wanted him to increase visitation, and they refused to consider any raise in his salary. Whether related to the Sampit incident or not, at the same time the state mission board reduced its three-hundred-dollar commitment to Georgetown by one-third. At the end of June a special deacons' meeting discussed the "existing conditions relative to church and pastor." A formal resolution of June 29 was delivered in writing to Jones: "Resolved, that in consideration of an unharmonious relation existing between pastor and church, we believe your usefulness as pastor has passed. We, therefore, ask your resignation as pastor of the First Baptist Church, the same to take effect with night service, July 11th, 1915."[62]

Josiah Doar, however, painted an entirely different picture of the process, claiming that the resignation had come as a "great surprise to the numerous friends of Pastor Jones' throughout the city." In the *Times's* version Jones had to make a personal plea before the church accepted his resignation. "Had he not done this his letter would have been promptly laid on the table." Jones, it was said, had the church and community's "love and respect . . . and it will be a long time before his place can be filled." Doar and "scores of others" held out hope that the pastor "may yet reconsider his determination to leave."[63] Given the attitudes of the deacons, that was not an option. Jones departed immediately.

A pulpit committee was appointed shortly thereafter, and in September they recommended J. C. Collum at a salary of one thousand dollars, parsonage and utilities, and a promise that "as conditions warrant" his salary would increase.[64] The church voted favorably. Collum asked for some time to talk with his wife in the Baraca Room, and they made a mutual decision to accept the church's offer.[65] By 1916 church revivals featured named evangelists, including Dr. J. W. Hickerson of the Southern Baptist Convention's home mission board and Dr. J. A. Ray of Chickasha, Oklahoma.[66] The latter was "a preacher of unusual oratorical power, possesses a most charming personality and a magnetism that only few public preachers enjoy."[67] Both of these evangelists brought along their own choirmasters. Collum continued Jones's tradition of listing his sermon topics in the newspaper, and the Ladies' Aid Society offered an array of dinners and entertainments. Oyster roasts were particularly popular, and the one in January 1916 was "most successful . . . , a good sum being raised."[68]

After the United States entered World War I in the spring of 1917, the tone of church activities changed to helping the war effort. The Sunday school held an "ice cream festival" for the Red Cross on a Saturday followed by "special patriotic services" at the church with Collum preaching on "the work and needs of the Red Cross."[69] Two weeks later, at another event, Mayor Olin Sawyer addressed the congregation. The young ladies of the church unfurled a "Service Flag" with eighteen stars to honor the members of the Sunday school in the military. The church was full, and "the whole service was of a most solemn and impressive nature."[70]

Pastor Collum was determined to volunteer for war work and offered his services to the Young Men's Christian Association. Collum passed the entrance examination in Columbia and was ordered to report to Blue Ridge, North Carolina, for training as a YMCA worker.[71] The church granted him a three-month leave, while expressing "so much regret to give him up even for a short time."[72] Collum never made that trip because the entire East Coast was swept with the great Spanish flu pandemic in the fall of 1918. Military camps were especially hard hit, and many towns in South Carolina banned all public meetings. Churches in Georgetown were not allowed to reopen until November 9, 1918. During the crisis Collum's orders were on hold until shortly after the armistice, when he reported for training. With the war over on November 11, he was soon back in Georgetown.[73] The veterans began coming home in the spring of 1919, and both races gave celebrations for the heroes. Three thousand people attended the African American celebration, and the white residents held theirs in the Indigo Society Hall, where Collum gave the benediction.[74] The following fall saw him preach his last sermon in Georgetown, having accepted a call to Augusta, Georgia.[75] He retired from his Georgetown pastorate after serving "four years faithfully and efficiently," as the church said in its laudatory resolution.[76]

It had been a rocky road for the church. A mere two decades into the new century, it had gone through one minister after another. The church remained dependent on its allotment from the state mission board and was in debt to the local bank. On a more positive note there was reason to feel blessed. The members must have been delighted to get out of their former building that never could be repaired or remodeled sufficiently. The church had also made a strategic move in uniting with the Southeast Association. There, their own leaders, R. Z. Robinett, H. C. Tallevast, P. H. Powell, and others, played important regional roles.

During this time the church experienced a rediscovery of its historic significance. John Waldo was the first to be honored thanks to an inquiry from Yates Snowden, a University of South Carolina professor who asked for support in investigating "the greatest book maker among the teachers of South Carolina in the nineteenth century."[77] The response to find Waldo's tombstone was enthusiastic, as was that of the women's groups of Georgetown "patriotic and otherwise." They found "Waldo's Bones" and published the entire inscription. Then Professor H. T. Cook of the Baptist State Historical Society took an interest, and he discovered Richard Furman's and Edmund Botsford's papers, which revealed Waldo's story: "Failed as Preacher: But John Waldo was Success as a Teacher. . . . Earned $1,500 a year by His School."[78] Their search in the cemetery, however, was not thorough; a few feet away was the lost marker of another important Baptist figure—Edmund Botsford.

In the spring of 1915 the ladies of the church sold ice cream and other refreshments for the benefit of the graveyard. The *Georgetown Times* thought this a great idea and urged everyone to participate in the "extensive improvements . . . to beautify the old burying ground." A carefully maintained cemetery, the editorial noted, "is the very best evidence that those who have gone before are not forgotten." In the course of clearing away the brush and vines none other than Edmund Botsford's tombstone was revealed. Much of the inscription on that ancient giant's simple marker was still visible, and for the first time in decades Georgetown was made aware of his contributions.[79] In 1918 Professor Cook returned to Georgetown, looking for information on William Screven, who, though a legend, was still relatively unknown historically. Cook's research spurred the *Baptist Courier*'s interest in locating Screven's grave. Elisha Screven's will specifically reserved a burial ground for his father, and it was determined that the spot was directly across from the office of the *Georgetown Times*. An eye witness to the discovery described it as "covered lightly with bricks, no name, stone, dates or any other work." Besides the street that bore his name, the writer for the *Baptist Courier* concluded that much of Screven's life as a minister "had faded out of the tradition," and he posed the question: "Would any other denomination neglect so completely their honored dead—

the progenitor even of the Convention itself?"[80] Decades would pass before a proper monument could be erected.

Another part of the church's identity involved its very name. Based on its last antebellum charter, it was the Baptist Church of Christ; locally it was simply the Baptist Church; in the association and state convention it was Georgetown; in legal documents the trustees still called it the Antipedo Baptist Church of Christ of Georgetown.[81] Some clarity was achieved in 1911 with a significant change in the bylaws: "This Church shall be known as the Georgetown Baptist Church until such a time as there may be another Baptist Church organized in the city. Thenafter such time as The First Baptist Church of Georgetown."[82] Possessed with a sense of history and a new sense of worth and tempered by nearly a century of suffering, the church was ready to earn that title.

ELEVEN

Maturity

IN THE FALL OF 1919 Pastor Collum received a call from Augusta, Georgia, and tendered his resignation, which the church accepted with regret. He departed Georgetown on October 1.[1] At the same time the church was preparing to participate in the Southern Baptist Convention's "Seventy-Five Million Campaign." Assisting in this effort was Dr. Robert Wilkins Lide from Charleston. While organizing the teams for the campaign, he preached in Georgetown in October, and the deacons immediately asked him to supply for two months at $125 per month. The appointment was made permanent, and Lide accepted a salary of $1,500 per year, of which $300 came from the state convention.[2] He enjoyed a long career in Georgetown, leading the church for the next twelve and a half years. From Darlington County, Lide had been preaching since 1875, holding pastorates at First Baptist of Darlington, First Baptist of Charleston, and others. At the age of sixty-seven he was well known and highly respected in the state and soon became the "dean of Georgetown's pastors."[3]

Assisting Lide was a group of strong leaders serving both the church and the Southeast Association. R. Z. Robinett was chairman of the board of deacons and longtime association moderator; P. H. Pow was the dedicated and meticulous clerk; E. E. Orvin served as church treasurer; T. G. Tedder led Sunday school, assisted by F. J. Tyson and B. W. Robinett. Other men who appear prominently in the records include J. W. Royal and H. C. Tallevast. Women continued to play a significant role. While the membership of the Ladies' Aid Society was never listed, the women of this group were presumably the same ones who led the Women's Missionary Union. These include Salley H. Joynes, Mrs. H. C. McKenney, Mrs. C. H. Whitten, Mrs. J. M. Layton, and Mrs. R. Z. Robinett.[4] These ladies were the successors to the aging Mary Butts who died on January 25, 1928. The women of the church, while excluded from senior positions, served in a variety of capacities. A 1922 account shows Miriam Tallevast as pianist, Janey Belle Royal as librarian, Mrs. J. E. Posey as superintendent of the Home Department, and Mrs. J. M. Layton as superintendent of the Cradle Roll. Of the thirteen Sunday-school classes, only two were led by men. The Berean (formerly Baraca) class for young men, led by R. Z. Robinett,

Dr. Robert W. Lide, pastor Georgetown Baptist, 1919–1932.
Courtesy of Georgetown First Baptist Church.

was especially active and well attended. A 1926 notice said the men's class "has been attracting considerable attention in Sunday-school circles, large attendance being reported every Sunday. Robinett's lectures have proved very interesting."[5] The men met monthly in private homes, and publicity director H. C. Tallevast said "these socials are growing more and more popular by drawing the members in closer touch with each other."[6] Under the leadership of T. J. Tedder, the Fidelis (formerly Philathea) class, for young women, grew dramatically, reporting seventy-one members in 1922. They too had socials and fundraisers and like the Bereans were divided into blue and red competing teams. One of the ladies' publicity efforts was a seven-stanza poem that concluded with

> We have class meetings and socials,
> Once in a while,
> To brighten us up and put
> On a new smile

We're going to expect you there,
Next Sunday with one friend or more,
You might get a surprise,
For we have one in store.[7]

The Baptist Young People's Union was also active with socials, where "games were played until a late hour" and "Winyah Punch" and cake were served.[8] Superintendent Tedder had made great strides by 1924, when enrollment hovered around three hundred. His "marvelous progress" was highlighted by the *Georgetown Times,* praising the school for receiving an A-1 Standard of Excellence. Out of 1,100 Baptist Sunday schools in the state, only eleven others had achieved that status.[9]

The new pastor put on a large revival in his first spring, bringing in T. V. McCaul from Bennettsville, South Carolina. Most striking about this event was the large advertisement in the *Times.* In this quarter-page announcement McCaul was termed "one of the Ablest Speakers of the State." Visitors were promised "Glorious Gospel Services; . . . Good Singing. Free Seats. Hearty Welcome."[10] The press reported "large congregations" and termed McCaul a "talented speaker and excellent singer."[11] The fall revival of 1921 was another success, with preaching twice a day for two weeks in early November. The evangelist was John R. Sampey, D.D., L.L.D., "one of the greatest men of the South among the Baptists." Accompanying Sampey was his music director, W. D. Spinx, "a gifted singer." Spinx had been a missionary in Africa and could sing songs in the language he had learned while there. On the first Sunday afternoon of the revival Spinx preached at Bethesda, the "colored church," where special seating was reserved for white guests.[12] Georgetown's biggest revival was an interdenominational effort, led by Lide as president of its executive committee. The revivalist was Gypsy Smith, Jr., son of the much better known father. Smith stayed three weeks for the meetings held in the Big Brick Tobacco Warehouse, which had been heated and could hold two thousand people. The revival brought people "from every section of the county and adjoining counties, pouring into Georgetown for night services."[13] When it was all over, the *Times* concluded that "Georgetown has experienced a most wonderful religious revival. Nothing like it has ever happened before in this section."[14]

One of Dr. Lide's special interests was missionary work, particularly in China, where he had children serving. His daughter, Florence, spent seven years without furlough in China, until she returned home in late 1920 to pursue academic studies. The son, Frank, preached in Georgetown that August, before he left to replace his sister in China.[15] Dr. Lide interested himself in the history of his new pastorate, and while surveying the grounds at Highmarket and Queen, where the old church once stood, he found the bell that had been installed after the Civil War. Aware that the foreign mission board was collecting bells for use in China, he arranged its donation.[16] By 1930 he had three children serving simultaneously there.[17]

Other early ideas by Lide included installing a "Kitchen Outfit" for use by church groups. Church leaders were receptive, and Deacon Tallevast observed there were "no other means that would promote interest in church work more than the social side."[18] The energetic pastor also upgraded the library for the Sunday school, and within two months the church purchased 117 books.[19] A telling advancement was Lide's decision to forego the state aid of $300 and live on the $1,500 the church paid. This milestone, a mark of real independence and sustainability, was possible because of increased giving, largely due to another of Lide's innovations, adopting the pledge envelopes.[20] Lide was also concerned about the plight of indigent members of the church, so a "poor committee" was appointed to raise funds "for taking care of the poor and sick."[21] His community work included urging the formation of a Boy Scout troop and of a Society for the Prevention of Cruelty to Animals.[22]

With all its progress, the church was hardly rich and deferred maintenance on the property had taken its toll. By 1921 the pews needed to be recovered or painted, the plaster was falling from the ceiling, the basement still flooded, and the roof on the parsonage still leaked. Once again it fell to the Ladies' Aid Society, and it was not an easy task. When they offered to pay half of the $120 to paint the pews, the deacons gave them "a free hand to do whatever they deem best," but the church was too poor to pay the other half.[23] Eventually it was up to the ladies to raise the money themselves: $64 for replastering, $100 for windows in the church and parsonage, and another $64 for window screens.[24] The ladies also attempted to have the parsonage roof repaired, but that effort was unsuccessful. Exasperated, Lide finally ordered the work done without knowing how to fund it. Assistant Sunday School Superintendent Tyson stepped forward and paid the $13 bill.[25]

Despite these stumbling blocks, the leaders were actively dreaming of what the church could become. One of Lide's aspirations was to obtain a pipe organ, a definite symbol of a proper church. In early 1922 he began to obtain price quotations, and factory representatives met with him and several of the ladies. The cost was three thousand dollars, to be paid in three years. The Ladies' Aid Society stood ready to raise the money, but the deacons decided to postpone discussion.[26] Three years later Lide resurrected the issue with the news that he had been offered a used organ from a Chicago church for seven hundred dollars. He felt strongly that with a good organ "church attendance and contributions would materially increase."[27] Unfortunately, by this time another buyer had taken the organ in Chicago. The deacons, however, had gotten the message and received church approval to borrow up to $3,500 and buy a new organ outright. The "large and beautiful" organ was installed in the first half of 1925, amid several notable changes: choir space was enlarged, an extra door added to the rear, and a front partition was replaced by large double doors to enhance access to the sanctuary.[28] In November the organ was highlighted in a special music program, followed by a free-will offering. That Christmas the church enjoyed its first cantata, which included the added talents of the West End Methodist choir.[29] The brass pipes are remembered as extending from "midway of the wall to the ceiling and from one side of the choir loft to the other."[30]

Lide's biggest ambition was a new church edifice. He broached the subject in early spring 1923 at a special deacons' meeting, noting that "the time was ripe for the undertaking, for the new building would strengthen the Baptist position in Georgetown."[31] Two weeks later the congregation heard a resolution presented by Deacon Tallevast. Upon a motion by F. J. Tyson, seconded by F. H. Sawyer, the church adopted the following:

> WHEREAS we believe that the time has come when the members of the First Baptist Church of Georgetown, South Carolina, should make a definite beginning looking to the erection of a new and beautiful house of worship on our lot on the corner of Highmarket and Cleland Streets.
> . . . THEREFORE BE IT RESOLVED:
> First—that the church . . . authorized the raising of a building fund, the minimum amount of which shall be $5,000.00, to be paid in full by October 1st, 1923. . . .
> Second—That committees be appointed . . . to canvas the entire membership of the church and obtain pledges and cash contributions. . . .
> Third—That when the $5,000.00 has been paid in full, the membership and other friends will be asked to pledge an additional $20,000.00.
> Fourth—That when the foregoing has been accomplished . . . we as a church will proceed to have built an auditorium to cost approximately $25,000.00.
> Fifth—that some lady member of this church be elected as treasurer of this fund, and that she be officially designated as the treasurer of the building fund.

The last resolution, placing a woman in a formal position of authority, is worth noting. Salley Joynes took the job as treasurer of the building fund, and when she asked which bank the church preferred as a depository, she was told that the matter was left entirely to her discretion.[32] She and the Ladies' Aid Society immediately began fundraising efforts. Teas were quite popular among the ladies of Georgetown, and the society held a Silver Tea, a Shamrock Tea, and a Halloween Tea.[33] Their biggest effort, however, became "Delicatessen" sales. These were held on Saturdays on Front Street, first at Robinett's store and later at the Didy Wyn Gift Shop. They offered "all kinds of homemade goodies . . . including cakes, candy, pies, and dressed chickens," with the slogan "come get something good for Sunday dinner."[34]

Despite high hopes and the efforts of Mrs. Joynes, progress was slow and funds were meager. For example, the 1928 operating budget totaled only $2,780, of which $2,100 went to the pastor's salary. Ironically, the church was raising a great deal of money, but it was designated for the Seventy-Five Million Campaign. Begun in 1919, this coordinated effort raised funds for general Baptists institutions and programs. The state goal for South Carolina was $5,500,000.[35] The Georgetown church's quota was $8,132, and when the program ended in 1924 the church had exceeded that goal by nearly $3,000, for a total of $10,863.08.[36]

This major effort to raise money for the Southern Baptist Convention meant that the field was thoroughly picked over. As the church's obligation to the Seventy-Five Million Campaign went over the top, the deacons decided that half of the money collected would be "set aside in a special fund for repairs and building."[37] The extent to which this new effort was successful is unknown. Pow, the church clerk, moved to Florida in early 1926, and subsequent minutes do not resume until 1928, when J. M. Powell took over the position. By then economic conditions had changed considerably. No new building projects took place during this time. In 1930, when Lide reflected on the last decade, he could only report that the church had been repaired and the pipe organ installed.[38] Moreover, the church suffered a significant decrease in membership. In 1924 there were 322 communicants; in 1928 there were only 255.[39] The church's financial status was similar to that of the entire region, where agriculture prices had dropped dramatically after World War I. The fatal blow came in the fall of 1928, when a great flood occurred and destroyed the crops in Georgetown's service area. Across the Pee Dee nearly all the banks failed, including those in Georgetown. As George C. Rogers, Jr., observed in his history of Georgetown county, "the closing of the banks was the greatest blow to the people of the county since the defeat in 1865."[40] Presumably, whatever money Mrs. Joynes had deposited was lost.[41]

Faced with this calamity, Dr. Lide offered his resignation on November 11, 1928. At that time the church was $175 behind in paying its bills, and the congregation, in Lide's absence, had a lengthy discussion on the situation. Their confidence in their pastor remained strong, and with a unanimous vote, the church asked him to withdraw his resignation.[42] Another indication of the poor economy was a resolution presented in late 1928, which declared "if any member of this Church shall absent himself from worship and shall fail to contribute to its expenses for three months, if physically and financially able to do so, shall thereby forfeit their membership."[43] The vote on this draconian resolution in church conference was by secret ballot and passed by a four to one margin.

After 1929 the entire country entered the Great Depression and the hard times in Georgetown grew harder. One local sign of the stress came in 1931, when Lide announced in church conference that he had received a "request from the Negro Church [Bethesda] to give them one of our old Bibles." Lide noted that the church had two that were not being used, and the church approved the donation.[44] In that same year budgetary constraints forced a reduction in Lide's salary from $2,100 to $1,800.

The church looked to its past for reassurance in such difficult times, and in April the church held its first Home-Coming Day. Dr. Lide gave a special sermon on the history of the church, taking his text from Hebrews 10:32: "Call to remembrance the former days." Lide focused on points on which "Baptists stand alone and differ from other Believers":

1. That the Bible is an all-sufficient guide. . . .
2. We reject the doctrine of infant baptism; . . . Every man must for himself repent and for himself believe.
3. The first religious duty which the Bible requires is repentance towards God and faith in our Lord Jesus Christ—therefore we reject infant baptism and every doctrine which recognizes in any way persons as members of the church of Christ who have not given evidence of personal repentance and faith.

The two key points involved "Baptism that is immersion and nothing else is Baptism." The other issue was closed communion in which "only Baptized believers are to partake—that there is no warrant to invite the unbaptized." It was not, Lide said, that Baptists questioned the piety of other denominations but that "we believe them to be unbaptized."[45]

Back in 1880, while Lide was serving at Antioch in Darlington County, he married Anna W. Wilson. When they reached their fiftieth anniversary in 1930, Georgetown put on a handsome celebration at R. Z. Robinett's home, providing coffee, tea, singing, and recitations. The ladies of the church made the wedding cake, "a beautiful pyramid of white iced layers, decorated with tiny white and yellow roses." The best present, however, was a cablegram from Lide's three children in China. The wire read simply Philippians 1:3. When Lide found it in his ever-handy Bible, he read, "I thank my God upon every remembrance of you."[46] Lide's health had begun to fail in 1926 when he went to Charleston to seek medical attention. He took most of that summer off to recuperate.[47] He managed to resume work for six more years, but by 1932 it was time for him to retire.

Dr. Charles A. Jones of Columbia was the special speaker for the occasion, and after service Lide called a church conference and asked Jones to moderate. He then departed the conference, leaving a message for R. Z. Robinett to read to the congregation. They felt "stress of great feeling" at the announcement of their pastor's resignation. The conference agreed with Robinett "that the Church faced a serious loss." The pastor's letter was brief, making his resignation effective the last Sunday in July 1932. His sole reason, he said, was "my strength is not sufficient for the pastorate, and so I am retiring from pastoral work all together, however, I shall hope to preach as opportunity may offer." In its formal tribute to Lide the church members praised his fifty-seven years in the ministry, which included 6,387 sermons, 875 baptisms, 400 marriage ceremonies, and 300 funerals. In his years at Georgetown he delivered 1,490 sermons, baptized 164, married 48, received into the church by letter 75, and preached at 51 funerals. The church's resolution concluded, "We bow in humble submission to the will of our Heavenly Father and in fervent prayer that this His beloved servant may be blessed in health and the riches of grace for many, many years to come."[48] The resolution as taken down by the clerk and was signed by deacons R. Z. Robinett, T. J. Tedder, J. M. Powell, H. H. Craven, B. E. McLeod, F. J. Tyson, J. W. Lawrimore, and B. W. Robinett.

Lide's successor was Maxie C. Collins, who was appointed in October 1933 and began his duties on December 1. Maxie came highly recommended. Born and raised near Lake City, he went to Furman and the Southern Baptist Seminary, and he served as student pastor at the University of Florida and assistant pastor at Highland Baptist Church, Louisville. Collins was also the brother of Henry C. Collins, the popular Methodist minister who had recently completed his appointment at West End Methodist. Nearly the whole town turned out to hear Maxie Collins's first sermon: "Every seat was filled, many sitting on the pulpit and numbers standing in the rear . . . ; a hundred or more people were turned away." The ministerial association had charge of the program to welcome Collins to Georgetown, and the title of his opening sermon was "Behold I Stand at the Door and Knock."[49]

Married with a small child, Collins moved his family into a completely renovated parsonage. Working for a salary of $1,200 per year, Collins made significant contributions, including holding sunrise Easter services on the church lawn; serving as the Boy Scout master and secretary of the ministerial association; preaching part-time at Johnson's Chapel, a small church located near

Brown's Ferry; and organizing the church's first Vacation Bible School. In the summer of 1934, suffering from a "painful ailment of the hip," Collins went to the Baptist hospital in Columbia for an operation.[50] On September 15, 1935, Collins offered his resignation, saying that he had been "called to a larger field that offered greater opportunities for service" in Batesberg, South Carolina.[51] At that time the church had 338 members, 450 Sunday-school pupils, five Baptist Young People's Unions with 190 members, and three brotherhoods totaling 146 men.[52]

Succeeding Maxie Collins was Henry Herbert Wells, Jr. A member of the old Bethel (Black River) Church in Sumter County, he had a Baptist pedigree that was impeccable. From his great-great-grandfather onward, his forbears served as deacons of that church. Two of his sisters became Baptist missionaries to China, and through his grandmother, Eliza Mary Mellichamp, he was the sixth great-grandson of none other than William Screven. He also was related to the Cuttinos by virtue of Thomas Mellichamp, who married Sarah Ludlow Cuttino in 1846. Like Collins he attended Furman and then the Southern Baptist Seminary in Louisville. He lived in Darlington County, South Carolina, prior to coming to Georgetown in early 1936, with a two-point charge at Black Creek and Antioch Baptist churches. When he moved to Georgetown he and his wife had an eight-month-old son, and another son was born in the parsonage in 1939.[53] An active sportsman, Wells enjoyed cabinet making as a hobby, and one of the family's treasures is a small chest for baby clothing given to him by Sheriff Henry B. Bruorton.[54] Another hobby the family adopted in Georgetown was the development of a fine coin collection. In the Great Depression many members were able to put only small change in the collection plate, and Wells traded out the Indian-head pennies and other old coins.[55] Working on a 1936 salary of $1,500, Wells also preached at Johnson's Chapel on the third and fourth Sunday afternoons.[56]

In the midst of economic stress the church had given up on its building plans and began focusing on reducing the church's indebtedness. At this time Salley Joynes was no longer leading the building-fund campaign but headed the debt payment effort. It was a great day on July 12, 1936, when R. Z. Robinett announced that the mortgage had been paid in full, and he and H. H. Craven, church treasurer, burned the papers before the entire congregation. Robinett also read a heartwarming letter from Dr. Lide, congratulating them on reaching the goal "you have been praying for these many years." The clerk J. M. Powell was asked to respond to Lide, and wrote "we know that this debt has been of great concern to you. . . . Your great interest in this matter inspired us to eliminate this obligation as quickly as possible."[57] A year later the church went back into debt for interior improvements and a new heating plant, the

Hot Air System, guaranteed to "give us a temperature of 60 degrees in the basement when 30 degrees on the outside and the Auditorium could be made as hot as desired."[58] The 1939 church budget totaled $4,009, including church contributions to the Baptist giving fund (the Cooperative Program) and debt payments. The pastor's salary was $1,800; the organist received $120 and the janitor $144.[59]

It had been twenty years since Lide's arrival, and they had been hard ones for the town and its churches. Bethesda, under the leadership of Pastor G. Goings Daniels, had struggled but was holding its own. In the summer of 1926 Daniels wrote an address to "the White Citizens of Georgetown," thanking them for their support toward the church building on Wood Street. He asked for additional contributions: "We need within 60 days $2,500."[60] Three years later Bethesda celebrated its sixty-fourth anniversary when the edifice was finished as "one of the most modern among colored people in the state." Church membership included 1,500 "intelligent colored people having members representing nearly every profession." Pastor Daniels had a highly regarded program of religious and social work, and he was currently building a job-training effort "along industrial as well as religious lines. He says he believes in the religion of work." In the two-week-long anniversary celebration white ministers spoke at Bethesda, including Henry Collins of West End Methodist and Dr. Lide. The public was also invited, and Daniels noted that "special arrangements have been made to accommodate the white friends who desire to attend."[61] The Depression slowed Bethesda's growth, with African Americans suffering miserably in the 1930s. By 1941 the church was far behind in paying Daniels's salary, and he resigned in May 1941, to be replaced by Thomas O. Mills.[62]

Georgetonians could take some solace in having their historic town recognized. In the spring of 1930 the South Carolina Society of Colonial Dames erected a monument, modestly called a "boulder," to Elisha Screven. This was a grand event, including members of the Colonial Dames, the Charleston Navy Band, and some five hundred school children. Dr. Lide delivered the invocation, Mayor Harold Kaminski welcomed the crowd, and Screven descendant Herbert Lee Smith gave the main address. Lillian Johnstone, another Screven descendant, unveiled the monument honoring Elisha Screven as the individual "who planned and founded Georgetown." Erected on the southeast corner of Screven and Prince Streets, it stood just a stone's throw from William Screven's grave.[63] This event seems to have spurred quite a bit of enthusiasm in the town, which soon began planning a civic homecoming featuring a parade, carnival, boat races, and an air show.[64] That February the church celebrated its own anniversary with an elaborate party, after which R. Z. Robinett read a church history written by C. G. Barr. That work, while incomplete, did use historic sources, and Barr was the first to correct the erroneous assumption around town that William Screven himself had founded the church. Barr understood enough to give the credit to Furman and Botsford. Another celebration came in the spring of 1941, when the Baptist State Convention erected a monument to William Screven at the corner of Cleland and Highmarket Streets. Pastor Wells led the dedication and unveiling service.[65]

During Wells's tenure, Georgetown began to emerge from the Depression. The key development was industry, and for Georgetown that was a paper company. Construction of the mill started in the fall of 1936 on the Sampit River, and the plant began operation the following spring, becoming "the largest kraft paper mill in the world."[66] The other development nationwide was the coming of World War II in September 1939, which boosted industrial production as part of the war preparedness effort. By 1940 the country had its first peacetime draft, and the United States entered the war with Pearl Harbor, December 7, 1941. Shortly thereafter, Georgetown and the entire coast were ordered blacked out at night against the threat of U-boat attacks.[67] Patriotism was high in the port city where the U. S. Navy was actively recruiting. When some of Wells's flock joined the navy, he heard about the lack of chaplains and decided to accept that challenge. He resigned his position with the church, who thanked him for his "six years of splendid and faithful services." Leaving Georgetown in November 1941, he was stationed at Jacksonville, Florida, when the Japanese attacked Pearl Harbor. Wells found his calling in the Chaplains Corps and made it a career. Rising from lieutenant junior grade, he retired in 1962 as a commander.[68]

From 1942 to 1946, Joseph (Joe) Haynesworth Darr, Jr., led the church. Born in 1906 in Sumter County, Darr also possessed an impressive lineage as a descendant of Botsford and the Cuttinos. After attending the Southern Seminary in Louisville, he preached in rural churches in Sumter County. He gave his trial sermon in Georgetown in late November 1941 and moved to town on March 13, 1942.[69] The ministerial association held a welcome for him at his first sermon, with the Episcopal rector giving the address.[70] The church experienced rapid growth under Darr. By 1945 his salary was $3,825, and there were 593 communicants, 573 Sunday-school students, and a church budget of $18,188.54.[71] Moreover, the church had purchased $24,000 in war bonds and had $2,442 in the bank.[72] Another development at Georgetown was the establishment of a Training Union, a Baptist version of an evening Sunday school.[73]

When Darr left in 1946 to pastor the First Baptist Church in Clinton, South Carolina, his successor was Verner V. Raines, whose primary contribution, in addition to continued growth, was the fulfillment of Lide's dream of

Henry Herbert Wells, Jr., pastor of Georgetown Baptist, 1936–1941,
after which he began his career as a U.S. Navy chaplain.
Courtesy of Georgetown First Baptist Church.

a new church facing Highmarket Street. This achievement reflects the general
growth and prosperity of Georgetown after the war. The laying of the cornerstone occurred at eleven o'clock, February 27, with the local Masonic order
acting as the "escort of honor." Pastor Raines read the scripture, and L. A.
Caulder and Hasford B. Jones gave prayers. Jones, who had been preaching in
area churches, was a special guest since it was under him that the 1914 church
was constructed. D. D. Lewis of the state Sunday-school board preached.[74]

The new sanctuary was incorporated into the older building, which had
been completely remodeled as the education department. At a total cost of
$175,000, the sanctuary featured a gallery and a new organ. Designed by for-
mer Georgetonian and architect F. Arthur Hazard of Augusta, Georgia, the
edifice was constructed by the Dawson Engineering Company of Charleston.
W. R. Weatherly was chairman of the building committee, which included

James F. Carter, Beverly H. Sawyer, R. Z. Robinett, Jody Hinds, and W. E. Skinner. The ribbon cutting occurred on September 11, 1949, at eleven o'clock. Local ministers from the Presbyterian, Episcopal, and Methodist churches participated, and Raines gave the benediction. The morning sermon was delivered by S. H. Jones, editor of the *Baptist Courier*. Another service began at a quarter after one and included B. B. Jernigan of Columbia and John Hamrick, pastor of First Baptist in Charleston. The Reverend H. L. Gross of Columbia gave the benediction. The evening closed with Training Union at seven o'clock, followed by worship and baptismal services.[75]

When the new facility opened, membership stood at 866 and Sunday school at 892. The church and the city of Georgetown had entered a new, modern age. With all the changes since the war, including an increase in industry and subsequent population growth, other Baptist churches began to develop nearby. No longer desperately poor by comparison to its earlier years, the First Baptist Church of Georgetown was now one of the largest and most vibrant churches in the association.

TWELVE

Missions and Memories

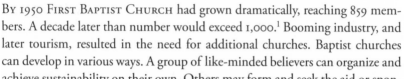

By 1950 First Baptist Church had grown dramatically, reaching 859 members. A decade later than number would exceed 1,000.[1] Booming industry, and later tourism, resulted in the need for additional churches. Baptist churches can develop in various ways. A group of like-minded believers can organize and achieve sustainability on their own. Others may form and seek the aid or sponsorship from a larger church. Finally, a well-established church may formally initiate a mission, buying land, building a structure, and providing a salary for a minister. The Baptists of Georgetown experienced each of these, and the first church to be founded after the war was named for William Screven.

Screven Baptist Church was the brainchild of Jessie and S. D. Miller, who lived across the Sampit River in the growing community of Maryville. Jessie Miller was an especially active member of First Church and of the Southeast Association, and on October 3, 1949, she organized an adult Training Union in her home on Sunday evenings. Twenty-one people attended the first meeting. On January 16, 1950, the group set up a Sunday school that met in the Richard Gibson building. Out of this grew the Southside Mission, eventually named Screven Baptist Church on March 26, 1950, with fifty-six charter members. At the organizational meeting, the pastor of First Baptist, Verner V. Raines, acted as moderator and delivered the sermon. L. A. Caulder, pastor of Hemingway, and A. L. Gross, of the state convention, also participated.[2] Although the term *mission* was used frequently, Screven Baptist was never funded by First Baptist. The March 19, 1930, report of the planning committee for the Southside effort read: "Due to the financial load which is upon the First Baptist Church . . . the newly organized church [will] not be given any financial assistance." The First Baptist Church had just built its new sanctuary at substantial cost, and all the members could do was "endorse the organization of the new church, [and] give it their good will and sincere prayers."[3]

Assistance did come from other churches. Andrews Baptist gave Screven its old building, which was moved to South Island Road where the church had purchased three lots. Screven Church bought the pews from Manning Baptist and held its first services on May 14, 1950. The Reverend J. K. Lawton, pastor at Andrews, became the new church's first minister, preaching on the second and fourth Sunday afternoons. For 1951 the church had an operating budget of four thousand dollars. Lawton soon gave up the pastorate and was succeeded by Hampton I. Perry on a supply basis. Catastrophe struck on February 28, 1951, when the entire edifice was destroyed by fire. In little more than a month ground was broken for a new educational building, and the church called Roy G. Ryan of Augusta, Georgia, as minister. He served until 1956 and was succeeded by Isaac C. Vassar. During Vassar's ministry a new sanctuary was constructed and dedicated in 1957, with First Baptist donating the pulpit furniture for Screven. In thanking First Church for the furniture, Vassar said it "shall remain as a lasting token of friendship, fellowship, and mutual devotion in serving our Lord in an even greater way."[4]

Raines left First Baptist in 1951 and was replaced by Dr. C. Earl Cooper. Cooper's pastorate lasted merely a year, and he was followed by Dr. Warren H. Clapp. He and his family moved to Georgetown in early October 1952, coming from the First Baptist Church of Willow Springs, Missouri. Rapid growth greeted his early ministry, and his first endeavor was replacing the old, deteriorated parsonage. The church purchased the relatively new home of Lester Weed, only one block away, and the pastor moved in with his family shortly afterward. Clapp also led a substantial upgrading of the sanctuary and educational building. Neither had air conditioning, and a $13,300 Westinghouse unit was installed to cool both, making First Baptist the first house of worship in Georgetown to be so equipped.[5] On January 8, 1956, the church held a special service to celebrate burning the mortgage on the sanctuary built seven years earlier.[6] A year later the church began broadcasting its revival services on the radio.[7]

During this period, at the request of the United Daughters of the Confederacy, the church granted permission to move the town's Confederate monument from the middle of Broad and Highmarket Streets, where it had become a traffic hazard, to the Antipedo Baptist Cemetery on Church Street. The grounds were put in order and the monument to William Screven relocated to the old cemetery.[8] Clapp's last noticeable achievement in Georgetown was the construction of a new educational building. Groundbreaking took place in 1958, and the aging R. Z. Robinett turned the first spade of dirt, marking his third such occasion for the church. The new building, priced at $142,000 and located on Cleland Street, was completed the following year.[9] Although the numbers were impressive and the church improved physically, Clapp resigned on July 17, 1960, to assume the pastorate at Southside Baptist Church in Spartanburg, South Carolina. The congregation responded with a heartfelt resolution, which read in part: "Dr. Clapp has served us with an awe-inspiring fervor, and under his challenging leadership we have seen our church grow both in stature and in Spirit. Through the precept of his noble character, we have been drawn together more closely in fellowship and in loyalty to our Savior, to His church, and our community."[10]

J. Mahlon Kirkland, from the First Baptist Church of Port Allen, Louisiana, filled the pulpit on August 28, 1960. Upon hearing him preach, the congregation immediately offered Kirkland a permanent position, a call he readily accepted.[11] He was a native of Georgia and educated at Brewton Parker Junior College and Mercer University. In his early career Kirkland was a high-school principal, basketball coach, and math instructor, in addition to filling part-time pastorates. He received his master's of theology in 1947 from the Baptist Seminary in New Orleans. In his long tenure at Georgetown, Kirkland served as moderator of the Southeast Association for two terms, spent five years as a trustee for the *Baptist Courier*, sat on the board of trustees for Charleston Southern University for ten years, and received an honorary doctor of divinity from that institution in 1975. He also served as president of the South Carolina Baptist Historical Society. In Georgetown he was an active community member: president of the Lions Club, president of the local cancer society, and on the board of the mental health association. Most significantly, in those difficult days of racial unrest, he was the first president of Georgetown's Bi-Racial Committee.[12] In his own account Kirkland cited five accomplishments of which he was most proud. He ordained four young men into the ministry, created a popular summer youth camp, built a new and fully equipped fellowship hall, initiated three missions that became churches, and set up an elementary school.[13] The last two have the greatest historical significance.

Because of his background in education, Kirkland led First Baptist in establishing an elementary school. Discussions began in 1966 and initial planning was to offer the first three grades, but the initiative soon expanded to include kindergarten through sixth grade.[14] Across the South, private white schools called segregation academies appeared in most areas. The First Baptist Church School prohibited admission to all African Americans, but children of non-European descent were admitted. Many Georgetown residents recall that families spent the night sleeping in their cars in order to enroll their children under the first-come, first-served policy.[15] Most of the operational records of the school have not survived, but a financial statement for September 1971 shows a budget of $13,039.62, with more than $6,000 in savings.[16]

Student handbooks and yearbooks were printed for the academic years 1971–1972 through 1988–1989. The initial books were mimeographed and stapled, but by 1972 quality improved considerably when the Olan Mills Company began handling the photography and printing. From its earliest publications, the school's mission statement remained consistent: "First Baptist Church School seeks to educate the whole child by combining the normal academic program of a school with the religious development so necessary for the development of a well-rounded person in today's world. The aesthetic development of our students is also encouraged by classes in Art and Music." What became the yearbook appeared in 1971 as the "Blue Blazers Booklet," a collection of poems and artwork by the fifth and sixth graders. By 1972 the church had an organized Blue Blazer athletic program with a football team, boys' basketball, and fifth- and sixth-grade cheerleader teams. In 1975 a girls' basketball team was added, but the football program had ended. The term *Blue Blazer* had disappeared by 1987, and the athletic teams were then known as the Saints. In 1986 the school sponsored five boys' basketball teams: Small Fry (two teams), Greyhounds, Deacons, and Saints. Another student organization, an environmental group called the Earth Patrol, appeared in 1979. The yearbook for 1972–1973 is the first to contain photographs of faculty, staff, and students.

Kirkland's other dramatic achievement in the 1960s was the establishment of official missions directly supported by First Baptist. In this effort he was aided by his father J. R. Kirkland, who served as First Baptist's mission pastor.[17] Working with the architectural department of the Southern Baptist Convention, the church developed a long-range planning process, and by 1963 was busily buying property and planning to purchase more.[18] On May 2, 1965, the church voted to start a mission in the Kensington–Lakewood area. That effort was carefully planned, and a group of forty First Baptist members created what is now Lakewood Baptist Church. The groundbreaking for Lakewood's $60,000 building occurred in September 19, 1965, with Kirkland presiding.[19] The 5,000-square-foot mission building, designed to accommodate 225 people, was dedicated on February 6, 1966.[20] In 1969 the church had 205 members, 245 Sunday-school students, and an annual budget of $28,987.[21] Months after the initiation of the Lakewood effort, First Baptist agreed to sponsor a mission at Pawleys Island. A house and three acres were purchased for $16,500 from Mrs. W. P. Bair, a member of First Baptist.[22] In 1966 a building for Pawleys was constructed, and Ranford A. Haselden served as the summer pastor. The state convention gave $2,000 to buy pews for Pawleys, and in 1969 the mission had fifty members. Everett Davidson was appointed pastor in 1971, followed by A. F. Smoak in 1972 who was ordained by the First Baptist Church. Also that year, heating and cooling were added to Pawleys.[23]

The story of a rural community on Andrews highway is a prime example of how local Baptist churches are organized and supported. In early 1966 a group began holding prayer services in the homes of the sick, inspiring the desire for a church. Dora Scott Jenkins donated the land, and the first organizational meetings were held at E. M. Jenkins's residence. The Reverend Franklin Low-rimore helped write the church covenant, and J. M. Kirkland of First Baptist was involved in selecting the name North Hampton Baptist Church. Initially meeting in Hardy's Store, the group began construction on an educational building in the spring of 1967. In early 1968 First Baptist agreed to sponsor North Hampton, and in 1971 the church became fully independent.[24] A 1969 local Baptist membership report gave the following numbers:

First Baptist......1,360
Lakewood 205
Pawleys 45
Screven 630
North Hampton 70

Total .... 2,312[25]

The 1970s were characterized by further growth and expansion. In 1972 the church voted to expand its facilities at the corner of Highmarket and Dozier Streets with the addition of a new recreational-educational building.[26] This facility included a church parlor, a bride's room, Sunday-school rooms, several classrooms, a kitchen and cafeteria capable of seating three hundred persons, a bell tower and carillon chimes, and covered walkways to connect the various buildings. The bell tower, which was freestanding and struck the hours from six until nine o'clock, was the only one of its kind in Georgetown.[27] The dedication for the new facility took place April 29, 1973, and former pastors J. H. Darr and C. E. Cooper delivered the morning and evening services, respectively. Pastor Kirkland officiated at the dedication, saying: "We as a part of God's total program for the world, for the winning of the lost, for the perfecting of the Saints, for the work of the ministry, for the edifying of the body of Christ, for his service, honor, and glory, in His name, in the name of His son, and the Holy Spirit, we dedicate this building."[28]

The following year another significant dedication took place, this time to honor William Screven by preserving his grave site. Elisha Screven had reserved the plot in his will, but over the years it had passed through several owners and the entrance to the plot had been closed. Eventually, it became the property of the county and was in danger of being paved over for parking. The George-town Garden Club, led by Mrs. H. D. Bull, wife of the late rector of Prince George Winyah, took responsibility for the site, and that work won an award for historical preservation from the South Carolina Council of Garden Clubs. In the fall of 1974 the club and First Baptist came together to celebrate the erection of a new brick wall and a handsome bronze plaque. Many local state notables attended the event, as well as key figures in historical circles, including

Dr. J. Glenwood Clayton, curator of the Baptist historical collection at Furman University, and Mrs. Ollin J. Owens, secretary of the South Carolina Baptist Historical Society. Dr. Kirkland gave the invocation and welcome, followed by brief remarks by Mayor O. M. Higgins and Court Council chairman Alfred Schooler. The Reverend Earl D. Crumpler, pastor of North Trenholm Baptist Church, gave the keynote address.[29] Since then, the grave has been maintained in pristine condition and is one of the must-see sights in historic Georgetown.

Kirkland served Georgetown First Baptist for an impressive eighteen years and provided a degree of consistency not experienced since the days of Robert Lide. In years of service Kirkland was exceeded only by Edmund Botsford, nearly two hundred years earlier. Dr. Kirkland resigned on the fourth Sunday in September 1978 and became director of the Agency on Aging for the Waccamaw Region. He also founded a new Baptist church, Messiah Baptist in the Maryville section. That structure, originally an Episcopal chapel, remains an active and beautiful church.

On August 26, 1979, Bob A. Teems of Huguenot Road Baptist in Richmond, Virginia, accepted the call to Georgetown. A native of Boone, North Carolina, Teems moved with his family to Sumter when he was fifteen, and there he graduated from Edmunds High School. After attending the University of South Carolina, he received bachelor's and master's degrees in divinity from Southwestern Baptist Seminary, earning a doctorate at Southeastern Baptist Seminary. In addition to serving as pastor of churches in Virginia and South Carolina, he and his wife worked as missionaries in the French West Indies. He stated upon arrival that "we feel there is a lot of potential here. I'm genuinely grateful for the nice way we have been received."[30] Dr. Teems already had in mind goals for his new church, such as a youth ministry and a Young at Heart club. He also had an avid interest in church history, and under his leadership, and that of church historian Virginia Skinner, a series of celebrations ensued. This work was aided considerably by the services of Robert Baker, professor of church history at Southwestern Baptist Theological Seminary in Fort Worth, Texas. In 1980 official historical markers honoring William and Elisha Screven were erected in Georgetown after approval by the South Carolina Department of Archives and History. This event coincided with the Georgetown County Lowcountry History Festival, and First Baptist hosted many of these celebratory events, including addresses by historians George C. Rogers, Jr., and Charles W. Joyner. A large crowd witnessed the unveiling on that bright Sunday afternoon of October 5, 1980, including U.S. senator Strom Thurmond and representatives from numerous states and national historical groups. One particularly welcome guest was Dr. David Cuttino, professor of music at Charleston Southern University and a descendant of Screven and former

Dr. Bob A. Teems, pastor of Georgetown First Baptist Church,
1979–1986, a period of growth and renewed interest in church history.
Courtesy of Georgetown First Baptist Church.

Georgetown Baptist pastors. Together Dr. Baker and Mayor Douglas L. Hinds removed the red covering from the markers. The whole affair, the newspaper said, represented "an assurance that will see the names of the two Screvens imprinted upon the ages of Georgetown's history for decades to come." [31]

Part of the festival included a tour of the ancient Belin Church at Black Mingo. In the twentieth century that area's population had dwindled, and the church fell upon hard times. By the 1920s it was all but abandoned. In 1936 the congregation of nearby Nesmith Baptist Church, which had grown out of Belin, undertook to restore the church and services were held there quarterly.[32] In 1951 membership was tiny, but the church was still open thanks to the support from the Southeast Association. By this time it was called variously Belin's Church, Old Belin, and Black Mingo. In 1960 the church was largely inactive and received the designation "historical" by the association, with periodic events and association meetings held there. In 1976 the church had services monthly, and in 1986 the association had on hand more than seven thousand dollars to support Black Mingo.[33] The publicity surrounding the Lowcountry History Festival included photographs of the interior, along with a substantial narrative of the church's history. Unfortunately, the efforts to save and celebrate this magnificent church were futile. It was completely destroyed by arsonists in 1992.

By this time Virginia Skinner had discovered the original records of the church at Furman University. Her first opportunity to discuss her findings publicly came in the fall of 1982 with the dedication of an original watercolor of the antebellum Antipedo Church. She and her siblings commissioned the work by Pawleys Island artist Pete Przekop to honor their parents, Sheriff H. Brightman and Reba Young Bruorton.[34] Skinner made another presentation on November 6, 1983, when a historical marker was unveiled at the old Baptist Cemetery.[35] A second watercolor of the church as it appeared in the 1890s was exhibited in 1984. This work, by local artist Nancy Bourne, honored Judge and Mrs. Herman Samuel Higgins, important members of the church in the early 1900s. The unveiling by Bourne and William Oliver Higgins occurred on Sunday, September 23, 1984, as part of the church's Historical Observance Day. For this occasion Mayor Douglas Lanford Hinds and Dr. Clifton Lide Williams, and their wives, sponsored the publication of a thirty-one page booklet containing Virginia Skinner's "Brief History of the Baptists of Georgetown, S.C. (1710–1984)."[36]

Teems considered 1980 to be an important year not only because of the historical interest generated, but also because of the arrival of Robbie Sox as minister of music and youth. Under Sox the music program made tremendous strides, building the church's reputation for quality performances and community involvement. Teems later wrote, "I consider this a key event in the ongoing development of FBC in the late twentieth century."[37] The best known outcome of Sox's work is the all-community "singing Christmas tree." First presented in 1990, the event has become a town tradition. With full-scale recreational and educational programs, the church grew rapidly, and in 1983 additional property was purchased at the corner of Cleland and Prince Streets. Another groundbreaking ceremony followed for the Family Life Center on October 6, 1985. The completion of this center signaled the end of Teems's pastorate at Georgetown First Baptist.[38]

A pulpit committee began its search for a replacement that same year, but it took two years to find another pastor. The church welcomed the family of Dr. Wilson Nelson in 1987, and in 1989 he organized a Master Plan Committee to study the needs of the church. Meanwhile, Nelson received his doctorate from Southeastern Baptist Theological Seminary in May 1991. He formed another plan, called "Reaching New Heights," in an effort to retire the church's debt. The church school became a casualty of this retrenchment. Like many private academies, the school faced a serious challenge in offering competitive teacher salaries, and in 1989 the church ended that part of its educational program. Nelson was successful in handling the church's debt, and soon he and the congregation were considering building a new sanctuary. In May 1992, however, Nelson tended his resignation and accepted a call to First Baptist in Greer, South Carolina. Dr. Lewis McCormick, former president of the South Carolina Baptist Historical Society, became interim pastor. During his service, Esta Rice, a devoted Baptist, commissioned artist Danny McLaughoin to create an oil painting of the 1914–1949 church; the painting hangs in the foyer with other art works.[39]

The church found a permanent pastor in Dr. Ronald G. Dillon, and he and his wife moved to Georgetown in June 1993, purchasing a home in Wedgefield Plantation. Serious debate continued about razing the 1949 sanctuary and beginning anew, and the decision to build passed by a narrow margin. Dillon called his expansion program "Together We Build." On June 22, 1994, the church hired the architectural firm of James, Durant, Matthews and Shelley of Sumter, South Carolina, and a year later contracted with the Wise Construction Company. The cost for this new house and related items was approximately $2.9 million and total indebtedness at completion was $1.5 million.[40] On September 28, 1997, the church dedicated its new worship center. It had been eight years in planning and two years in construction, and its completion was proclaimed "a momentous occasion in Georgetown church history."[41] Totaling 15,800 square feet, the sanctuary featured a soaring roof, red-carpeted floors, and beautiful stained-glass windows. With a capacity of 740, the church was full for the dedication led by Pastor Dillon. The program included preachers from other denominations, among them representatives from Bethel AME and Bethesda Missionary Baptist.[42] The celebrations stretched into the following year and were concluded on June 3, 1998, with the dedication of a cornerstone box.[43] While Dillon's pastorate showed no significant changes in church membership, a notable achievement was in serving children with special needs. To that end, the church constructed a prayer chapel on the campus called Grace Church. In August 1999 Dr. Dillon ended his work in Georgetown and accepted the pastorate of First Baptist Church in Mount Pleasant, South Carolina.[44] The Reverend Hiram McElrath served diligently as interim minister and was asked to stay on as associate pastor after the church hired its current pastor.

Dr. Ted Sherrill, pastor of Georgetown First Baptist Church
since 2000. Courtesy of Georgetown First Baptist Church.

Ted Allen Sherrill arrived in Georgetown on September 1, 2000. He had
received his undergraduate degree from Clemson University in 1980 and then
became the youth and activities minister at First Baptist Church in Greer,
South Carolina. Having earned a master of divinity degree in 1986, he began
his pastorate at St. Matthews Baptist that same year. He left St. Matthews in
June 1991 for Pierpont Baptist Church in Charleston, South Carolina, and
while there he earned a doctor of ministry from Southeastern Baptist Theological Seminary in 1999. Noted for developing evangelistic ministries, he initiated
the Upward Sports Ministry in 2003, which promoted salvation, character, and
self-esteem for children kindergarten through sixth grade. Another ministry
followed in 2005 called FAITH Evangelism, a visitation program.[45]

With the advent of the twenty-first century, many churches and denominations experienced substantial shifts both in doctrine and in practice. First
Baptist is a good example of these changes in terms of music. The doxology is
no longer required in every service, and drums, guitars, and electronic sound

systems have appeared. The terms that Baptists and other churches use for these services are *traditional, contemporary,* and *blended.* As J. Holmes, minister of music since 1996 said of the contemporary style, "same message; different beat."[46]

A more recent improvement has transpired in the Antipedo Baptist Cemetery, where the church initiated a restoration effort. The tombstones were faded, cracked, broken, and often illegible. Virginia Skinner's historical committee obtained approval to construct an obelisk containing the names of those interred there. Today, the seven-thousand-pound pedestal, dedicated on June 8, 2003, stands near the front of the cemetery.[47] A year later a special inscribed stone was placed by Edmund Botsford's grave.[48] The final addition to the beautiful grounds of the cemetery was a proper fence of wrought iron and

Entrance to the Antipedo Baptist Cemetery adjacent to the church that was built about 1805. Photo by Isaac Dusenbury.

Interior of the present-day First Baptist Church of Georgetown.
Courtesy of Georgetown First Baptist Church.

brickwork. A dream for many years, the fence was completed in the spring of 2007, another fine addition to historic sites in Georgetown.[49]

The church's biggest celebration in 2010 marked the arrival of William Screven in Winyah three hundred years earlier. Virginia Skinner and the newly formed Georgetown Baptist Historical Society sponsored a series of events to commemorate three centuries of their church's history, involving a children's historical sketch, teas for the ladies, breakfast for the men, a commissioned logo, along with lapel pins, ornaments, and plates. The most lasting contribution was the creation of the church archives. Interest in the celebration brought contributions of artifacts, family histories, and other significant documents from near and far. With paintings and photographs lining the walls and antique documents under glass around every corner, First Baptist has made it a priority to honor those who helped make the church what it is today. The capstone of that effort is this publication, made possible by the contributions of the Georgetown Baptist Historical Society. What a fitting conclusion for a congregation that struggled for many years and suffered so much but emerged as a well-respected church with beautiful, well-maintained buildings and grounds, an excellent, committed staff, and a genuine spirit-filled membership dedicated to spreading the gospel at home and abroad.

Present-day First Baptist Church of Georgetown.
Courtesy of Georgetown First Baptist Church.

Notes

First Baptist Church of Georgetown Archives   FBCG
South Carolina Baptist Historical Collection   SCBHC
South Carolina Department of Archives and History   SCDAH
South Caroliniana Library   SCL

Chapter 1: From Somerset to Kittery

1. Henry F. Brown, *Baptism through the Centuries* (Mountain View, Calif.: Pacific Press Publishing Association, 1965), 75–90. An excellent account of early forms of baptism is Peter Cramer, *Baptism and Change in the Early Middle Ages, c.200–c.1150* (Cambridge: Cambridge University Press, 1993).

2. Patrick Collinson, *The Reformation: A History* (New York: Modern Library, 2006), 49–64, 173–78.

3. Hans J. Hillerbrand, ed., *The Oxford Encyclopedia of the Reformation* (New York: Oxford University Press, 1996), s.vv. "Anabaptists," "Baptists." A scholarly and informative source on Anabaptists and other radical religious sects is George Huntston Williams, *The Radical Reformation*, 3rd ed. (Kirksville, Mo.: Sixteenth Century Journal Publishers, 1992).

4. William Henry Brackney, *The Baptists* (Westport, Conn.: Greenwood Press, 1988), xvii–xxii, 3–7.

5. James M. Renihan, "John Spilsbury, 1593c.–1662/1668," in *The British Particular Baptists, 1638–1910*, ed. Michael A. G. Haykin (Springfield, Mo.: Particular Baptist Press, 1998), 1:20–37.

6. Diarmaid MacCulloch, *The Reformation: A History* (New York: Penguin Group, 2004), 253–69, 280–303; Brackney, *Baptists*, 5–6.

7. MacCulloch, *The Reformation*, 502–45.

8. "The Confession of Faith, Of those Churches which are commonly (though falsly) called Anabaptists . . . ," in *Baptist Confessions of Faith*, ed. William L. Lumpkin (Philadelphia: Judson Press, 1959), 153–71.

9. Brackney, *Baptists*, 7–9.

10. Michael N. Ivey, *A Welsh Succession of Primitive Baptist Faith and Practice* (n.p.: M. N. Ivey, 1994), 29–42.

11. Edwin S. Gaustad, *Roger Williams* (New York: Oxford University Press, 2005), 1–16, 52–53.

12. Robert A. Baker, *The First Southern Baptists* (Nashville: Broadman Press, 1966), 3–7.

13. Nathan E. Wood, *The History of the First Baptist Church of Boston* (1899; repr., New York: Arno Press, 1980), 55–71.

14. Baker, *First Southern Baptists*, 7–8.

15. There are several spellings for William Screven's surname, including Scriven, Sereven, Screeven, Scrivine, and Scrivener. With the exception of quotations from primary sources, Screven is used.

16. Robert A. Baker, "More Light on William Screven," *Journal of the South Carolina Baptist Historical Society* 6 (November 1980): 19.

17. Joseph Ivimey, *A History of the English Baptists* (n.p.: London, 1814), 2:520.

18. "A Confession of the Faith of Several Churches of Christ In the County of Somerset . . . ," in Lumpkin, *Baptist Confessions of Faith*, 203–18.

19. Baker, *First Southern Baptists*, 3, 13.

20. On September 29, 1685, Joseph Atwell was adopted by the Screvens. Robert Cutt, Bridgett's youngest brother, had been entrusted to them upon the death of Bridgett's father. For more on the Cutt Family, see Cecil Hampden Cutts Howard, *Genealogy of the Cutts Family in America* (Albany: J. Munsell's Sons, 1892).

21. Robert E. Moody, ed., *Province and Court Records of Maine* (Portland: Maine Historical Society, 1947), 2:306–7.

22. Sybol Noyes, Charles Thornton Libby, and Walter Goodwin Davis, eds., *Genealogical Dictionary of Maine and New Hampshire* (1928–1939; repr., Baltimore: Genealogical Publishing, 1972), s.v. "Scriven."

23. Joshua Millet, *A History of the Baptists in Maine; Together with Brief Notices of Societies and Institutions, and a Dictionary of the Labors of Each Minister* (Portland: Charles Day, 1845), 24.

24. William Willis, ed., *Collections of the Maine Historical Society* (Portland, 1865), 1:400–401; Moody, *Records*, 3:xiii.

25. Wood, *First Baptist Church of Boston*, 179.

26. Morgan Edwards, *Materials Towards a History of the Baptists* (1770; repr., Danielsville, Ga.: Heritage Papers, 1984), 2:122–23; "Historical Sketch of the First Baptist Church," in *Year Book* (N.p.: Charleston, 1881), 316; Noyes, Libby, and Davis, *Genealogical Dictionary*, s.v. "Scriven"; William G. Whilden, "Reverend William Screven," *New-England Historical and Genealogical Register* 43 (October 1889): 356.

27. Henry S. Burrage, *History of the Baptists in Maine* (Portland: Marks Printing House, 1904), 22; Leah Townsend, *South Carolina Baptists, 1670–1805* (1935; repr., Baltimore: Genealogical Publishing, 1974), 6.

28. Baker, *First Southern Baptists*, 17–22.

29. Isaac Backus, *A History of New England with Particular Reference to the Denomination of Christians Called Baptists* (Newton, Mass.: Backus Historical Society, 1871), 1:401. Isaac Backus was a well-known Baptist preacher in New England and one of the only historians to read the original letters of the First Baptist Church of Boston. He reprinted them in their entirety in *History of New England.*
30. Ibid., 401–2.
31. Ibid., 402–3.
32. Moody, *Records,* 3:161–62.
33. Ibid., 3:3, 33, 165–66, 177.
34. Ibid., 3:404.
35. Ibid., 3:181.
36. Wood, *First Baptist Church of Boston,* 181–82. According to the church covenant, the congregation consisted of ten men and seven women. William Screven, Humphrey Churchwood, Robert Williams, John Morgradge, Richard Cutt, Timothy Davis, Leonard Drown, William Adams, Humphrey Axtell, and George Litten signed the covenant. The names of the seven women are not listed.
37. Moody, *Records,* 3:120, 181–82.
38. Thomas Armitage, *A History of the Baptists: Traced by their Vital Principles . . .* (New York: Bryan, Taylor, 1887), 704; Backus, *History of New England,* 1:467, 2:480; David Benedict, *A General History of the Baptist Denomination in America and Other Parts of the World* (New York: Lewis Colby, 1848), 701–2; Burrage, *History of the Baptists in Maine,* 21; Henry Toliver Cook, *The Story of the Baptists in All Ages and Countries* (New York: Wiley Brothers, 1884), 254–55; Edwards, *Materials,* 2:123; "Historical Sketch," 316; Basil Manly, *Mercy and Judgment: A Discourse Containing Some Fragments of the History of the Baptist Church in Charleston, S.C.* (Charleston: Press of Knowles, Vose, 1837), 11; Edward McGrady, *The History of South Carolina Under the Proprietary Government, 1670–1719* (New York: Macmillan, 1897), 326; Elizabeth Anne Poyas, *The Olden Time of Carolina by the Octogenarian Lady of Charleston, S.C.* (Charleston: Courtenay, 1855), 112; H. A. Tupper, ed., *Two Centuries of the First Baptist Church of South Carolina, 1683–1883* (Baltimore: R. H. Woodward, 1889), 52, 70; Henry C. Vedder, *A Short History of the Baptists* (Philadelphia: American Baptist Publication Society, 1891), 301; Whilden, "Reverend William Screven," 356.
39. Townsend, *South Carolina Baptists,* 6.
40. Moody, *Records,* 3:14, 90, 149, 219, 303.
41. Baker, *First Southern Baptists,* 34–38, 67–68.
42. Designated as Charles Town when the city was founded in 1670, the name changed to Charleston in 1783. The modern spelling is used here.
43. Baker, *First Southern Baptists,* 39–44.
44. Walter Edgar, *South Carolina: A History* (Columbia: University of South Carolina Press, 1998), 86–94. For samples of promotional literature, see H. Roy Merrens, ed., *The Colonial South Carolina Scene: Contemporary Views, 1697–1774,* tricentennial ed. (Columbia: University of South Carolina Press, 1977).

45. Baker, *First Southern Baptists,* 42–46.

46. Robert A. Baker, Paul J. Craven, Jr., and R. Marshall Blalock, *History of the First Baptist Church of Charleston, South Carolina, 1682–2007,* 325th anniversary ed. (Springfield, Miss.: Particular Baptist Press, 2007), 74–78; Alexander S. Salley, Jr., ed., *Warrants for Land in South Carolina, 1672–1711* (Columbia: Historical Commission of South Carolina, 1915), 134–36; Henry A. M. Smith, "Some Forgotten Towns in Lower South Carolina," *South Carolina Historical and Genealogical Magazine* 14 (July 1913): 134–36.

47. Baker, Craven, and Blalock, *First Baptist Church of Charleston,* 74–78; Salley, *Warrants for Land,* 134–36; Smith, "Some Forgotten Towns," 134–36. According to land records, Screven also secured 260 acres in Berkeley County. See Proprietary Grants, 38:386, 401, and McCrady Plat 05859, SCDAH.

48. Baker, *First Southern Baptists,* 78–82.

CHAPTER 2: CHARLESTON

1. Walter Edgar, *South Carolina: A History* (Columbia: University of South Carolina Press, 1998), 43–62.

2. Arthur Henry Hirsch, *The Huguenots of Colonial South Carolina* (Columbia: University of South Carolina Press, 1999), 3–46.

3. James William Hagy, *This Happy Land: The Jews of Colonial and Antebellum Charleston* (Tuscaloosa: University of Alabama Press, 1993), 5–27.

4. Robert M. Weir, *Colonial South Carolina: A History* (New York: KTO Press, 1983), 65–67.

5. Edgar, *South Carolina,* 93–94.

6. Alexander S. Salley, Jr., *Narratives of Early Carolina, 1650–1708* (New York: Charles Scribner's Sons, 1911), 221–23.

7. Daniel Defoe, "Party-Tyranny: or, An Occasional Bill in Miniature. . . . ," in Salley, *Narratives,* 237, 243.

8. "Letters of Rev. Samuel Thomas, 1702–1710," *South Carolina Historical and Genealogical Magazine* 4 (July 1903): 226.

9. Edgar, *South Carolina,* 82–97; Loulie Latimer Owens, "South Carolina Baptists and the American Revolution," *Journal of the South Carolina Baptist Historical Society* 1 (November 1975): 31–33.

10. Weir, *Colonial South Carolina,* 210.

11. Owens, "South Carolina Baptists," 33–35.

12. Robert A. Baker, Paul J. Craven, Jr., and R. Marshall Blalock, *History of the First Baptist Church of Charleston, South Carolina, 1682–2007,* 325th anniversary ed. (Springfield, Miss.: Particular Baptist Press, 2007), 80.

13. Conveyance Book, 1:60–62, SCDAH; Henry A. M. Smith, "The Baronies of South Carolina," *South Carolina Historical and Genealogical Magazine* 15 (October 1914): 159.

14. Morgan Edwards, *Materials Towards a History of the Baptists* (1770; repr., Danielsville, Ga.: Heritage Papers, 1984), 2:120.

15. Loulie Latimer Owens, *Saints of Clay: The Shaping of South Carolina Baptists* (Columbia: R. L. Bryan, 1971), 25.

16. The only time Screven may have met resistance was when he lost his Charleston home to a fire in 1700 and the Commons House of Assembly refused to compensate him for the damages. On February 28, 1700, the lower house ordered the public receiver, Captain Thomas Smith, to pay William Screven twenty pounds "in consideration of the great damages he sustained by the loss of his House and Goods by fire, and that this Order be sent to the Upper House for their Concurrence," but the upper house denied Screven's claim. While the logic behind this decision is unknown, Screven's faith may have been one reason his suit failed. The real tragedy for historians is the loss of Screven's books and papers in the fire. Absent that, we would know much more about his life and works. *Journal of the Commons House of Assembly,* February 28, 1700, SCDAH.

17. Robert E. Moody, ed., *Province and Court Records of Maine* (Portland: Maine Historical Society, 1947), 3:xxxvii.

18. Ibid.

19. Ibid., 3:xxxvii–xxxviii.

20. Hirsch, *Huguenots of Colonial South Carolina,* 309.

21. Baker, Craven, and Blalock, *First Baptist Church of Charleston,* 85.

22. Robert Goodwyn Rhett, *Charleston: An Epic of Carolina* (Richmond: Garrett and Massie, 1940), 55. Screven estimated that his congregation numbered ninety members, a figure that is significantly lower than the figures provided by Anglicans. See Baker, Craven, and Blalock, *First Baptist Church of Charleston,* 90–94; Edwards, *Materials,* 2:121.

23. Bill J. Leonard, *Baptists in America* (New York: Columbia University Press, 2005), 65–90.

24. Baker, Craven, and Blalock, *First Baptist Church of Charleston,* 81; Terry A. Chrisope, "William Screven, 1629–1713," in *A Noble Company: Biographical Essays on Notable Particular-Regular Baptists in America,* ed. Terry Wolever (Springfield, Miss.: Particular Baptist Press, 2006), 1:218–21; Edwards, *Materials,* 120; Leah Townsend, *South Carolina Baptists, 1670–1805* (1935; repr., Baltimore: Genealogical Publishing, 1974), 2:9.

25. Some studies do not recognize the General Baptist presence in South Carolina but instead group everyone together as Particular Baptists. For early Baptist statistics in South Carolina, see Robert G. Gardner, "South Carolina Baptist Statistics, 1672–1790: A Table," *Journal of the South Carolina Baptist Historical Society* 9 (November 1983): 34.

26. W. T. Whitley, ed., *Minutes of the General Assembly of the General Baptist Churches in England* (London: Kingsgate Press, 1909–1910), 1:75.

27. *Journal of the Commons House of Assembly,* May 1, 1745, SCDAH.

28. Basil Manly, *Mercy and Judgment: A Discourse Containing Some Fragments of the History of the Baptist Church in Charleston, S.C.* (Charleston: Press of Knowles, Vose, 1837), 25.

29. Baker, Craven, and Blalock, *First Baptist Church of Charleston,* 107–9, 114–20; Edwards, *Materials,* 2:120–22; Townsend, *South Carolina Baptists,* 9–17.

30. Edwards, *Materials,* 2:123.

31. Manly, *Mercy and Judgment,* 70–71. The Baptist minister Isaac Backus preserved a few of Screven's letters held by the First Baptist Church of Boston. In 1796 Backus sent the letters to Colonel Thomas Screven, William Screven's great-grandson. Basil Manly reprinted the letters in their entirety in *Mercy and Judgment.*

32. Ibid., 72–73.

33. Ibid., 73.

34. Edwards, *Materials,* 2:123.

35. Frank J. Klingberg, ed., *The Carolina Chronicle of Dr. Francis Le Jau* (Berkeley: University of California Press, 1956), 122.

36. Manly, *Mercy and Judgment,* 309.

37. Baker, Craven, and Blalock, *First Baptist Church of Charleston,* 94–95.

CHAPTER 3: THE SETTLING OF GEORGETOWN

1. Robert A. Baker, Paul J. Craven, Jr., and R. Marshall Blalock, *History of the First Baptist Church of Charleston, South Carolina, 1682–2007* (Springfield, Miss.: Particular Baptist Press, 2007), 94–95, 104; George C. Rogers, Jr., *The History of Georgetown County, South Carolina* (Columbia: University of South Carolina Press, 1970), 1–8.

2. Members of the First Baptist Church of Charleston who secured land in the Winyah region prior to William Screven's arrival included James Child, Lawrence Dennis, Mary Grimball, and the Parmenter family. For the land records of Lawrence Dennis, Mary Grimball, and Aaron Screven, see Proprietary Grants, 38:486, 506, 533, SCDAH. For Robert Baker's summary of these land grants, including direct quotations, see Baker, "The Founding of Georgetown," 2–3, FBCG.

3. Charleston Deeds, LL:256–65, SCDAH. William Screven's April 13, 1709, purchase of one hundred acres in Winyah is mentioned in a land record dated March 11 and 12, 1752, and concerns the sale of some property in Craven County by his grandson, Robert Screven. A memorial dated April 21, 1733, also refers to Screven's purchase. See Memorial Book, 4:365–71, SCDAH.

4. H. Roy Merrens, ed., *The Colonial South Carolina Scene: Contemporary Views, 1697–1774,* tricentennial ed. (Columbia: University of South Carolina Press, 1977), 60–61.

5. Robert K. Ackerman, *South Carolina Colonial Land Policies* (Columbia: University of South Carolina Press, 1977), 26–29.

6. Royal Grants, 39:107–8, SCDAH.

7. Ackerman, *South Carolina Colonial Land Policies,* 12–35, 97.

8. Royal Grants, 39:286–87, SCDAH.

9. James Glen, "An Attempt Towards an Estimate of the Value of South Carolina, for the Right Honourable the Lords Commissioners for Trade and Plantations," in Merrens, *Colonial South Carolina Scene,* 180.

10. Charleston Deeds, LL:256–65, and Memorial Book, 4:365–71, SCDAH.

11. Suzanne Cameron Linder and Marta Leslie Thacker, *Historical Atlas of the Rice Plantations of Georgetown County and the Santee River* (Columbia: South Carolina Department of Archives and History, 2001), 725, 433.

12. Henry A. M. Smith, "Georgetown: The Original Plan and the Earliest Settlers," *South Carolina Historical and Genealogical Magazine* 9 (April 1908): 85.

13. Proprietary Grants, 38:516–18, SCDAH.

14. The terms *peppercorn* and *one ear of Indian corn* were used to represent token payments. See Ackerman, *South Carolina Colonial Land Policies,* 18, 25, 27, 56.

15. Office of the Historical Commission Grant Book (1707–1711), 217–23, SCDAH.

16. Charleston County Wills, 1:6–7, SCDAH.

17. Smith, "Georgetown," 86. At some point the entire holdings of the Perrie family were conveyed to John Perrie. His will of 1708 stipulated that his daughter Mary was to receive all of his Winyah property, including the 2,500 acres formerly belonging to his brother and sister.

18. Isaac Motte vs. John Perrie, Judgment Roll, 2D, 68A, SCDAH.

19. Robert A. Baker, The First Southern Baptists (Nashville: Broadman Press, 1966), 64.

20. Edwards, *Materials,* 2:123. Morgan Edwards was the only Baptist historian to see "An Ornament for Church Members." He printed this segment in *Materials Towards a History of the Baptists.*

21. For memorials of William Screven's will, see Memorial Book, 1:280, 287; 5:335, SCDAH. For more on memorials, see Katie-Prince Ward Esker, *South Carolina Memorials, 1731–1776* (Cottonport, La.: Polyanthos, 1973), v.

22. Memorial Book, 1:73, SCDAH.

23. Smith, "Georgetown," 88.

24. Rogers, *History of Georgetown,* 33; Smith, "Georgetown," 88; Merrens, *Colonial South Carolina Scene,* 114.

25. Miscellaneous Records, 2:262–63, SCDAH.

26. Ibid., 2:264–77.

27. In October 1732 Elias Horry advertised his property for sale: "Lot No. 23, at Georgetown, Winyah, Fronting the Bay," *South Carolina Gazette.*

28. "A New Voyage to Georgia. By A Young Gentlemen. Giving an Account of his Travels to South Carolina, and Part of North Carolina.," in Merrens, *Colonial South Carolina Scene,* 114.

29. Miscellaneous Records, 2:277, SCDAH.

30. Charleston County Wills, 3:238–39, SCDAH.

31. November 23–30, 1734, *South Carolina Gazette.* Elisha Screven's advertisement was reprinted in subsequent editions of the *Gazette,* including December 14–21, December 21–28, and December 28–January 4, 1734/1735.

32. Miscellaneous Records, 2:280–81, SCDAH.

33. July 5, 1735, *South Carolina Gazette.*

34. Charleston Deeds, MM:260–65; Miscellaneous Records, Part 1, 59–64; Charleston County Wills, 8:489, SCDAH.

35. July 5–12, 1735, *South Carolina Gazette.*
36. Charleston Deeds, MM:243–49, SCDAH.
37. Charleston Deeds, Y:262–75, SCDAH.
38. Charleston Deeds, MM:1–27, SCDAH.
39. Miscellaneous Records, 2:276–80, SCDAH. Although no revised plan is attached to the indenture, a plan of Georgetown dated 1798 and signed by John Hardwick reflects the Clelands' alterations.
40. Renunciation of Dower, 1:23–31, SCDAH.
41. August 6–13, 1737, *South Carolina Gazette.*
42. David Ramsay, *The History of South Carolina, From its First Settlement in 1670 to the Year 1808* (Charleston: David Longworth, 1809), 2:591.
43. Charleston Deeds, QQ:609–13, SCDAH.
44. Charleston County Wills, 8:190–95, SCDAH; "Historical Notes," *South Carolina Historical and Genealogical Magazine* 16 (April 1915): 94.

CHAPTER 4: EQUALITY OR NOTHING

1. Willtown on Black Mingo Creek should not be confused with Willtown, also known as New London, on the Edisto River. For the history of New London, see Henry A. M. Smith, "Willtown or New London," *South Carolina Historical and Genealogical Magazine* 10 (January 1909): 20–32.
2. J. W. Nelson Chandler, "Willtown, Black Mingo: The Rise and Fall of an Early Village in the South Carolina Lowcountry," *South Carolina Historical Magazine* 105 (April 2004): 108–18.
3. William H. Chandler, "Some Historic Churches in Williamsburg County," *Names in South Carolina* 18 (Winter 1971): 28–29.
4. Charleston County Wills, 8:190–95, SCDAH; "Historical Notes," *South Carolina Historical and Genealogical Magazine* 16 (April 1915): 94.
5. Black Mingo Meeting House was also known as the Black River Church, the Brick Church, and the Wyneau Congregation.
6. Chandler, "Willtown," 130. When Georgetown became a district in 1769, its boundary lines enveloped Black Mingo. Georgetown lost Black Mingo when the General Assembly carved Williamsburg District out of the western half of Georgetown in 1804.
7. William Willis Boddie, *History of Williamsburg: Something about the People of Williamsburg County, South Carolina, from the First Settlement by Europeans about 1705 until 1923* (Columbia: State Company, 1923), 48–49.
8. Ibid., 35; Chandler, "Some Historic Churches," 28–29; John Renning Phillips, *The Good Intent: The Story and Heritage of a Fresno Family* (n.p.: Magnolia Group Press, 2007), 417; James P. Hayes, *James and Related Sea Islands* (Charleston: Hayes, 1978), 129; Gordon B. Jenkinson, *A History of the Homes and People of Williamsburg District* (Charleston: History Press, 2007), 56; Carol Thalimer and Dan Thalimer, *Country Roads of South Carolina* (Oaks, Pa.: Country Roads Press, 1996), 56.

9. Charleston County Wills, 8:190, SCDAH.

10. Hart to Richard Furman, undated, Oliver Hart Papers, SCBHC.

11. Hart to Furman, April 18, 1794, Oliver Hart Papers, SCBHC.

12. Harvey Toliver Cook, *Rambles in the Pee Dee Basin South Carolina* (Columbia: State Company, 1926), 148.

13. James A. Wallace, *History of Williamsburg Church* (Salisbury, N.C.: Bell and James Printers, 1856), 21.

14. David Benedict, *Fifty Years Among the Baptists* (New York: Sheldon, 1860), 75.

15. Boddie, *History of Williamsburg,* 48.

16. Ibid., 148.

17. Charleston County Wills, 5:113, SCDAH.

18. Ibid., 5:126.

19. Cook, *Rambles,* 148. According to Cook, the old Black Mingo Meeting House was located within two miles of the parsonage of Prince Frederick Church. Its successor, which Cook claims was built about 1741, was located within six miles of the parsonage.

20. Chandler, "Willtown," 119.

21. George Howe, *History of the Presbyterian Church in South Carolina* (Columbia: Duffie and Chapman, 1870), 1:282.

22. Cook, *Rambles,* 151.

23. Lionel Francis Baxter and John William Baxter, *A Baxter Family from South Carolina: Scotch Irish Pioneers from Ulster* (St. Petersburg: Genealogy Publication Service, 1989), 17–18.

24. Howe, *History of the Presbyterian Church,* 1:204, 255, 283, 323, 410, 469–70; 2:74, 249.

25. Louis P. Towles, "Township Plan," in *The South Carolina Encyclopedia,* ed. Walter Edgar (Columbia: University of South Carolina Press, 2006), 973–74.

26. James Fowler Cooper, *An Historical Sketch of Indiantown Presbyterian Church in Williamsburg County, S.C., 1757–1957* (n.p., 1957). The records of the Indiantown Presbyterian Church note that on June 20, 1824, "Mrs. Margaret McConnell was received into this Church on reputable testimony of her having been an acceptable member of the Black Mingo Church, this church now being extinct."

27. Chandler, "Some Historic Churches," 29.

28. Boddie, *History of Williamsburg,* 49.

29. Chandler, "Some Historic Churches," 31.

30. Charleston County Wills, 8:94, SCDAH.

31. Chandler, "Some Historic Churches," 31.

32. Boddie, *History of Williamsburg,* 58.

33. Charles Woodmason, *The Carolina Backcountry on the Eve of the Revolution: The Journal and Other Writings of Charles Woodmason, Anglican Itinerant,* ed. Richard J. Hooker (Chapel Hill: University of North Carolina Press, 1953), 43.

34. Loulie L. Owens, "Oliver Hart and the American Revolution," *Journal of the South Carolina Baptist Historical Society* 1 (November 1975): 3–4.

35. Loulie Latimer Owens, *Oliver Hart, 1723–1795: A Biography* (Greenville: South Carolina Baptist Historical Society, 1966), 1–12.

36. Owens, "Oliver Hart and the American Revolution," 3–5.

37. Walter Edgar, *South Carolina: A History* (Columbia: University of South Carolina Press, 1998), 223.

38. Journal of Oliver Hart, August 12, 1775, Oliver Hart Papers, SCL.

39. Edgar, *South Carolina,* 223–24, 241.

40. Welsh Neck Church Book, March 8, 1776, SCBHC.

41. Owens, "Oliver Hart and the American Revolution," 35–38.

42. William Tennent, "Petition to the South Carolina House of Assembly," January 11, 1777, William Tennent Papers, SCL.

43. William Tennent, "Speech to the South Carolina House of Assembly," January Baptists and the American Revolution," *Journal of the South Carolina Baptist Historical Society* 1 (November 1975): 35–38. Charleston Baptist Association, Minutes, 1777, SCBHC. Hart to Furman, February 12, 1777, Oliver Hart 11, 1777, SCL.

44. Loulie Latimer Owens, "South Carolina Baptists and the American Revolution," *Journal of the South Carolina Baptist Historical Society* 1 (November 1975): 35–38.

45. Charleston Baptist Association, Minutes, 1777, SCBHC.

46. Hart to Furman, February 12, 1777, Oliver Hart Papers, SCBHC.

47. Owens, "South Carolina Baptists and the American Revolution," 37–38. The 1790 constitution extended religious equality to all denominations, including Catholics.

48. Leah Townsend, *South Carolina Baptists, 1670–1805* (1935; repr., Baltimore: Genealogical Publishing, 1974), 278–79, 176–78. Townsend collated a list of Baptist ministers and prominent laymen who aided the Patriot side: Francis Boykin, James Crowder, David Golightly, John Greer, John Hart (Oliver Hart's son), George Hicks, the Reverend Henry Holcombe, Abel Kolb, Robert Lide, Benjamin Moseley, William Murphy, Benjamin Neighbors, Samuel Newman, Benjamin Nix, the Reverend Drury Pace, Joshua Palmer, John Putman, Jeremiah Rhame, Alexander Scott, Arthur Simkins, James Smart, Tristram Thomas, Thacker Vivian, John Webb, Jonathan Wise, and William Woodward. Many of these men, along with other Baptists, went on to fill political positions when the war ended.

49. Morgan Edwards, *Materials Towards a History of the Baptists* (1770; repr., Danielsville, Ga.: Heritage Papers, 1984), 2:159.

50. Henry Laurens, *The Papers of Henry Laurens: Jan. 5, 1776–Nov. 1, 1777,* ed. David R. Chesnutt and C. James Taylor (Columbia: University of South Carolina Press, 1988), 11:197–98.

51. Owens, *Oliver Hart,* 19–30.

52. Wood Furman, *A Biography of Richard Furman,* ed. Harvey T. Cook (Greenville: Baptist Courier Job Rooms, 1913), 11.

53. James A. Rogers, *Richard Furman: Life and Legacy* (Macon: Mercer University Press, 2001), 1–100.

54. Townsend, *South Carolina Baptists,* 176–77.

55. James Foster Broome, Jr., "A Model of Regular Baptist Ministry in South Carolina" (Master's thesis, Southern Baptist Theological Seminary, 1985), 10–33.

56. Edgar, *South Carolina,* 245–46.

57. George C. Rogers, Jr., *The History of Georgetown County, South Carolina* (Columbia: University of South Carolina Press, 1970), 118, 121–74.

58. Francisco de Miranda, *The New Democracy in America: Travels of Francisco de Miranda in the United States, 1783–1784,* trans. Judson P. Wood and ed. John S. Ezell (Norman: University of Oklahoma Press, 1963), 16.

59. Martin to John Martin, Jr., Georgetown, February 16, 1788, John Martin Papers, South Carolina Historical Society.

60. Chandler, "Willtown," 121.

61. Antipedo Baptist Church, Minutes, April 9, 1805, FBCG.

Chapter 5: A Work of Grace

1. Furman to Samuel Pearce, February 12, 1791, Richard Furman Papers, SCL.

2. John Martin to John Martin, Jr., February 16, 1788, John Martin Papers, South Carolina Historical Society.

3. Antipedo Baptist Church, Minutes, April 9, 1805, FBCG.

4. Edmund Botsford to Furman, December 27, 1798, Edmund Botsford Papers, SCBHC.

5. Antipedo Baptist Church, Minutes, April 9, 1805, FBCG.

6. G. P. Cuttino, *History of the Cuttino Family* (Atlanta: Emory University Office of Publications, 1982), 7–17.

7. Journal of Oliver Hart, April 28, 1780, Oliver Hart Papers, SCL.

8. Leah Townsend, *South Carolina Baptists, 1670–1805* (1935; repr., Baltimore: Genealogical Publishing, 1974), 58–59; David Benedict, *A General History of the Baptist Denomination in America and Other Parts of the World* (Boston: Manning and Loring, 1813), 2:151–52.

9. Furman to Sarah Furman Haynsworth, June 29, 1788, Richard Furman Papers, SCBHC.

10. Furman to Hart, July 4, 1788, Richard Furman Papers, SCBHC.

11. Hart to Furman, September 28, 1789, Richard Furman Papers, SCBHC.

12. Furman to Haynsworth, October 29, 1788, Richard Furman Papers, SCBHC. See also in the Richard Furman Papers, Furman to Haynsworth, February 12, 1789; Furman to Hart, April 12, 1789; Haynsworth to Furman, June 20, 1789; Furman to Rachel Brodhead Furman, undated.

13. Furman to Pearce, February 12, 1791, Richard Furman Papers, SCBHC.

14. Hart to Furman, May 8, 1790, Richard Furman Papers, SCBHC.

15. Ibid., July 15, 1790. For a biography of Henry Smalley, see William B. Sprague, *Annals of the American Pulpit; or, Commemorative Notices of Distinguished American Clergymen of Various Denominations . . .* (New York: Robert Carter and Brothers, 1860), 6:281–82.

16. Furman to Hart, August 27, 1790, Richard Furman Papers, SCBHC.

17. Manning to Furman, February 15, 1791, Richard Furman Papers, SCBHC.

18. Furman to Broadhead Furman, October 9, 1792, Richard Furman Papers, SCBHC.

19. Furman to Broadhead Furman, November 23, 1792, Richard Furman Papers, SCBHC.

20. Waldo to Furman, December 11, 1792, Richard Furman Papers, SCBHC.

21. Botsford to Furman, April 27, 1793, Richard Furman Papers, SCBHC.

22. Hart to Furman, May 30, 1793, Richard Furman Papers, SCBHC.

23. Joseph A. Conforti, *Samuel Hopkins and the New Divinity Movement: Calvinism, the Congregational Ministry, and Reform in New England between the Great Awakenings* (Grand Rapids: Christian University Press, 1981).

24. Hart to Furman, August 27, 1793, Oliver Hart Papers, SCBHC.

25. Furman to Hart, September 23, 1793, Richard Furman Papers, SCBHC.

26. S. W. Lynd, ed., *Memoir of the Rev. William Staughton, D. D.* (Boston: Lincoln, Edmands, 1834), 27–28.

27. Ibid., 28–29.

28. Dunscombe to Furman, July 28, 1793, Richard Furman Papers, SCBHC.

29. Pearce to Furman, England, July 2, 1794, Richard Furman Papers, SCBHC

30. Waldo to Furman, November 6, 1793, Richard Furman Papers, SCBHC.

31. Hinton to Furman, May 1, 1794, Richard Furman Papers, SCBHC.

32. Furman to Brodhead Furman, December 18, 1793, SCBHC.

33. Waldo to Furman, November 22, 1793, Richard Furman Papers, SCBHC.

34. Lynd, *Memoir,* 35.

35. Ibid., 33–34.

36. Charleston Baptist Association, Minutes, 1794, SCBHC.

37. Lynd, *Memoir,* 35.

38. Botsford to Furman, April 14, 1795, Edmund Botsford Papers, SCBHC.

39. Lynd, *Memoir,* 36–37. Botsford's recommendation can be found in the same volume:

> If the bearer, my much esteemed friend, the Rev. William Staughton, should providentially meet with any of the brethren in the ministry, or others to whom I am known, I wish to inform them that I received from my very respectable friend, Rev. James Hinton, of Oxford, Old England, a very honorable recommendation of him, as a pious christian, and a gentleman of abilities in the ministry. I am happy to declare, and which I think my duty, from a personal acquaintance with him, that I think him highly deserving the excellent character given him. I doubt not those who may be favored with his acquaintance, will think themselves thereby obliged. Any favor shown to my friend will be esteemed as done to myself.

40. James A. Rogers, *Richard Furman: Life and Legacy* (Macon: Mercer University Press, 2001), 82.

41. Lynd, *Memoir,* 35.

42. Charleston Baptist Association, Minutes, 1795.

43. Rogers, *Furman: Life and Legacy,* 31.

44. Botsford to Furman, April 10, 1796, Edmund Botsford Papers, SCBHC.

45. Botsford to Furman, July 18, 1796, Edmund Botsford Papers, SCBHC.

46. Botsford to Furman, October 12, 1796, Edmund Botsford Papers, SCBHC.

47. Charles D. Mallary, ed., *Memoirs of Elder Edmund Botsford* (1832; repr., Springfield, Miss.: Particular Baptist Press, 2004), 14. Mallary, a well-known Baptist minister in Georgia, was married to Botsford's granddaughter and in 1832 published the collection of Botsford's manuscripts and letters cited above. Botsford's memoirs and most of the letters Mallary cites are not in Botsford's papers at Furman University.

48. Ibid., 16.

49. James Foster Broome, "Edmund Botsford a Model of Regular Baptist Ministry in South Carolina" (Ph.D. diss., Southern Baptist Theological Seminary, 1985) 10–25.

50. Journal of Oliver Hart, March 14, 1773, Oliver Hart Papers, SCL. Hart recorded in his journal: "On Lords Day March ye 14th 1773 I assisted Rev. Mr. Frances Pelot in the Ordination of Mr. Edmund Botsford to the work of the Ministry."

51. For the history of the Baptist church at Welsh Neck, see *Historical Sketch of the Welsh Neck Baptist Church, Society Hill, S.C.: Two Hundred and Twenty Fifth Anniversary, March 3, 1963* (Columbia: State Company, 1963).

52. Mallary, *Memoirs,* 41.

53. Broome, "Edmund Botsford," 26–33.

54. Botsford to Furman, August 20, 1797, Edmund Botsford Papers, SCBHC.

55. Minutes, Charleston Baptist Association, 1796–1800, SCBHC.

56. Botsford to Furman, March 15, 1798, Edmund Botsford Papers, SCBHC.

57. Charleston Baptist Association, Minutes, 1796–1800. From 1794 to 1800 annual contributions from the Georgetown church ranged from six pounds to twenty pounds. No contribution was made in 1799.

58. The term *Antipedo* is spelled variously as *Antipado* and *Antiædo.* The modern spelling will be used for clarity.

59. General Assembly Petitions, nos. 180 and 181, 342–47, SCDAH.

60. General Assembly Committee Reports, no. 144, SCDAH.

61. General Assembly Petitions, nos. 124, 106–11, SCDAH.

62. General Assembly Committee Reports, no. 125, SCDAH.

63. "An Act to Incorporate the Antipædo Baptist Church, in the Town of Georgetown," in *The Statutes at Large of South Carolina,* ed. Thomas Cooper and David J. McCord (Columbia: A. S. Johnson, 1840), 8:213–14.

64. Furman to Hart, June 2, 1792, Richard Furman Papers, SCBHC.

65. Furman to Brodhead Furman, October 9, 1792, SCBHC.

66. Botsford to Furman, July 27, 1798, Edmund Botsford Papers, SCBHC.

67. Botsford to Furman, December 27, 1798, SCBHC.

68. Antipedo Baptist Church, Minutes, April 9, 1805, Georgetown FBCG.

69. Botsford to Furman, February 28, 1802, Edmund Botsford Papers, SCBHC.
70. Botsford to John M. Roberts, August 17, 1802, Edmund Botsford Papers, SCBHC.
71. Botsford to Furman, April 21, 1803, Edmund Botsford Papers, SCBHC.
72. Antipedo Baptist Church, Minutes, February 28 and March 29, 1805, FBCG.
73. Benedict, *General History of the Baptist Denomination*, 2:152.

CHAPTER 6: THE ANTIPEDO BAPTIST CHURCH

1. Elmer T. Clark, J. Manning Potts, and Jacob S. Payton, eds., *The Journal and Letters of Francis Asbury* (Nashville: Abingdon Press, 1958), 2:423–24; 1:505, 667.
2. David Benedict, *Fifty Years Among the Baptists* (New York: Sheldon, 1860), 76.
3. Edmund Botsford, "Reflection Fifth," undated manuscript, Edmund Botsford Papers, SCBHC.
4. Amy Lee Mears, "Worship in Selected Churches of the Charleston Baptist Association, 1682–1795" (PhD diss., Southern Baptist Theological Seminary, 1995), 73–74.
5. Robert Andrew Baker and Paul J. Craven, *Adventure in Faith: The First 300 Years of First Baptist Church, Charleston, South Carolina* (Madison, Wis.: Broadman Press, 1982), 284.
6. Charles D. Mallary, ed., *Memoirs of Elder Edmund Botsford* (1832; repr., Springfield, Miss.: Particular Baptist Press, 2004), 54.
7. Mears, "Worship in Selected Churches," 85.
8. Ibid., 69.
9. *Georgetown Gazette,* May 30, 1804.
10. First Baptist Church of Georgetown, Minutes, 1805–1821, FBCG.
11. Botsford to Cathy Botsford, July 30, 1811, Edmund Botsford Papers, SCBHC.
12. Clark, Potts, and Payton, *Journal and Letters of Francis Asbury,* 2:423–24.
13. Benedict, *Fifty Years Among the Baptists,* 79–80.
14. H. A. Tupper, ed., *Two Centuries of the First Baptist Church of South Carolina, 1683–1883* (Baltimore: R. H. Woodward, 1889), 297.
15. David W. Music, "Congregational Song Practices in Southern Baptist Churches: A Historical Overview," *Southern Baptist Church Music Journal* 9 (1992): 13.
16. Furman to Botsford, June 11, 1793, Richard Furman Papers, SCBHC.
17. Mallary, *Memoirs,* 215.
18. Botsford to Furman, March 3, 1798, Edmund Botsford Papers, SCBHC.
19. Botsford, "Reflection Fifth."
20. Baker and Craven, *Adventure in Faith,* 284.
21. Mears, "Worship in Selected Churches," 175, 181.
22. Ibid., 81–82.
23. Botsford to Furman, 1796, Edmund Botsford Papers, SCBHC.
24. Mallary, *Memoirs,* 132.
25. Ibid., 85–86.
26. Botsford, "Reflection Fifth."

27. For more on Botsford and baptism, see "Reasons for Renouncing Infant Baptism in a Letter to a Friend" and his unpublished manuscript entitled "Examination" in the Edmund Botsford Papers at Furman University.

28. Joe Madison King, *A History of South Carolina Baptists* (Columbia: General Board of the South Carolina Baptist Convention, 1964), 150–51.

29. Charleston Baptist Association, Minutes, 1799, SCBHC.

30. John B. Boles, *The Great Revival: Beginnings of the Bible Belt* (Lexington: University Press of Kentucky, 1996), 70.

31. John Rippon, *The Baptist Annual Register, For 1790, 1791, 1792, and Part of 1793. Including Sketches of the State of Religion Among Different Denominations of Good Men at Home and Abroad* (London: Dilly, Button, and Thomas, 1793–1802), 104–08.

32. Botsford to John M. Roberts, November 24, 1802, Edmund Botsford Papers, SCBHC.

33. Botsford to John M. Roberts, August 17, 1802, Edmund Botsford Papers, SCBHC.

34. Mallary, *Memoirs,* 64, 116, 132, 29. Botsford's wives were Susannah Nun (m. 1773; d. 1790), Catharine Evans (m. 1791; d. 1796), Ann Deliesseline (m. 1799; d. 1801), and Hannah Goff (m. 1803; d. 1821).

35. Mears, "Worship in Selected Churches," 71.

36. Antipedo Baptist Church, Minutes, January 1805, FBCG. Furman wrote Botsford in 1805: "Your arrangement in the Choice of Officers for the Church as a Corporation, I think was very well made. Hope it will be followed with a blessing." Furman to Botsford, February 10, 1805, Richard Furman Papers, SCBHC.

37. Antipedo Baptist Church, Minutes, January 1805, FBCG.

38. Charleston Baptist Association, "A Summary of Church-Discipline Shewing the Qualifications and Duties of the Officers and Members of a Gospel Church," 1813, 6–10, SCBHC.

39. Leah Townsend, South Carolina Baptists, 1670–1805 (1935; repr., Baltimore: Genealogical Publishing, 1974), 290–91.

40. Benedict, *Fifty Years Among the Baptists,* 78.

41. Charleston Baptist Association, "A Summary of Church-Discipline," 6, 13–14, 25.

42. Townsend, *South Carolina Baptists,* 293.

43. Botsford to Furman, December 27, 1798, Edmund Botsford Papers, SCBHC.

44. Antipedo Baptist Church, Minutes, February 28 and April 9, 1805, April 8, 1806, February 5, 1821, FBCG.

45. Cuttino's epitaph reads: "In him were united those virtues which produced respect from his fellow Citizens from his numerous family and esteem from the Church of which he was a member nearly 40 years and to promote which and the interest of Religion in general he was a very liberal and benevolent benefactor."

46. *Charleston Courier,* September 16, 1806.

47. Mallary, *Memoirs,* 73–74.

48. Botsford to Furman, April 21, 1803, Edmund Botsford Papers, SCBHC.

49. Mallary, *Memoirs,* 64.

50. Botsford to Cathy Botsford, September 5, 1808, Edmund Botsford Papers, SCBHC.

51. Furman to Hart, January 26, 1785, Richard Furman Papers, SCBHC.

52. Townsend, *South Carolina Baptists,* 27.

53. Rippon, *The Baptist Annual Register,* 104–8.

54. Ibid., 105.

55. Mallary, *Memoirs,* 151–52.

56. Botsford to Furman, May 26, 1812, Edmund Botsford Papers, SCBHC.

57. Ibid.

58. Annie Hughes Mallard, "Religious Work of South Carolina Baptists among the Slaves from 1781–1830" (Master's thesis, University of South Carolina, 1946), 32, 37, 55.

59. Botsford to Cathy Botsford, June 17, 1811, Edmund Botsford Papers, SCBHC.

60. Mallary, *Memoirs,* 85–86.

61. Botsford to Unknown, November 1, 1809, Edmund Botsford Papers, SCL.

62. Furman to Botsford, March 10, 1817, Richard Furman Papers, SCBHC.

63. H. Cuthbert, *Life of Richard Fuller, D. D.* (New York: Sheldon and Company, 1879), 20.

64. Townsend, *South Carolina Baptists,* 255.

65. Welsh Neck Church Book, July 31 and September 4, 1790, SCBHC.

66. James A. Rogers, *Ebenezer: The Story of a Church* (Columbia: R. L. Bryan, 2001), 50–51.

67. Mallard, "Religious Work of South Carolina Baptists," 51.

68. Journal of Peter Horry, August 17, 1812, Guignard Family Papers, SCL.

69. Mallard, "Religious Work of South Carolina Baptists," 75.

70. David Benedict, *A General History of the Baptist Denomination in America and Other Parts of the World* (Boston: Lincoln and Edmands, 1813), 2:210.

71. Sally E. Hadden, *Slave Patrols: Law and Violence in Virginia and the Carolinas* (Cambridge: Harvard University Press, 2001), 110.

72. For more on South Carolina slave laws, see John Belton O'Neall, *The Negro Law of South Carolina* (Columbia: John G. Bowman, 1848).

73. Thomas Cooper and David J. McCord, eds., *The Statutes at Large of South Carolina* (Columbia: A. S. Johnson, 1840), 7:343, 354, 364–65, 385, 389–99, 410, 440–41.

74. General Assembly Petition, 1801, no. 123, SCDAH; King, *History of South Carolina Baptists,* 125–26.

75. Cooper and McCord, *Statutes at Large,* 7:448–49.

76. Susan Markey Fickling, "Slave-Conversion in South Carolina, 1830–1860" (Master's thesis, University of South Carolina, 1924), 31–32.

77. Clark, Potts, and Payton, *Journal and Letters of Francis Asbury,* 2:186.

78. George C. Rogers, Jr., *The History of Georgetown County, South Carolina* (Columbia: University of South Carolina Press, 1970), 193.

79. Mallard, "Religious Work of South Carolina Baptists," 3–4, 14.

80. Mallary, *Memoirs,* 209, 132.
81. Benedict, *General History of the Baptist Denomination,* 2:207.
82. Charleston Baptist Association, Minutes, 1794–1831, SCBHC.
83. Mallary, *Memoirs,* 38.
84. Botsford to Furman, January 11, 1789, Edmund Botsford Papers, SCBHC.
85. Data taken from the U.S. Department of the Interior, Census Office, First, Second, Third, Fourth, and Fifth Census, 1790–1830, Winyaw, Georgetown District, South Carolina, Ancestry.com. According to Leah Townsend, of the 661 possible Baptists in the 1790 census, 433 or two-thirds were nonslaveholders. Most of these nonslaveholding whites resided in the backcountry. Out of the 228 slaveholders, only 21 owned more than 20 slaves. Townsend, *South Carolina Baptists,* 281.
86. Valerie Quinney, "Decisions on Slavery, the Slave-Trade and Civil Rights for Negroes in the Early French Revolution," *Journal of Negro History* 55 (April 1970): 117; William Baker, "William Wilberforce on the Idea of Negro Inferiority," *Church History* 31 (July–September 1970): 1–4.

CHAPTER 7: BOTSFORD'S DILEMMA

1. Andrew Lee Feight, "Edmund Botsford and Richard Furman: Slavery in the South Carolina Lowcountry, 1766–1825," *Journal of the South Carolina Baptist Historical Society* 19 (November 1993): 7.
2. David Benedict, *A General History of the Baptist Denomination in America and Other Parts of the World* (Boston: Lincoln and Edmands, 1813), 2:210.
3. Ibid.
4. Botsford to John M. Roberts, March 30, 1812, Edmund Botsford Papers, SCBHC.
5. Richard Furman, *Exposition of the Views of the Baptists Relative to the Coloured Population of the United States in Communication to the Governor of South-Carolina* (Charleston: A. E. Miller, 1838), 6, 8, 16, 20, 24. For an earlier piece on slavery written by Furman, see the circular letter entitled "On Religious and Civil Duties" in the 1800 Charleston Baptist Association minutes at Furman.
6. Richard Furman, "Questions on Slavery," 1807, SCBHC.
7. Edmund Botsford, "Essay on Slavery," undated, SCBHC. For more on the differences between Furman's and Botsford's perspectives on slavery, see Feight, "Edmund Botsford and Richard Furman," 1–22.
8. Botsford to Furman, October 15, 1801, Edmund Botsford Papers, SCBHC.
9. Edmund Botsford, *Sambo and Toney: A Dialogue between Two Servants* (Georgetown: Francis M. Baxter, 1808).
10. Ibid., 12, 19.
11. Botsford to Furman, October 15, 1808, Edmund Botsford Papers, SCBHC. Botsford explained his intentions thusly: "The Dialogues will show to the master, what we wish to inculcate, and may be the means of removing prejudice from his mind; which will be in favor of the slave: and I have not the least doubt of their being useful to the serious blacks. It is very difficult to simplify the terms and phrases of divinity to their capacities; I have, however, attempted it; how I have

succeeded, time will discover. If my performance is productive of any good, God shall have the praise. My Inglesby shall be considered the author of the invention; and Botsford the writer; and if it should be despised, Botsford is perfectly willing to bear the blame, for this very good reason, he really meant well. Besides, this is the first piece, as far as I know, that ever was published for the use of the blacks. If it should induce any person to write a better, still I shall have cause to be thankful." Charles D. Mallary, ed., *Memoirs of Elder Edmund Botsford* (1832; repr., Springfield, Miss.: Particular Baptist Press, 2004), 91.

12. Botsford to Furman, October 15, 1808, Edmund Botsford Papers, SCBHC.

13. Botsford to Furman, February 20, 1809, Edmund Botsford Papers, SCBHC.

14. Botsford to Furman, circa 1809, Edmund Botsford Papers, SCBHC

15. Botsford to Furman, October 25, 1814. Edmund Botsford Papers, SCBHC.

16. Mallary, *Memoirs,* 142, 153, 118, 144–45, 204.

17. Ibid., 127, 142–44, 185, 203, 206.

18. James A. Rogers, *Richard Furman: Life and Legacy* (Macon: Mercer University Press, 2001), 77, 216.

19. Amy Lee Mears, "Worship in Selected Churches of the Charleston Baptist Association, 1682–1795" (Ph.D. diss., Southern Baptist Theological Seminary, 1995), 40.

20. Furman to Pearce, February 12, 1791, Richard Furman Papers, SCBHC.

21. Botsford to Furman, February 20, 1809, Edmund Botsford Papers, SCBHC.

22. Leah Townsend, *South Carolina Baptists, 1670–1805* (1935; repr., Baltimore: Genealogical Publishing, 1974), 118–19, 161–62; Rogers, *Life and Legacy,* 118–23.

23. Charleston Baptist Association, Minutes, 1800, SCBHC.

24. Mallary, *Memoirs,* 65–68, 77–81.

25. Journal of Peter Horry, November 22, 1812, Guignard Family Papers, SCL.

26. Mallary, *Memoirs,* 154.

27. Botsford to Cook, April 15, 1813, Edmund Botsford Papers, SCBHC.

28. Botsford to Cook, November 8, 1818, Edmund Botsford Papers, SCBHC.

29. Furman to Wood Furman, June 21, 1808, and Furman to Dorothea Furman, November 8, 1813, Richard Furman Papers, SCBHC; Mallary, *Memoirs,* 194.

30. Furman to Botsford, May 12, 1810, Richard Furman Papers, SCBHC.

31. James Foster Broome, "Edmund Botsford: A Model of Regular Baptist Ministry in South Carolina" (Ph.D. diss., Southern Baptist Theological Seminary, 1985), 74.

32. Mallary, *Memoirs,* 168–69.

33. Botsford to William B. Johnson, October 19, 1809, Edmund Botsford Papers, SCBHC.

34. Mallary, *Memoirs,* 89, 143.

35. Botsford to Furman, October 15, 1801, Edmund Botsford Papers, SCBHC.

36. Furman to Botsford, undated, Richard Furman Papers, SCBHC.

37. Botsford to John M. Roberts, February 28, 1812, Edmund Botsford Papers, SCBHC.

38. Furman to Dorothea Furman, July 11, 1814, Richard Furman Papers, SCBHC.

39. Botsford to William Inglesby, May 23, 1816, Edmund Botsford Papers, SCBHC.
40. Furman to Botsford, January 24, 1817, Richard Furman Papers, SCBHC.
41. Mallary, *Memoirs,* 191.
42. Botsford to Furman, April 15, 1818, Edmund Botsford Papers, SCBHC.
43. Mallary, *Memoirs,* 191–92.
44. Botsford to John Roberts, October 29, 1818, Edmund Botsford Papers, SCBHC.
45. Mallary, *Memoirs,* 198–99.
46. Botsford to Furman, July 17, 1819, Edmund Botsford Papers, SCBHC.
47. Mallary, *Memoirs,* 69, 89–90, 143, 189.
48. *Southern Evangelical Intelligencer,* January 1, 1820. See also *Charleston City Gazette and Daily Advertiser,* January 7, 1820; *New-Hampshire Gazette,* January 18, 1820; *Hartford Times,* January 25, 1820. According to the *City Gazette,* death notices for Botsford appeared in the "Winyaw Intelligencer, and in different papers in this city."
49. Charleston Baptist Association, Minutes, 1820, SCBHC. Several sources cite Botsford's age at death as seventy-five; however, this is incorrect given his birth date of November 1, 1745.
50. According to Charles Mallary, Lee Compere preached the sermon at Botsford's interment. Mallary, *Memoirs,* 217.
51. Rogers, *Life and Legacy,* 254.
52. Botsford to Furman, January 11, 1789, Edmund Botsford Papers, SCBHC.
53. Furman to Botsford, January 24, 1817, Richard Furman Papers, SCBHC.
54. Richard Furman, *The Crown of Life Promised to the Truly Faithful: A Sermon Saved to the Memory of the Rev. Edmund Botsford, A. M. Late Pastor of the Baptist Church in Georgetown, S. C.* (Charleston: W. M. Riley, 1822), 29–30, 33–34. For the original draft of *The Crown of Life,* see "Tribute to Botsford" in the Richard Furman Papers at Furman University.
55. Rogers, *Life and Legacy,* 253.
56. The Cuttino family remained active members and leaders in the Georgetown church throughout the nineteenth century. In 1816 Botsford wrote the following about Peter Cuttino and his siblings: "As you have seen Mr. Cook you have heard of the Baptism of Mr. Cuttino & his wife. . . . The other three Sons of Mr. Cuttino appear to be seriously attentive, I hope & pray it may not wear off. . . . Mr. Cuttino I hope will make a useful Member, he not only is anxious for prayer meetings but engages in prayer, Mr. Waldo also, so that we begin to look up a little." Botsford to Furman, 1816, Edmund Botsford Papers, SCBHC.
57. Cook to Furman, June 16, 1820, Richard Furman Papers, SCBHC.
58. Grosvenor's publications include *Slavery vs. The Bible: A Correspondence Between the General Conference of Maine, and the Presbytery of Tombecbee, Mississippi and Baptist Anti-Slavery Correspondent* (n.p.: Worcester, 1840).
59. Charleston Baptist Association, Minutes, 1820–1825, SCBHC.
60. *Georgetown Times,* March 12 and 26, 1913.
61. Botsford to John M. Roberts, November 29, 1814, Edmund Botsford Papers, SCBHC. On another occasion Botsford wrote Furman: "Mr. Waldo is in a poor

state of health, I much fear he will not stand it long. I think he is too much of a Quack to be healthy, & quacks are generally very opinionated." Botsford to Furman, May 22, 1815, Edmund Botsford Papers, SCBHC.

62. Journal of Peter Horry, September 19, 1812, Guignard Family Papers, SCL.

63. *Georgetown Gazette,* January 1, 1817.

64. Charleston Baptist Association, Minutes, 1826, SCBHC.

65. Botsford to Furman, May 22, 1815, and Botsford to Furman, undated, Edmund Botsford Papers, SCBHC.

66. John M'Clintock and James Strong, *Cyclopædia of Biblical, Theological, and Ecclesiastical Literature,* vol. 5 (New York: Harper and Brothers, 1883), s.v. "Peter Ludlow."

67. In 1801 the General Assembly granted the church incorporation for a period of ten years. Botsford reapplied for incorporation in 1812, with the specific request that it be perpetual. The committee denied the request but extended incorporation for an additional fourteen years. In 1827 Georgetown was perpetually incorporated "with all the privileges and powers heretofore granted, by the name and style of 'The Baptist Church of Christ, in Georgetown, South Carolina.'" General Assembly Petitions, nos. 115 and 116, 341–46; General Assembly Committee Reports, no. 154; General Assembly Petitions, nos. 104 and 105, 819–28, SCDAH; Thomas Cooper and David J. McCord, eds., *The Statutes at Large of South Carolina* (Columbia: A. S. Johnson, 1840), 8:353.

68. Charleston Baptist Association, Minutes, 1826–1830, SCBHC.

CHAPTER 8: THE ANTEBELLUM CHURCH

1. *Winyaw Intelligencer,* February 19, 1835.

2. Sherman L. Ricards and George M. Blackburn, "A Demographic History of Slavery: Georgetown County, South Carolina, 1850," *South Carolina Historical and Genealogical Magazine* 76 (October 1975): 216.

3. Charleston Baptist Association, Minutes, 1857, SCBHC.

4. Ibid., 1831.

5. Ibid., 1832.

6. Ibid., 1833.

7. Harvey Toliver Cook, *The Life Work of James Clement Furman* (n.p.: Greenville, 1926), 30. James Clement Furman is best known as the longtime president of Furman University.

8. Charleston Baptist Association, Minutes, 1834, SCBHC.

9. Ibid., 1835.

10. Ibid., 1836.

11. Ibid., 1837.

12. Ibid., 1838.

13. Ibid., 1840.

14. Ibid., 1840–1841.

15. *Georgetown American,* February 10, 1841. Mrs. Blyth, a wealthy rice planter, also left money to the Methodist church, enough to paint the building and fence and

install proper housing for the church bell. George C. Rogers, Jr., *The History of Georgetown County, South Carolina* (Columbia: University of South Carolina Press, 1970), 354.

16. *Winyah Observer,* February 5, 1842.

17. Ibid., May 7, 1842.

18. Charleston Baptist Association, Minutes, 1842, SCBHC. In 1843 the prestigious Winyah Indigo Society (founded 1757) celebrated its anniversary at the Baptist church. Childers delivered the sermon, after which "the Society sat down to a sumptuous dinner . . . which they moistened with old wine." See *Winyah Observer,* May 6, 1843. In 1844 Georgetown District's Washington Temperance Society named Childers a delegate to the convention in Charleston. See *Winyah Observer,* January 31, 1844.

19. *Winyah Observer,* March 16, 1844.

20. "Broadway Baptist Church," in *The Encyclopedia of Louisville,* ed. John E. Kleber (Lexington: University Press of Kentucky, 2001); "First Baptist Church, Penns Grove, NJ," Church Index, Historical Society of Penns Grove, Carneys Point; Henry R. Stiles, *A History of the City of Brooklyn* (Brooklyn: Published by Subscription, 1870), 3:770–71; William Allen Wilbur, *Chronicles of Calvary Baptist Church in the City of Washington* (Washington: Judd and Detweiler, 1914), 27.

21. *Winyah Observer,* January 18, 1845.

22. Ibid., January 25, 1845.

23. Ibid.

24. Ibid., April 5, 1845.

25. Ibid., November 29, 1845.

26. Southeast Baptist Association, Minutes, 1943, SCBHC; Margorie Rhem, "Willtown and Old Belin's," undated, FBCG.

27. *Winyah Observer,* November 8, 1843.

28. Southeast Baptist Association, Minutes, 1943, SCBHC. Belin was involved in a lawsuit lasting several years over the public use of the road, landing, and dock, on his premises. The public gained rights to the road and landing, while Belin kept the dock as his personal property. *Winyah Observer,* April 26, 1848.

29. H. I. Hester, *They That Wait: A History of Anderson College* (Anderson: Anderson College, 1969), 8–9; Joe Madison King, *A History of South Carolina Baptists* (Columbia: General Board of the South Carolina Baptist Convention, 1964), 216–19; Robert A. Baker, *The Southern Baptist Convention and Its People, 1607–1972* (Nashville: Broadman Press, 1974), 164–65. See also Hortense Woodson, *Giant in the Land: A Biography of William Bullein Johnson* (Nashville: Broadman Press, 1950); Doug Watson, "William Bullein Johnson: The First President of the Southern Baptist Convention and His Portrayal of the Baptist Identity," *Journal of the South Carolina Baptist Historical Society 26* (November 2000): 11. The Georgetown press followed Johnson's role in the creation of the Southern Baptist Convention: *Winyah Observer,* May 8, and May 19, 1841; May 10, May 17, and May 24, 1845; October 20, 1847.

30. Charleston Baptist Association, Minutes, 1846, SCBHC.
31. Ibid., 1846–1847.
32. Ibid., 1849.
33. Ibid., 1850.
34. Ibid., 1851.
35. Ibid., 1852.
36. Ibid., 1853.
37. Ibid., 1854.
38. Ibid., 1856.
39. South Carolina Baptist Convention, Minutes, 1886, SCBHC.
40. Charleston Baptist Association, Minutes, 1856, SCBHC.
41. Ibid., 1857.
42. As an adult, David William Cuttino III lived and worked in Sumter, where he was moderator of the Santee Association and known throughout the state for his leadership in the temperance movement and charitable endeavors. He died in 1886, the same year as his father. Their obituaries are in the South Carolina Baptist Convention minutes of that year.
43. Charleston Baptist Association, Minutes, 1858, SCBHC.
44. Ibid., 1859; South Carolina Baptist Convention, Minutes, 1886, SCBHC.
45. South Carolina Baptist Convention, Minutes, 1886, SCBHC.
46. King, *History of South Carolina Baptists,* 255. In 1860 Beaufort Baptist Church's membership totaled 3,713, and of that number 3,557 were African American. One of the black deacons was Jacob White. John Allen Middleton, *Directory and Pre-1900 Historical Survey of South Carolina's Black Baptists,* (Columbia: J. A. Middleton and Associates, 1992), 3:1. Carter G. Woodson cites Silver Bluff Baptist Church on the Savannah River in South Carolina as the first black Baptist church in America, founded in the early 1770s. Woodson, *The History of the Negro Church,* 2nd ed. (Washington: Associated Publishers, 1921), 41. See also Walter H. Brooks, "The Evolution of the Negro Baptist Church," *Journal of Negro History* 7 (January 1922): 15. More recently, Leroy Fitts noted the continuing disagreement over the first independent black Baptist church. Some argue that the oldest was the First Colored Baptist Church in Savannah, Georgia, organized January 20, 1788. Leroy Fitts, *A History of Black Baptists* (Nashville: Broadman Press, 1985), 33.
47. The church in Georgetown had by far the highest percentage of African American members of any church in the Charleston Association. The only churches that could challenge Georgetown were those in Beaufort and St. Helena in the Savannah River Association. Lawrence S. Rowland, *The History of Beaufort County, South Carolina* (Columbia: University of South Carolina Press, 1996), 1:356–58.
48. Charleston Baptist Association, Minutes, 1854, SCBHC.
49. Data taken from the U.S. Department of the Interior, Census Office, Fifth, Sixth, Seventh, and Eighth Census, 1830–1860, Georgetown, Williamsburg, Clarendon, and Charleston Districts, South Carolina; Wells Family Papers, FBCG. One of

D. W. Cuttino's slaves, a teenage girl named Fillis, was given to him by his father-in-law upon his second marriage for the nominal cost of five dollars.

50. In 1845 the wealthy Georgetown planter Robert F. W. Allston wrote that the Georgetown Baptists "admit preachers of color." See Daniel Elliott Huger, *Proceedings of the Meeting in Charleston, S. C., May 13–15, 1845, on the Religious Instruction of the Negroes* (Charleston: B. Jenkins, 1845), 36.

51. This argument totaled nine different pieces and appeared in the pages of the *Georgetown American* on February 17, March 3, 10, and 24, 1841.

52. The terminology and roles of black leaders are clearly explained in Susan Markey Fickling, "Slave-Conversion in South Carolina, 1830–1860" (Master's thesis, University of South Carolina, 1924). For a list of black leaders in the Methodist Church in Georgetown, see Rogers, *History of Georgetown*, 350–51.

53. Huger, *Proceedings of the Meeting in Charleston*, 34.

54. Ibid., 35–37. From November to May, Glennie worked two parish churches and ten plantations. He preached at each of the plantations twice a month, visiting four on Sundays and six during the week. He noted that slaves from seven plantations were close enough to walk to a parish church and at one black attendance often reached two hundred. Glennie, as well as the Methodists and Baptists, used the oral, rote method, "the negroes soon learning to repeat, understandingly, the responses, and uniting in the chants with much satisfaction." For more on Glennie, see Charles Joyner, *Down by the Riverside: A South Carolina Slave Community* (Urbana: University of Illinois Press, 1984), 154–63.

55. Huger, *Proceedings of the Meeting in Charleston*, 49. The catechism was William Capers's *Catechism for Little Children and for Use on the Missions to the Slaves in South Carolina*. Capers was superintendent of Methodist missions in South Carolina and the driving force in slave conversion. See Donald G. Matthews, *Slavery and Methodism: A Chapter in American Morality, 1780–1845* (Princeton: Princeton University Press, 1965), 69–79. The Methodists in Georgetown organized a Sabbath school for black children in late 1838. By 1844, 150 children were enrolled. On the anniversary of its founding, they and their parents formed a great procession to go to the church for a special ceremony. *Winyah Observer*, May 25, 1844. Leah Townsend, in her *South Carolina Baptists*, termed black Baptists as constituting a "church by themselves." Townsend, *South Carolina Baptists, 1670–1805* (1935. Reprint, Baltimore: Genealogical Publishing, 1974), 256. The classic work is Albert J. Raboteau, *Slave Religion: The "Invisible Institution" in the Antebellum South* (New York: Oxford University Press, 1978). Margaret W. Creel's *"A Peculiar People": Slave Religion and Community-Culture among the Gullahs* (New York: New York University Press, 1988) deals with the Sea Islands south of Georgetown. William Dusinberre, *Them Dark Days: Slavery in the American Rice Swamps* (New York: Oxford University Press, 1996), offers little on slave religion. The voluminous slave narratives collected by WPA workers in the 1930s, while enlightening in so many respects, have no details regarding Georgetown Baptists.

56. Charleston Baptist Association, Minutes, 1859, 1860, 1872, SCBHC.

Chapter 9: Recovery

1. For a report on Georgetown refugees in Conwayboro and on the fear of Federal gunboats on the river, see William Wyndham Malet, *An Errand to the South in the Summer of 1862* (London: Richard Bentley, 1863), 277.

2. Louis P. Towles, ed., *A World Turned Upside Down: The Palmers of South Santee, 1818–1881* (Columbia: University of South Carolina Press in cooperation with the Caroline McKissick Dial South Caroliniana Library Endowment Fund and the South Caroliniana Sociey, 1996), is the fascinating tragic story of a great family on the South Santee ruined by the war and Reconstruction.

3. George C. Rogers, Jr., *The History of Georgetown County, South Carolina* (Columbia: University of South Carolina Press, 1970), 416–62.

4. Joe Madison King, *A History of South Carolina Baptists* (Columbia: General Board of the South Carolina Baptist Convention, 1964), 247.

5. After the rice industry died the Bobolinks changed their migratory pattern and were seen no more. Coverage of the Bobolinks and the rice-bird industry runs throughout the *Georgetown Times* from the 1880s into the twentieth century. In the 1890s Georgetown hoped it had found a new industry by shipping the birds to New York where they were a delicacy, but the Progressive Era's concern over health soon ended that prospect.

6. Charleston Baptist Association, Minutes, 1871, SCBHC.

7. Joel Williamson, *After Slavery: The Negro in South Carolina during Reconstruction, 1861–1877* (Chapel Hill: University of North Carolina Press, 1965), 180.

8. Ibid. Williamson concludes: "After the war secession movements by Negroes within white-dominated churches were opposed by Southern whites of all denominations. The Baptists shared this general desire to keep Negroes in their 'accustomed place in the galleries.'"

9. *Georgetown Times,* November 21, 1891. Another Bethesda pastor was G. W. Raiford (also spelled Rayford), who preached there in the 1880s before leaving in 1891. *Georgetown Enquirer,* March 7 and 14, 1888. On social activities at Bethesda, see also *Georgetown Enquirer,* May 16 and 30, 1888. On a "little colored girl" evangelist at Bethesda in 1896 when R. B. Salters was pastor, see *Georgetown Times,* February 1, 1896. The legendary African American preacher of the area was undoubtedly James Small, said to have been born about 1814. He was living on the Waccamaw when he died in 1894. Only the year before, he had constructed a new church at Black River. His funeral was "the largest ever seen on the Waccamaw," with as many as twelve hundred people in attendance. The mile-long procession contained fifty buggies, and four preachers officiated. "A good man is gone," according to the *Georgetown Times.*

10. John Allen Middleton, *Directory and Pre-1900 Historical Survey of South Carolina's Black Baptists* (Columbia: J. A. Middleton and Associates, 1992), 3:1–2.

11. Charleston Baptist Association, Minutes, 1871, SCBHC.

12. Williamson, *After Slavery,* 193–95.

13. Charleston Baptist Association, Minutes, 1871, SCBHC.
14. Middleton, *Directory,* 3:1–2.
15. King, *History of South Carolina Baptists,* 255.
16. South Carolina Baptist Convention, Minutes, 1877, SCBHC.
17. Leroy Fitts, *A History of Black Baptists* (Nashville: Broadman Press, 1985), 194–95. Northern Baptists, through the work of the American Baptist Home Mission Board, were especially active in helping African American churches and educational institutions develop. In the case of Benedict, the land in Columbia was donated by Mrs. B. A. Benedict of Providence, Rhode Island, and the American Baptists established the school. Benedict opened in 1871 with the Reverend Timothy D. Dodge as president.
18. South Carolina Baptist Convention, Minutes, 1889, 1891, and 1902, SCBHC. The effort of the state convention to work with the black Missionary Baptist Convention continued into the 1930s. King, *History of South Carolina Baptists,* 312. See also Charleston Baptist Association, Minutes, 1904, SCBHC.
19. Charleston Baptist Association, Minutes, 1904, SCBHC.
20. Ibid., 1872 and 1873. C. T. Wright was the clerk and deacon. He died in 1872 and was replaced by James C. Logan.
21. Charleston Baptist Association and South Carolina Baptist Convention, Minutes, 1872, SCBHC. An interesting part of Charleston's minutes is the use of the designation *the First Baptist Church in Georgetown.* Legally the church remained the Baptist Church of Christ in Georgetown but was consistently referred to simply as the Baptist Church.
22. Charleston Baptist Association, Minutes,1873, SCBHC.
23. A church historian, writing in 1930, said that the church likely stayed closed until "about 1884 (by 'closed,' I mean without any permanent pastor)." First Baptist Church of Georgetown, Minutes, January 30, 1930, FBCG.
24. Charleston Baptist Association, Minutes, 1871, SCBHC.
25. Ibid., 1875.
26. The first notice of Oliver preaching in Georgetown is *Georgetown Times,* February 8, 1877. For his other visits, see *Georgetown Times and Comet,* August 14, 1879, and November 14, 1883; *Georgetown Enquirer,* November 8, 1882, February 14, 1882, December 5, 1883, and February 29, 1888. In the state convention's list of pastors' addresses, Oliver is placed at Georgetown in 1877, 1878, 1883, 1887, and 1889. See Charleston Baptist Association, Minutes, 1876, SCBHC.
27. South Carolina Baptist Convention, Minutes, 1876, SCBHC.
28. Charleston Baptist Association, Minutes, 1876, SCBHC; Charleston Baptist Association, Minutes, 1877, SCBHC.
29. *Georgetown Times and Comet,* August 14, 1879; *Georgetown Enquirer,* February 14 and December 5, 1883. For the rest of his life Oliver preached in many churches in the Pee Dee, especially in and around Florence. He died suddenly in 1913 in Byromville, Georgia. "The Reverend Hugh Forsyth Oliver, August 18, 1852–July 28, 1913," FBCG; *Georgetown Times,* July 30, 1913; Oliver Family Papers, FBCG.

30. *Georgetown Enquirer,* April 5, 1882; July 22, August 12, and September 16, 1885.
31. South Carolina Baptist Convention, Minutes, 1886, SCBHC.
32. Rogers, *History of Georgetown,* 464–73, 511.
33. First Baptist Church of Georgetown, Minutes, January 30, 1930, FBCG.
34. In 1886 Bailey became secretary-treasurer of the General Board of the South Carolina Baptist Convention. He served until 1909 and died in 1923. King, *History of South Carolina Baptists,* 251, 298, 303.
35. *Georgetown Enquirer,* July 22, August 12, and September 16, 1885.
36. South Carolina Baptist Convention, Minutes,1886, SCBHC.
37. *Georgetown Enquirer,* May 7, 1887.
38. *Georgetown Times,* May 12, 1900. This obituary credits Butts with having the church "repaired at his own expense."
39. *Georgetown Times,* November 14, 1891. Mustard died in 1891.
40. Charleston Baptist Association, Minutes, 1888, SCBHC.
41. *Georgetown Enquirer,* March 21, 1888.
42. The first notice of Carroll preaching in Georgetown came in the *Georgetown Enquirer,* April 11, 1888.
43. The Sampit church was constituted in 1888 but lasted no more than a few years. The value of the building was only one hundred dollars. The last missionary there was J. M. Kirton. Charleston Baptist Association, Minutes, 1889–1890, SCBHC.
44. *Georgetown Enquirer,* March 21, 1888.
45. *Georgetown Times,* December 8, 1889.
46. Ibid., February 8, March 15, and March 22, 1890.
47. Charleston Baptist Association, Minutes, 1890, SCBHC.
48. *Georgetown Times,* May 10, May 24, June 14, September 20, October 4, and October 11, 1890; March 8, 1891. Regarding social ills in Georgetown, especially drunkenness and violations of the Sabbath, see the editorial in the *Georgetown Times,* February 28, 1891.
49. *Georgetown Times,* April 18, April 25, and May 23, 1891.
50. The remarks of the *Times* are reported in *Georgetown Enquirer,* February 9, 1887.
51. Ibid.
52. *Georgetown Times,* May 10, 1890, and March 28, 1891.
53. Charleston Baptist Association, Minutes, 1890, SCBHC. The association began tracking church values in 1890. Citadel Square and First Baptist, both of Charleston, had by far the most valuable churches, $60,000 and $40,000 respectively. The next highest were two churches worth $1,800, followed by Georgetown's $1,300. Four churches, including Sampit, were valued at only $100.
54. *Georgetown Times,* June 6, 1891.
55. Ibid., February 27 and June 11, 1892.
56. Ibid., June 20, October 7, and November 21 and 28, 1891.
57. Charleston Baptist Association, Minutes, 1892, SCBHC.
58. *Georgetown Times,* January 23, February 6, March 26, and April 2, 1892.

59. Ibid., June 18, 1892.

60. Ibid., November 19, 1892.

61. Charleston Baptist Association, Minutes, 1892, SCBHC.

62. *Georgetown Times,* December 3, 1892.

63. Ibid., July 1, 1893, December 8, 1894, and April 20, 1895.

64. Ibid., February 7, 1894. See also January 31, and February 3, 1894.

65. Ibid., April 18, 1894. See also April 25, May 2, May 5, and May 9, 1894.

66. Ibid., May 9, 1894.

67. Ibid., February 26, 1896.

68. South Carolina Baptist Convention, Minutes, 1896, SCBHC.

69. On Jones, see *Georgetown Times,* June 20, June 21, July 4, July 18, August 26, and October 7, 1896. Jones later became secretary of the state mission board.

70. Charleston Baptist Association, Minutes, 1897, SCBHC. On Wells's arrival, see *Georgetown Times,* March 27, April 13, April 14, and April 17, 1897.

71. *Georgetown Times,* November 24, 1897.

72. Ibid., June 16, 1897. For events of late 1897, see December 1, December 4, December 8, December 15, and December 29, 1897.

73. Ibid., May 12, 1900.

Chapter 10: Growing Pains

1. On the Atlantic Coast Lumber Company and Georgetown at the turn of the century, see Roy Talbert, Jr., *No Greater Legacy: The Centennial History of Willcox, McLeod, Buyck & Williams, 1895–1995* (Columbia: Benchmark, 1995), 37–46; George C. Rogers, Jr., *The History of Georgetown County, South Carolina* (Columbia: University of South Carolina Press, 1970), 498–500.

2. On tobacco, see Eldred E. Prince, *Long Green: The Rise and Fall of Tobacco in South Carolina* (Athens: University of Georgia Press, 2000).

3. For a few years after 1900 Georgetown had another paper, the *Georgetown Outlook,* also valuable, especially regarding economic development.

4. Charleston Baptist Association, Minutes, 1900, SCBHC. Georgetown still received two hundred dollars a year from the association, along with Forreston, Eutawville, Cannon Street, Citadel Square Mission, Providence, and Summerville.

5. Rogers, *History of Georgetown,* 513–14.

6. *Georgetown Times,* January 22, 1908.

7. Ibid., November 13, 1901.

8. Ibid., March 30, 1902.

9. Ibid., September 30, 1903.

10. *Georgetown Outlook,* May 9, 1903.

11. *Georgetown Times,* May 20, 1903.

12. *Georgetown Outlook,* May 30, 1903.

13. Ibid., March 29, 1903.

14. Ibid., May 23, 1903.

15. Ibid., January 2, 1904.
16. Ibid., December 31, 1904.
17. Charleston Baptist Association, Minutes, 1903, SCBHC.
18. The Knights of Pythias was established in 1864 and continues to remain active; *Georgetown Outlook,* May 7, 1904.
19. *Georgetown Outlook,* April 30, 1904.
20. *Georgetown Outlook,* August 27, 1904; *Georgetown Times,* August 31, 1904.
21. Charleston Baptist Association, Minutes, 1904, SCBHC.
22. Ibid., 1904–1907.
23. *Georgetown Times,* March 16, 1907.
24. *Georgetown Outlook,* August 17, 1907.
25. *Georgetown Times,* December 18, 1907. In its annual report that fall, Georgetown church members called this period "a crisis in their life." Charleston Baptist Association, Minutes, 1907, SCBHC.
26. *Georgetown Times,* January 13, 1909.
27. First Baptist Church of Georgetown, Minutes, October 10, 1909, FBCG.
28. Ibid., December 1, 1909.
29. Ibid., December 5, and December 26, 1909.
30. *Georgetown Times,* September 28, 1910.
31. First Baptist Church of Georgetown, Minutes, January 16, 1910, FBCG.
32. The record of economic difficulties is spread throughout the church minutes from 1910 to 1914.
33. "Associational Letter," September 30, 1910, FBCG.
34. Ibid.
35. First Baptist Church of Georgetown, Minutes, March 6–August 14, 1910, FBCG.
36. Ibid., February 13, 1917.
37. Ibid., October 30, 1910, FBCG. Turner's salary was $800 including a $150 grant from the state mission board.
38. *Georgetown Times,* January 3 and January 6, 1912. First Baptist Church of Georgetown, Minutes, November 12 and November 19, 1911, FBCG.
39. First Baptist Church of Georgetown, Minutes, May 15, 1912, FBCG.
40. *Georgetown Times,* May 20 and May 23, 1914.
41. Ibid., June 8 and June 15, 1912.
42. Ibid., December 21, 1912.
43. Ibid., November 27, 1912.
44. Joe Madison King, *A History of South Carolina Baptists* (Columbia: General Board of the South Carolina Baptist Convention, 1964), 432–33; Elaine Y. Eaddy, "Black Mingo Baptist Church Located Near Deserted Willtown," *Three Rivers Chronicle* 1 (Fall 1981): 3–4; "History of Nesmith Baptist Church," FBCG; Margorie Rhem, "Willtown and Old Belin's," FBCG.
45. For membership in the Southeast Association, see King, *South Carolina Baptists,* 432–33.
46. *Georgetown Times,* September 18, 1912.

47. Ibid., January 17, 1914. While Bellonby was in town, Bethesda's pastor, W. W. Carter, also hoped to draw up a contract for a new church. That, however, did not materialize.
48. *Georgetown Times,* April 9, 1913.
49. Ibid., March 11, 1914.
50. Charleston Baptist Association, Minutes, 1909, SCBHC.
51. *Georgetown Times,* October 10, 1914.
52. Ibid., April 8, 1914.
53. Ibid., May 13, 1914.
54. Ibid., October 10, 1914.
55. Ibid., October 10, November 7, and November 21, 1914, February 13 and February 20, 1915. Notes of appreciation to W. B. Arnhalter of the Peerless Theatre and to W. D. Morgan of the Steele Opera House, dated April 16, 1919, are in church minutes, FBCG.
56. *Georgetown Times,* January 30, 1915.
57. Ibid., March 27, 1915.
58. Ibid., March 31, 1915.
59. Ibid., March 27, 1915.
60. Ibid., July 15, 1914.
61. First Baptist Church of Georgetown, Minutes, January 31, 1915, FBCG. The church minutes of the first half of 1915 are filled with indications of a conflict with the pastor.
62. Ibid., June 29, 1915.
63. *Georgetown Times,* July 7, 1915.
64. First Baptist Church of Georgetown, Minutes, September 12, 1915, FBCG.
65. *Georgetown Times,* September 8, September 15, and September 22, 1915; First Baptist Church of Georgetown, Minutes, September 12, 1915, FBCG.
66. *Georgetown Times,* April 16, May 29, and May 3, 1916.
67. Ibid., November 4 and November 18, 1916.
68. Ibid., January 29, 1916.
69. Ibid., May 18, 1918.
70. Ibid., June 5, 1918.
71. The Reverend J. C. McLemore, former pastor in Georgetown, was also in YMCA work at Camp Jackson in Columbia. *Georgetown Times,* December 17, 1918.
72. *Georgetown Times,* October 9, 1918. See also September 21, 1918.
73. On the flu, see *Georgetown Times,* November 9, and December 7, 1918. For the flu in South Carolina, see Talbert, *No Greater Legacy.*
74. *Georgetown Times,* May 3, May 10, and July 2, 1919.
75. Ibid., October 1, 1919.
76. "Resolution," September 12, 1919, FBCG.
77. *Georgetown Times,* March 8, 1913.
78. Ibid., March 12 and 26, 1913.
79. Ibid., May 22, 1955.

80. Ibid., March 23, 1918. The *Baptist Courier* article is reprinted here, along with a description of Cook's visit.
81. The last use of *Antipedo* officially came in a legal document involving the replacement of a lost deed. See First Baptist Church of Georgetown, Minutes, March 17, 1918, FBCG.
82. First Baptist Church of Georgetown, Minutes, February 12, 1911, FBCG. The complete bylaws dated February 12, 1911, are in the church minutes.

CHAPTER 11: MATURITY

1. First Baptist Church of Georgetown, Minutes, September 12, 1919, FBCG; *Georgetown Times,* October 1, 1919.
2. *Georgetown Times,* October 12 and November 2, 1919; Ibid., November 5, 1919.
3. Ibid., October 24, 1924. See also July 1, 1932.
4. These names appear frequently in the church and association minutes, along with many others.
5. *Georgetown Times,* July 2, 1926.
6. Ibid., February 23, 1923.
7. Ibid., April 5, 1923.
8. Ibid., July 2, 1926.
9. Ibid., October 24, 1924.
10. This announcement appeared in *Georgetown Times,* April 9 and April 16, 1920.
11. Ibid., April 23, 1920.
12. Ibid., October 29 and November 4, 1921.
13. Ibid., November 23, 1923.
14. Ibid., December 14 1923. See also May 18, and November 16, 1923.
15. Ibid., August 6 and October 5, 1920.
16. First Baptist Church of Georgetown, Minutes, November 14, 1920, FBCG.
17. *Georgetown Times,* December 19, 1930.
18. First Baptist Church of Georgetown, Minutes, January 9, 1921, FBCG.
19. Ibid., March 13, 1921.
20. The last mention of state aid is in the First Baptist Church of Georgetown minutes, December 8, 1919, FBCG. At the same meeting Lide recommended the duplex system. On implementation, see First Baptist Church of Georgetown, Minutes, October 5, 1920, FBCG.
21. Ibid., May 7, 1920.
22. *Georgetown Times,* September 25, 1925.
23. First Baptist Church of Georgetown, Minutes, July 8, 1921, FBCG.
24. These continuing needs are addressed in First Baptist Church of Georgetown, Minutes, July 8, 1921 to January 6, 1922, FBCG.
25. Ibid., January 11, 1923, FBCG.
26. Ibid., February 10 and February 12, 1922, March 10, March 12, and March 19, 1922.
27. Ibid., February 2, 1925.
28. *Georgetown Times,* July 31, 1925.

29. Ibid., November 13 and December 18, 1925. See also December 20, December 29, and December 15, 1933.

30. First Baptist Church of Georgetown, Minutes, December 9, 1928, and February 2, February 8, and February 22, 1925, FBCG; "First Baptist Church, Commemorative Service," September 27, 1992, 15, FBCG.

31. First Baptist Church of Georgetown, Minutes, April 30, 1923, FBCG.

32. Ibid., June 10 and July 8, 1923.

33. *Georgetown Times,* February 4, March 27, and November 6, 1925.

34. Ibid., April 4, 1924.

35. On the Seventy-Five Million Campaign, see Joe Madison King, *A History of South Carolina Baptists* (Columbia: General Board of the South Carolina Baptist Convention, 1964), 280, 284, 295, 298, 300, 301.

36. First Baptist Church of Georgetown, Minutes, December 31, 1924, FBCG.

37. Ibid., November 21, 1924.

38. Ibid., October 26, 1930.

39. Southeastern Baptist Association, Minutes, 1924–1928, SCBHC. One of the members who left the church in 1928 was H. C. Tallevast.

40. George C. Rogers, Jr., *The History of Georgetown County, South Carolina* (Columbia: University of South Carolina Press, 1970), 501–2.

41. Ibid., 502. On bank closures, see Roy Talbert, Jr., *So Much to be Thankful For: The Conway National Bank and the Economic History of Horry County* (Columbia: R. L. Bryan, 2003), 185; John G. Sproat and Larry Schweikart, *Making Change: South Carolina Banking in the Twentieth Century* (Columbia: South Carolina Bankers Association, 1990), 60. Georgetown began experiencing bank failures in the spring of 1924 followed by a series of closings and reopenings. By 1932 there were no banks. *Georgetown Times,* January 23, 1927, and January 15, 1932.

42. First Baptist Church of Georgetown, Minutes, November 11, and December 2, 1928, FBCG.

43. Ibid., December 9, 1928.

44. Ibid., March 8, 1931.

45. Information about the April festivities is attached to the church minutes of October 12, 1930, FBCG.

46. *Georgetown Times,* December 9, 1930.

47. Ibid., June 18 and July 23, 1926.

48. First Baptist Church of Georgetown, Minutes, June 26, 1932, FBCG. The complete resolution also appeared in *Georgetown Times,* July 15, 1932.

49. *Georgetown Times,* December 9, 1932. See also September 20, 1935.

50. On Collins's ailment, see *Georgetown Times,* July 13, July 17, August 3, August 17, and August 31, 1934. On his other activities, see April 14, September 1, and September 22, 1933; June 1, and July 13, 1934; First Baptist Church of Georgetown, Minutes, September 25, 1935, FBCG.

51. First Baptist Church of Georgetown, Minutes, September 15, September 20, and September 25, 1935, FBCG.

52. Southeast Baptist Association, Minutes, 1934, SCBHC.

53. The Wells family papers in the church archives include an excellent biographical sketch by his son. See also *Georgetown Times,* January 10 and February 21, 1936.

54. Henry B. Bruorton, the "high sheriff," was one of the most powerful men of his day, and stories of his exploits are still told in Georgetown. He is the father of Virginia Skinner.

55. Wells Family Papers, FBCG.

56. Southeast Baptist Association, Minutes, 1938, SCBHC.

57. Lide's letter from Greenville, July 3, 1936, and Powell's response, August 9, 1936, are in the First Baptist Church of Georgetown minutes.

58. First Baptist Church of Georgetown, Minutes, November 21, 1937, FBCG.

59. Ibid., December 11, 1938. The Cooperative Program began shortly after the completion of the Seventy-Five Million Campaign.

60. *Georgetown Times,* July 16, 1926.

61. Ibid., March 15, 1929.

62. Ibid., November 28, 1941.

63. Ibid., April 4, 1925, and May 2, 1930.

64. Ibid., June 13 and August 8, 1930.

65. Ibid., May 23, 1941.

66. Rogers, *History of Georgetown,* 503.

67. *Georgetown Times,* March 6, 1942.

68. Wells Family Papers, FBCG.

69. Darr Family Papers, FBCG.

70. *Georgetown Times,* March 13, 1942.

71. Southeast Baptist Association, Minutes, 1945, SCBHC.

72. Darr Family Papers, FBCG.

73. Southeast Baptist Association, Minutes, 1943–1944, SCBHC.

74. *Georgetown Times,* February 25, 1949.

75. The original programs for the cornerstone laying and the dedication ceremony are in FBCG.

CHAPTER 12: MISSIONS AND MEMORIES

1. Southeast Baptist Association, Minutes, 1950 and 1960, SCBHC.

2. *Georgetown Times,* March 26, 1950.

3. "Report of the Planning Committee for the Southside Mission," March 19, 1950, FBCG. In 1950 First Baptist's indebtedness amounted to forty-three thousand dollars. See Southeast Baptist Association, Minutes, 1950, SCBHC.

4. Isaac C. Vassar to First Baptist, September 16, 1957, FBCG. First Baptist approved buying the pulpit fixtures on May 8, 1957. At that time S. D. Miller was Screven's clerk and E. C. Britt served as treasurer. A February 15, 1953, Screven church bulletin announced a baptismal service at First Church after the evening service. See FBCG.

5. First Baptist Church of Georgetown, Minutes, March 7, 1954, FBCG.

6. Ibid., January 8, 1956.

7. Ibid., March 6, 1957.

8. Ibid., May 8, June 10, and December 11, 1957. On moving Screven's monument, see W. H. Clapp to Mrs. A. P. Ward, December 13, 1957, FBCG.

9. Planning for the new educational building began in 1955. First Baptist Church of Georgetown, Minutes, November 2, 1955, FBCG. Progress reports are included in subsequent minutes. The church accepted the $142,000 bid from Kingstree Building Supply Company on January 26, 1958. *Georgetown Times,* August 15, 1957; *Baptist Courier,* March 20, 1958.

10. First Baptist Church of Georgetown, Minutes, August 8, 1960, FBCG. The Warren Clapp file in the church archives contains an October 14, 1956, church bulletin celebrating his work to that date. It also has an undated handwritten sketch of Clapp's contributions. His letter of resignation, dated July 17, 1960, is in the church minutes. He gave his last sermon in Georgetown on August 14. Years later, in 1997, Clapp returned to Georgetown and lived there until his death.

11. First Baptist Church of Georgetown, Minutes, August 24 and 28 and October 6, 1960, FBCG. Kirkland's salary for 1961 was $7,800, and the total church budget was $92,984.13. First Baptist Minutes, November 9, 1960. The 1965 budget was $108,312. Minutes, November 8, 1964. A year later it reached $120, 245.88. Minutes, October 31, 1965.

12. *Georgetown Times,* June 5, 1975.

13. J. M. Kirkland, no date, "The Facts and Dates of my Preaching at First Baptist Church of Georgetown," FBCG. Discussion of the summer youth program began in the spring of 1964. See First Baptist Church of Georgetown, Minutes, May 13, 1964, FBCG. Another first for the church was the purchase of a bus. See Minutes, November 4, 1964. A garage was built in 1966. See Minutes, April 4, 1966. By 1972 the church had an operational bus ministry. Minutes, January 12, 1972.

14. Minutes, First Baptist Church of Georgetown, June 8, 1966, FBCG. See also November 6, 1968.

15. Bob A. Teems, "Major Events at FBC Georgetown during the Ministry of Bob A. Teems," FBCG; First Baptist Church of Georgetown, Minutes, May 26, 1998, FBCG.

16. The 1971 budget is attached at the end of the 1971 church minutes.

17. On J. R. Kirkland, see the dedication program for Lakewood, February 6, 1966, and First Baptist Church directory, 1969, FBCG.

18. Discussions of property and planning are throughout the 1963 church minutes.

19. *Georgetown Times,* September 23, 1965.

20. The program for the dedication of the Lakewood mission is in FBCG. The mission was further aided by a $141.25 contribution from First Baptist Lide Sunday School Class. The Reverend and Mrs. J. R. Kirkland donated a new piano. Screven Baptist Church gave a beautiful pulpit Bible.

21. "A Brief History of First Baptist Church," First Baptist Church of Georgetown Church Directory 1969, FBCG. See also Minutes, September 10, 1969, FBCG. Aid also came from the state convention in the amount of seventy-five dollars per month. See State Baptist Convention, Minutes, May 12 and June 23, 1965, SCBHC.

22. *Georgetown Times,* September 23, 1965.

23. On Pawleys, see First Baptist Church of Georgetown, Minutes, March 9 and May 4, 1966; February 12, 1969, July 7, 1971; January 12, May 7, and December 6, 1972, FBCG. The program for the August 21, 1966, dedication ceremony is in FBCG.

24. "North Hampton Baptist, 1966–1994," FBCG. See also First Baptist Church of Georgetown Church Directory 1969, and minutes of the First Baptist Church of Georgetown, August 4, 1971, FBCG.

25. The 1969 membership numbers are attached at the end of the 1972 First Baptist Church of Georgetown minutes.

26. First Baptist Church of Georgetown, Minutes, April 5, 1972, FBCG.

27. *Georgetown Times,* April 13 and May 4, 1972, January 4, 1973; "First Baptist Church News," April 13, 1972, FBCG.

28. First Baptist Church of Georgetown Dedication Service Program, April 29, 1973, FBCG; First Baptist Church of Georgetown Commemorative Service Brochure, September 27, 1992, FBCG.

29. *Georgetown Times,* October 10 and 22, 1974. The program for the occasion is in the FBCG.

30. *Georgetown Times,* September 11, 1979.

31. Ibid., October 9, 1980. Dr. Baker received a key to the city. Dr. Teems recalled that Baker became an "honorary" member of First Baptist. See Teems, "Major Events," FBCG. For planning of the event, see *Georgetown Times,* July 31, 1980. For another report, see *Baptist Courier,* October 23, 1980. A *Georgetown Times* special supplement to the September 25, 1980, issue has a full description of the Lowcountry History Festival. The program for the Screven memorial service, "The March of Christian History," is in the FBCG.

32. *Georgetown Times,* October 9, 1980.

33. References to Belin/Black Mingo run throughout the Southeast Association minutes from the 1950s.

34. *Georgetown Times,* October 14 and 21, 1982. See also First Baptist Church of Georgetown Newsletter, October 14, 1982, FBCG.

35. First Baptist Church of Georgetown Newsletter, November 3, 1983, FBCG.

36. *Georgetown Times,* September 28, 1984; *Myrtle Beach Sun News,* September 29, 1984. Both paintings remain on exhibit in the church. The booklet for the commemorative service is in the FBCG.

37. Teems, "Major Events," FBCG.

38. Virginia Bruorton Skinner, "A Brief History of the Baptists of Georgetown, S.C. (1710–1984)," 2007, FBCG.

39. Accounts of Nelson's pastorate are in Skinner's "Brief History" and in "First Baptist Church Unveiling Service," September 30, 2007, FBCG. On the painting, see First Baptist Church of Georgetown Newsletter, September 24, 1992, FBCG; *Georgetown Times,* October 1, 1992. For the welcoming of Nelson and his family, see First Baptist Church of Georgetown Newsletter, July 9, 1987, FBCG. On the reception for his farewell, see First Baptist Church of Georgetown Newsletter, May 14, 1992, FBCG.

40. "A Brief Review of the Ministry of Ronald G. Dillon, Pastor," FBCG.

41. *Georgetown Times,* September 29, 1997. The program for the dedication service is in the FBCG.

42. For another description of the opening of the new sanctuary, see *Baptist Courier,* October 23, 1997.

43. The items placed in the cornerstone box are listed in Skinner, "Brief History," FBCG.

44. Ibid.

45. Sherrill's pastorate to 2007 is detailed in Skinner, "Brief History," FBCG.

46. This quotation and others were taken from oral histories conducted by Roy Talbert, Jr., and Meggan A. Farish. Notes and transcripts are available in the FBCG.

47. *Georgetown Times,* June 6, 2003; "The Messenger," June 3, 2003, FBCG.

48. "The Messenger," May 4, 2004, FBCG. Skinner, "Brief History."

49. *Georgetown Times,* June 27, 2007. The handsome invitations and the dedication program are in FBCG.

Bibliography

MANUSCRIPTS

First Baptist Church of Georgetown Archives, Georgetown, South Carolina
Antipedo Baptist Church Minutes
Church Bulletins
Church Directories
Church Programs
Church Annual Reports
Darr Family Papers
First Baptist Church of Georgetown Minutes
Miscellaneous Items
Oliver Family Papers
Oral Histories
Virginia Skinner, "A Brief History of the Baptists
    of Georgetown, S.C. (1710–1984)"
Wells Family Papers

South Carolina Baptist Historical Collection, James B. Duke Library,
    Furman University
Edmund Botsford Papers
Charleston Baptist Association Minutes
Richard Furman Papers
South Carolina Baptist Convention Minutes
Southeast Baptist Association Minutes
Welsh Neck Church Books

South Carolina Department of Archives and History
Charleston County Wills
Conveyance Books
General Assembly Committee Reports
General Assembly Petitions
Journal of the Commons House of Assembly
Judgment Rolls

Memorial Books
Miscellaneous Records
Plats for State Land Grants
Proprietary Grants
Renunciation of Dower
Royal Grants
Will Transcripts

Historical Society of Penns Grove, Carneys Point and Oldmans,
Penns Grove, New Jersey
Church Index

South Carolina Historical Society
John Martin Papers

South Caroliniana Library, Columbia, South Carolina
Richard Furman Papers
Guinard Family Papers
Oliver Hart Papers
William Tennent Papers

OFFICIAL RECORDS

Cooper, Thomas, and David J. McCord, eds. *The Statutes at Large of South Carolina.* 10 vols. Columbia: A. S. Johnson, 1836–1841.
United States Bureau of the Census. *A Century of Population Growth, From the First Census of the United States to the Twelfth, 1790–1900.* Baltimore: Genealogical Publication, 1967.

NEWSPAPERS

Baptist Courier
Charleston City Gazette and Daily Advertiser
Georgetown American
Georgetown Enquirer
Georgetown Gazette
Georgetown Outlook
Georgetown Times
Georgetown Times and Comet
Hartford Times
Myrtle Beach Sun News
New-Hampshire Gazette
South Carolina Gazette
Southern Evangelical Intelligencer
Winyaw Intelligencer
Winyaw Observer

ARTICLES AND ESSAYS

Baker, Robert A. "More Light on William Screven." *Journal of the South Carolina Baptist Historical Society* 6 (November 1980): 18–33.

Baker, William. "William Wilberforce on the Idea of Negro Inferiority." *Church History* 31 (July–September 1970): 433–40.

Brooks, Walter H. "The Evolution of the Negro Baptist Church." *Journal of Negro History* 7 (January 1922): 11–22.

Chandler, J. W. Nelson. "Willtown, Black Mingo: The Rise and Fall of an Early Village in the South Carolina Lowcountry." *South Carolina Historical Magazine* 105 (April 2004): 107–34.

Chandler, William H. "Some Historic Churches in Williamsburg County." *Names in South Carolina* 18 (Winter 1971): 28–29.

Chrisope, Terry A. "William Screven, 1629–1713." In *A Noble Company: Biographical Essays on Notable Particular-Regular Baptists in America.* Edited by Terry Wolever, 2:218–21. Springfield, Miss.: Particular Baptist Press, 2006.

Eaddy, Elaine Y. "Black Mingo Baptist Church Located Near Deserted Willtown." *Three Rivers Chronicle* 1 (Fall 1981): 3–4.

Feight, Andrew Lee. "Edmund Botsford and Richard Furman: Slavery in the South Carolina Lowcountry, 1766–1825." *Journal of the South Carolina Baptist Historical Society* 19 (November 1993): 2–22.

Gardner, Robert G. "South Carolina Baptist Statistics, 1672–1790: A Table." *Journal of the South Carolina Baptist Historical Society* 9 (November 1983): 34.

"Historical Notes." *South Carolina Historical and Genealogical Magazine* 16 (April 1915): 93–95.

"Historical Sketch of the First Baptist Church." In *Year Book.* N.p., Charleston, 1881.

"Letters of Rev. Samuel Thomas, 1702–1710." *South Carolina Historical and Genealogical Magazine* 4 (July 1903): 221–30.

McCulloch, Samuel Clyde. "The Foundation and Early Work of the Society for the Propagation of the Gospel in Foreign Parts." *Huntington Library Quarterly* 8 (May 1945): 241–58.

Music, David W. "Congregational Song Practices in Southern Baptist Churches: A Historical Overview." *Southern Baptist Church Music Journal* 9 (1992): 10–20.

Owens, Loulie Latimer. "Oliver Hart and the American Revolution." *Journal of South Carolina Baptist Historical Society* 1 (November 1975): 2-17.

———."South Carolina Baptists and the American Revolution." *Journal of the South Carolina Baptist Historical Society* 1 (November 1975): 31–45.

Quinney, Valerie. "Decisions on Slavery, the Slave-Trade and Civil Rights for Negroes in the Early French Revolution." *Journal of Negro History* 55 (April 1970): 117–30.

Renihan, James M. "John Spilsburg, 1593c.–1662/1668." In *The British Particular Baptists, 1638–1910,* 1:20–37. Edited by Michael A. G. Haykin. Springfield, Mo.: Particular Baptist Press, 1998.

Ricards, Sherman L., and George M. Blackburn. "A Demographic History of Slavery: Georgetown County, South Carolina, 1850." *South Carolina Historical and Genealogical Magazine* 76 (October 1975): 215–24.

Smith, Henry A. M. "The Baronies of South Carolina." *South Carolina Historical and Genealogical Magazine* 15 (October 1914): 149–65.

———. "Georgetown: The Original Plan and the Earliest Settlers." *South Carolina Historical and Genealogical Magazine* 9 (April 1908): 85–101.

———. "Some Forgotten Towns in Lower South Carolina." *South Carolina Historical and Genealogical Magazine* 14 (July 1913): 134–46.

———. "Willtown or New London." *South Carolina Historical and Genealogical Magazine* 10 (January 1909): 20–32.

Towles, Louis P. "Township Plan." In *The South Carolina Encyclopedia*. Edited by Walter Edgar, 973–74. Columbia: University of South Carolina Press, 2006.

Watson, Doug. "William Bullein Johnson: The First President of the Southern Baptist Convention and His Portrayal of the Baptist Identity." *Journal of the South Carolina Baptist Historical Society* 26 (November 2000): 11.

Whilden, William G. "Reverend William Screven." *New-England Historical and Genealogical Register* 43 (October 1889): 356–57.

BOOKS

Ackerman, Robert K. *South Carolina Colonial Land Policies.* Columbia: University of South Carolina Press, 1977.

Armitage, Thomas. *A History of the Baptists: Traced by their Vital Principles. . . .* New York: Bryan, Taylor, 1887.

Backus, Isaac. *A History of New England with Particular Reference to the Denomination of Christians Called Baptists,* 2 vols. Newton, Mass.: Backus Historical Society, 1871.

Baker, Robert A. *The First Southern Baptists.* Nashville: Broadman Press, 1966.

———. *The Southern Baptist Convention and Its People, 1607–1972.* Nashville: Broadman Press, 1974.

Baker, Robert A., and Paul J. Craven, Jr. *Adventure in Faith: The First 300 Years of First Baptist Church, Charleston, South Carolina.* Madison, Wis.: Broadman Press, 1982.

Baker, Robert A., Paul J. Craven, Jr., and R. Marshall Blalock. *History of the First Baptist Church of Charleston, South Carolina, 1682–2007.* Springfield, Miss.: Particular Baptist Press, 2007.

Baxter, Lionel Francis, and John William Baxter. *A Baxter Family from South Carolina: South Irish Pioneers from Ulster.* St. Petersburg: Genealogical Publication Service, 1989.

Benedict, David. *Fifty Years Among the Baptists.* New York: Sheldon, 1860.

———. *A General History of the Baptist Denomination in America and Other Parts of the World.* 2 vols. Boston: Lincoln and Edmands, 1813.

Boddie, William Willis. *History of Williamsburg: Something about the People of Williamsburg County, South Carolina, from the First Settlement by Europeans about 1705 until 1923.* Columbia: State Company, 1923.

Boles, John B. *The Great Revival: Beginnings of the Bible Belt.* Lexington: University Press of Kentucky, 1996.

Botsford, Edmund. *Sambo and Toney: A Dialogue between Two Servants.* Georgetown: Francis M. Baxter, 1808.

Brackney, William Henry. *The Baptists.* Westport, Conn.: Greenwood Press, 1988.

Brown, Henry F. *Baptism through the Centuries.* Mountain View, Calif.: Pacific Press Publishing Association, 1965.

Burrage, Henry S. *History of the Baptists in Maine.* Portland: Marks Printing House, 1904.

Clark, Elmer T., J. Manning Potts, and Jacob S. Payton, eds. *The Journal and Letters of Francis Asbury.* 3 vols. Nashville: Abingdon Press, 1958.

Collinson, Patrick. *The Reformation: A History.* New York: Modern Library, 2006.

Conforti, Joseph A. *Samuel Hopkins and the New Divinity Movement: Calvinism, the Congregational Ministry, and Reform in New England between the Great Awakenings.* Grand Rapids: Christian University Press, 1981.

Cook, Harvey Toliver. *The Life Work of James Clement Furman.* N.p.: Greenville, 1926.

—————. *Rambles in the Pee Dee Basin South Carolina.* Columbia: State Company, 1926.

—————. *The Story of the Baptists in All Ages and Countries.* New York: Wiley Brothers, 1884.

Cooper, James Fowler. *An Historical Sketch of Indiantown Presbyterian Church in Williamsburg County, S.C., 1757–1957.* N.p., 1957.

Cramer, Peter. *Baptism and Change in the Early Middle Ages, c.200–c.1150.* Cambridge: Cambridge University Press, 1993.

Creel, Margaret W. *"A Peculiar People": Slave Religion and Community-Culture among the Gullahs.* New York: New York University Press, 1988.

Cuthbert, H. *Life of Richard Fuller, D. D.* New York: Sheldon and Company 1879.

Cuttino, G. P. *History of the Cuttino Family.* Atlanta: Emory University Office of Publications, 1982.

Dusinberre, William. *Them Dark Days: Slavery in the American Rice Swamps.* New York: Oxford University Press, 1996.

Edgar, Walter. *South Carolina: A History.* Columbia: University of South Carolina Press, 1998.

Edwards, Morgan. *Materials Towards a History of the Baptists.* 2 vols. 1770. Reprint, Danielsville, Ga.: Heritage Papers, 1984.

Esker, Katie-Prince Ward. *South Carolina Memorials, 1731–1776.* Cottonport: Polyanthos, 1973.

Fitts, Leroy. *A History of Black Baptists.* Nashville: Broadman Press, 1985.

Ford, Lacy K. *Deliver Us from Evil: The Slavery Question in the Old South.* New York: Oxford University Press, 2009.

Furman, Richard. *The Crown of Life Promised to the Truly Faithful: A Sermon Saved to the Memory of the Rev. Edmund Botsford, A. M. Late Pastor of the Baptist Church in Georgetown, S. C.* Charleston: W. M. Riley, 1822.

————. *Exposition of the Views of the Baptists Relative to the Coloured Population of the United States in Communication to the Governor of South-Carolina.* Charleston: A. E. Miller, 1838.

Furman, Wood. *A Biography of Richard Furman.* Edited by Harvey T. Cook. Greenville: Baptist Courier Job Rooms, 1913.

Gaustad, Edwin S. *Roger Williams.* New York: Oxford University Press, 2005.

Grosvenor, Cyrus Pitt, ed. *Slavery vs. The Bible: A Correspondence between the General Conference of Maine, and the Presbytery of Tombecbee, Mississippi.* N.p., Worcester, 1840.

Hadden, Sally E. *Slave Patrols: Law and Violence in Virginia and the Carolinas.* Cambridge: Harvard University Press, 2001.

Hagy, James William. *This Happy Land: The Jews of Colonial and Antebellum Charleston.* Tuscaloosa: University of Alabama Press, 1993.

Hayes, James P. *James and Related Sea Islands.* Charleston: Hayes, 1978.

Hester, H. I. *They That Wait: A History of Anderson College.* Anderson: Anderson College, 1969.

Hillerbrand, Hans J., ed. *The Oxford Encyclopedia of the Reformation.* New York: Oxford University Press, 1996.

Hirsch, Arthur Henry. *The Huguenots of Colonial South Carolina.* Columbia: University of South Carolina Press, 1999.

Historical Sketch of the Welsh Neck Baptist Church, Society Hill, S. C.: Two Hundred and Twenty Fifth Anniversary, March 3, 1963. Columbia: State Company, 1963.

Howard, Cecil Hampden Cutts. *Genealogy of the Cutts Family in America.* Albany: J. Munsell's Sons, 1892.

Howe, George. *History of the Presbyterian Church in South Carolina.* 2 vols. Columbia: Duffie and Chapman, 1870.

Huger, Daniel Elliott. *Proceedings of the Meeting in Charleston, S.C., May 13–15, 1845, on the Religious Instruction of the Negroes.* Charleston: B. Jenkins, 1845.

Ivey, Michael N. *A Welsh Succession of Primitive Baptist Faith and Practice.* N.p.: M. N. Ivey, 1994.

Ivimey, Joseph. *A History of the English Baptists.* Vol. 2. N.p., London, 1814.

Jenkinson, Gordon B. *A History of the Homes and People of Williamsburg District.* Charleston: History Press, 2007.

Joyner, Charles. *Down by the Riverside: A South Carolina Slave Community.* Urbana: University of Illinois Press, 1984.

King, Joe Madison. *A History of South Carolina Baptists.* Columbia: General Board of the South Carolina Baptist Convention, 1964.

Kleber, John E., ed. *The Encyclopedia of Louisville.* Lexington: University Press of Kentucky, 2001.

Klingberg, Frank J., ed. *The Carolina Chronicle of Dr. Francis Le Jau.* Berkeley: University of California Press, 1956.

Laurens, Henry. *The Papers of Henry Laurens: Jan. 5, 1776-Nov. 1, 1777,* vol. 11. Edited by David R. Chesnutt and C. James Taylor. Columbia: University of South Carolina Press, 1988.

Leonard, Bill J. *Baptists in America.* New York: Columbia University Press, 2005.

Linder, Suzanne Cameron, and Marta Leslie Thacker. *Historical Atlas of the Rice Plantations of Georgetown County and the Santee River.* Columbia: South Carolina Department of Archives and History, 2001.

Lumpkin, William L., ed. *Baptist Confessions of Faith.* Philadelphia: Judson Press, 1959.

Lynd, S. W., ed. *Memoir of the Rev. William Staughton, D. D.* Boston: Lincoln, Edmands, 1834.

MacCulloch, Diarmaid. *The Reformation: A History.* New York: Penguin Group, 2004.

Malet, William Wyndham. *An Errand to the South in the Summer of 1862.* London: Richard Bentley, 1863.

Mallary, Charles D., ed. *Memoirs of Elder Edmund Botsford.* 1832. Reprint, Springfield, Miss.: Particular Baptist Press, 2004.

Manly, Basil. *Mercy and Judgment: A Discourse Containing Some Fragments of the History of the Baptist Church in Charleston, S.C.* Charleston: Press of Knowles, Vose, 1837.

Matthews, Donald G. *Slavery and Methodism: A Chapter in American Morality, 1780–1845.* Princeton: Princeton University Press, 1965.

McBeth, H. Leon. *A Sourcebook for Baptist Heritage.* Nashville: Broadman Press, 1990.

M'Clintock, John, and James Strong. *Cyclopædia of Biblical, Theological, and Ecclesiastical Literature.* 12 vols. New York: Harper and Brothers, 1883.

McGrady, Edward. *The History of South Carolina Under the Proprietary Government, 1670–1719.* New York: Macmillan, 1897.

Merrens, H. Roy, ed. *The Colonial South Carolina Scene: Contemporary Views, 1697–1774.* Tricentennial edition. Columbia: University of South Carolina Press, 1977.

Middleton, John Allen. *Directory and Pre-1900 Historical Survey of South Carolina's Black Baptists,* vol. 3. Columbia: J. A. Middleton and Associates, 1992.

Millet, Joshua. *A History of the Baptists in Maine; Together with Brief Notices of Societies and Institutions, and a Dictionary of the Labors of Each Minister.* Portland: Charles Day, 1845.

Miranda, Francisco de. *The New Democracy in America: Travels of Francisco de Miranda in the United States, 1783–1784.* Edited by John S. Ezell. Translated by Judson P. Wood. Norman: University of Oklahoma Press, 1963.

Moody, Robert E., ed. *Province and Court Records of Maine* 5 vols. Portland: Maine Historical Society, 1947.

Morgan, Philip D. *Slave Counterpoint: Black Culture in the Eighteenth-Century Chesapeake and Lowcountry.* Chapel Hill: University of North Carolina Press, 1998.

Noyes, Sybol, Charles Thornton Libby, and Walter Goodwin Davis, eds. *Genealogical Dictionary of Maine and New Hampshire.* 1928–1939. Reprint, Baltimore: Genealogical Publishing, 1972.

O'Brien, Michael. *Conjectures of Order: Intellectual Life and the American South, 1810–1860.* 2 vols. New York: Cambridge University Press, 2005.

O'Neall, John Belton. *The Negro Law of South Carolina.* Columbia: John G. Bowman, 1848.

Owens, Loulie Latimer. *Oliver Hart, 1723–1795: A Biography.* Greenville: South Carolina Baptist Historical Society, 1966.

———. *Saints of Clay: The Shaping of South Carolina Baptists.* Columbia: R. L. Bryan, 1971.

Phillips, John Renning. *The Good Intent: The Story and Heritage of a Fresno Family.* N.p.: Magnolia Group Press, 2007.

Poyas, Elizabeth Anne. *The Olden Time of Carolina by the Octogenarian Lady of Charleston, S.C.* Charleston: Courtenay, 1855.

Prince, Eldred E. *Long Green: The Rise and Fall of Tobacco in South Carolina.* Athens: University of Georgia Press, 2000.

Raboteau, Albert J. *Slave Religion: The "Invisible Institution" in the Antebellum South.* New York: Oxford University Press, 1978.

Ramsay, David. *The History of South Carolina, From its First Settlement in 1670 to the Year 1808,* 2 vols. Charleston: David Longworth, 1809.

Rhett, Robert Goodwyn. *Charleston: An Epic of Carolina.* Richmond: Garrett and Massie, 1940.

Rippon, John. *The Baptist Annual Register, For 1790, 1791, 1792, and Part of 1793. Including Sketches of the State of Religion Among Different Denominations of Good Men at Home and Abroad.* London: Dilly, Button, and Thomas, 1793–1802.

Rogers, George C., Jr. *The History of Georgetown County, South Carolina.* Columbia: University of South Carolina Press, 1970.

Rogers, James A. *Ebenezer: The Story of a Church.* Columbia: R. L. Bryan, 1978.

———. *Richard Furman: Life and Legacy.* Macon: Mercer University Press, 2001.

Rowland, Lawrence S. *The History of Beaufort County, South Carolina,* vol. 1. Columbia: University of South Carolina Press, 1996.

Salley, Alexander S., Jr., ed. *Narratives of Early Carolina, 1650–1708.* New York: Charles Scribner's Sons, 1911.

———. *Warrants for Land in South Carolina, 1672–1711.* Columbia: Historical Commission of South Carolina, 1915.

Smith, Mark M., ed. *Stono: Documenting and Interpreting a Southern Slave Revolt.* Columbia: University of South Carolina Press, 2005.

Sprague, William B. *Annals of the American Pulpit; or, Commemorative Notices of Distinguished American Clergymen of Various Denominations . . .* 9 vols. New York: Robert Carter and Brothers, 1857–1869.

Sproat, John G., and Larry Schweikart. *Making Change: South Carolina Banking in the Twentieth Century.* Columbia: South Carolina Bankers Association, 1990.

Stiles, Henry R. *A History of the City of Brooklyn.* Brooklyn: Published by Subscription, 1870.

Talbert, Roy, Jr. *No Greater Legacy: The Centennial History of Willcox, McLeod, Buyck & Williams, 1895–1995.* Columbia: Benchmark, 1995.

————. *So Much to be Thankful For: The Conway National Bank and the Economic History of Horry County.* Columbia: R. L. Bryan, 2003.

Thalimer, Carol, and Dan Thalimer. *Country Roads of South Carolina.* Oaks, Pa.: Country Roads Press, 1996.

Towles, Louis P., ed. *A World Turned Upside Down: The Palmers of South Santee, 1818–1881.* Columbia: University of South Carolina Press in cooperation with the Caroline McKissick Dial South Caroliniana Library Endowment Fund and the South Caroliniana Sociey, 1996.

Townsend, Leah. *South Carolina Baptists, 1670–1805.* 1935. Reprint, Baltimore: Genealogical Publishing, 1974.

Tupper, H. A., ed. *Two Centuries of the First Baptist Church of South Carolina, 1683–1883.* Baltimore: R. H. Woodward, 1889.

Vedder, Henry C. *A Short History of the Baptists.* Philadelphia: American Baptist Publication Society, 1891.

Wallace, James A. *History of Williamsburg Church.* Salisbury, N.C.: Bell and James Printers, 1856.

Weir, Robert M. *Colonial South Carolina: A History.* New York: KTO Press, 1983.

Whitley, W. T., ed. *Minutes of the General Assembly of the General Baptist Churches in England.* 2 vols. London: Kingsgate Press, 1909.

Wilbur, William Allen. *Chronicles of Calvary Baptist Church in the City of Washington.* Washington: Judd & Detweiler, 1914.

Williams, George Huntston. *The Radical Reformation.* 3rd ed. Kirksville, Mo.: Sixteenth Century Journal Publishers, 1992.

Williamson, Joel. *After Slavery: The Negro in South Carolina during Reconstruction, 1861–1877.* Chapel Hill: University of North Carolina Press, 1965.

Willis, William, ed. *Collections of the Maine Historical Society,* 2 vols. Portland, 1865.

Wood, Nathan E. *The History of the First Baptist Church of Boston.* 1899. Reprint, New York: Arno Press, 1980.

Woodmason, Charles. *The Carolina Backcountry on the Eve of the Revolution: The Journal and Other Writings of Charles Woodmason, Anglican Itinerant.* Edited by Richard J. Hooker. Chapel Hill: University of North Carolina Press, 1953.

Woodson, Carter G. *The History of the Negro Church.* 2nd ed. Washington: Associated Publishers, 1921.

Woodson, Hortense. *Giant in the Land: A Biography of William Bullein Johnson.* Nashville: Broadman Press, 1950.

Young, Jeffrey Robert. *Domesticating Slavery: The Master Class in Georgia and South Carolina, 1670–1837.* Chapel Hill: University of North Carolina Press, 1999.

THESES AND DISSERTATIONS

Broome, James Foster, Jr. "A Model of Regular Baptist Ministry in South Carolina." Ph.D. diss., Southern Baptist Theological Seminary, 1985.

Fickling, Susan Markey. "Slave-Conversion in South Carolina, 1830–1860." Master's thesis, University of South Carolina, 1924.

Henry, H. M. "The Police Control of the Slave in South Carolina." Ph.D. diss., Vanderbilt University, 1914.

Mallard, Annie Hughes. "Religious Work of South Carolina Baptists among the Slaves from 1781–1830." Master's thesis, University of South Carolina, 1946.

Mears, Amy Lee. "Worship in Selected Churches of the Charleston Baptist Association, 1682–1795." Ph.D. diss., Southern Baptist Theological Seminary, 1995.

Index

About the Authors

Roy Talbert, Jr., is a professor of history at Coastal Carolina University, where he has taught since 1979. Talbert's publications include *FDR's Utopian: Arthur Morgan of the TVA*, which led to his appearance on the History Channel, and the award-winning *Negative Intelligence: The Army and the American Left, 1917–1941*. He is also the author of *Coastal Carolina University: The First 50 Years* and *So Much to Be Thankful For* and coeditor of *The Journal of Peter Horry, South Carolinian: Recording the New Republic, 1812–1814* (University of South Carolina Press).

Meggan A. Farish is a graduate of Coastal Carolina University and a history doctoral candidate at Duke University. Farish was a research assistant for the Waccamaw Center for Cultural and Historical Studies and an archives processor at the South Caroliniana Library at the University of South Carolina. She is the coeditor of *The Journal of Peter Horry, South Carolinian: Recording the New Republic, 1812–1814* (University of South Carolina Press).